DICTATORS NEVER DIE

DICTATORS
NEVER DIE

A PORTRAIT OF
NICARAGUA AND THE
SOMOZA DYNASTY

BY

EDUARDO CRAWLEY

ST. MARTIN'S PRESS · NEW YORK

Library of Congress Cataloguing in Publication Data

Crawley, Eduardo D
    Dictators never die.

    Bibliography: p.
    1. Nicaragua—Politics and government—1937-
2. Somoza, Anastasio, Pres. Nicaragua, 1896-1956.   I. Title.
F1527.C7 1979   320.9'7285'05   78-31151
ISBN 0-312-20007-2

CONTENTS

	Preface	xi
	Introduction: Dictators never die	1
I.	The Emerald Colony	10
II.	From Hernán Cortés to Henry Morgan	15
III.	Enter Horatio Nelson: Independent Nicaragua	24
IV.	From William Walker to José Santos Zelaya	32
V.	The Brown Brothers' Republic	40
VI.	Enter the U.S. Marines	49
VII.	A rebel called Sandino	58
VIII.	'Nicaraguanisation' of the war	65
IX.	The Americans pull out	70
X.	The end of Sandino	79
XI.	The rise of Somoza I	87
XII.	'Our son of a bitch'	95
XIII.	The Argüello interlude	101
XIV.	Three little wars	109
XV.	Somoza is dead, long live Somoza!	115
XVI.	Playing the American card	123
XVII.	From Somoza II to Somoza III	129
XVIII.	Nicaragua in the late nineteen-sixties	136
XIX.	President and businessman	141
XX.	The earthquake and the spectre of Sandino	148
XXI.	Cracks in the edifice	155
XXII.	One man against a nation	162
	Glossary of Spanish terms used in text	169
	Select Bibliography	170
	Index	172

MAPS

Central America (Chapters 1 and 2)	vii
Nicaragua	viii-ix
Central America in the 20th Century	x

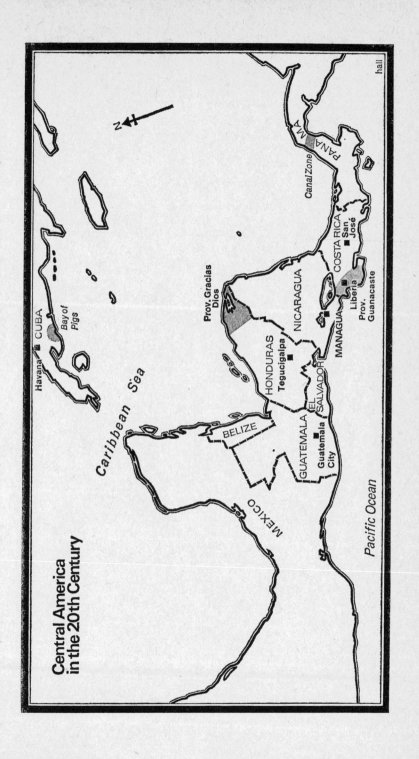

Central America
in the 20th Century

MEXICO

Caribbean Sea

CUBA
Havana

Bay of
Pigs

BELIZE

GUATEMALA
Guatemala
City

EL SALVADOR

HONDURAS
Tegucigalpa

Prov. Gracias
Dios

NICARAGUA

MANAGUA

Liberia
Prov.
Guanacaste

COSTA RICA
San
José

Canal Zone

PANAMA

Pacific Ocean

N

hall

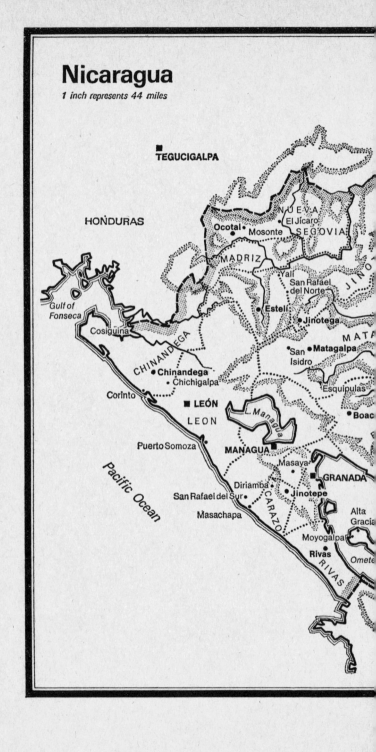

Nicaragua

1 inch represents 44 miles

TEGUCIGALPA

HONDURAS

NUEVA
Ocotal • El Jícaro
Mosonte SEGOVIA

MADRIZ

Gulf of
Fonseca

Yalí
San Rafael
del Norte

Estelí

Jinotega

JINO

Cosigüina

CHINANDEGA

MATA

San
Isidro

Matagalpa

Chinandega
Chichigalpa

Esquipulas

Corinto

LEÓN

L. Managua

Boac

LEON

Puerto Somoza

MANAGUA

Masaya

GRANADA

Pacific Ocean

Diriamba

Jinotepe

San Rafael del Sur

CARAZO

Alta
Gracia

Masachapa

Moyogalpa

Rivas

Omete

RIVAS

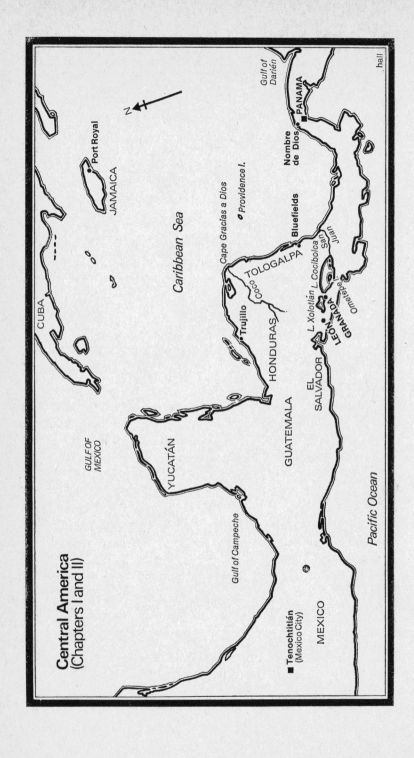

Central America
(Chapters I and II)

GULF OF MEXICO

MEXICO

■ Tenochtitlán (Mexico City)

Gulf of Campeche

YUCATÁN

GUATEMALA

EL SALVADOR

HONDURAS

Trujillo

Coco

TOLOGALPA

Cape Gracias a Dios

Providence I.

Bluefields

Nombre de Dios

PANAMA ■

Gulf of Darién

L. Xolotlán L. Cocibolca

LEÓN

GRANADA

Ometepe I.

San Juan

CUBA

JAMAICA

Port Royal

Caribbean Sea

Pacific Ocean

N

hall

PREFACE

Besides the printed sources listed on page 170-2, the most important contributions to the writing of this book came in the form of a series of interviews conducted during four visits to Nicaragua between 1975 and 1978. Among those whom I interviewed were President Anastasio Somoza Debayle, the late Pedro Joaquín Chamorro, Colonel László Pataky, Doña Margarita Debayle de Pallais and several other members of the Somoza family, an administrator of one of the Somoza enterprises, sympathisers and members of the Frente Sandinista de Liberación Nacional, and two Guardia officers (as with the source I came to know as 'Puntos Suspensivos'* I have either undertaken, or considered it prudent to maintain the anonymity of some of these informants).

Many details of the Sandino campaign and later developments in Central American politics were provided in long conversations with the Peruvian politicans Víctor Raúl Haya de la Torre (once a courier for Sandino) and Andrés Townsend Ezcurra (also an expert on the early history of independent Central America), with the former Guatemalan President Juan José Arévalo, and with the former Costa Rican President Daniel Oduber. Some of the references to Cuba arise from conversations held in 1968 with the Cuban diplomats Guido Sánchez and Santiago Díaz.

To all these individuals, named and unnamed, I would like to express my thanks.

Press reports, far too numerous to be listed, have also aided me in the reconstruction of the Somoza era in Nicaragua : the Nicar aguan newspapers *La Prensa* and *Novedades,* the press cuttings and other material in the archives of the inter-American magazine *Visión,* the collection of *sandinista* publications and communiqués in the reconstruction of the Somoza era in Nicaragua : the Nicaraguan newspapers *La Prensa* and *Novedades,* the press cuttings Riding, Leonard Greenwood, Nicholas Asheshov, Robert Rosenhouse, Bernard Diederich, Karen de Young and Filadelfo Martínez.

London, November 1978   E.C.

---

* Literally the three dots [. . .] used in punctuation.

DICTATORS NEVER DIE

Go too close to a dictator and you risk being overwhelmed by ambiguity. Only from a distance can you see the ruthlessness and cynicism, the greed and amorality, the supreme disdain for the many who have suffered deprivation and degradation for his sake. This black and white picture, however, is true in the sense that a caricature is true and false only inasmuch as it fails to register the fact that no man, no situation, is wholly bad all the time.

These thoughts stuck in my mind after I had met Anastasio Somoza Debayle, 'Tachito', General and President, third ruler of Nicaragua in a family that had wielded power since 1936. I had arrived in the capital, Managua, in mid-1975, only six months after a group of urban guerrillas, the Frente Sandinista de Liberación Nacional, had shocked the city by bursting into a reception and holding hostage seventeen of the régime's most prominent figures, including the President's brother-in-law and his cousin. On that fateful December 27th, Somoza had had to swallow his pride, pay ransom for the captives and let the guerrillas fly out, scot-free, to Havana. This insolent challenge to the régime's authority threw Tachito into a rage and the affluent of Managua into a panic, neither of which had abated by the time of my arrival.

Repression had been severe and was reportedly continuing. Even worse, the whole of Central America was alive with rumours that the police investigation was linking many of the younger set of Nicaragua's bourgeoisie with guerrilla activities. The story had been leaked of how the *sandinistas* had tried to coax Bianca Jagger (the local girl who became an international celebrity when she married the pop star Mick Jagger) into making the December 27th raid even more of a sensation by getting herself invited to the party and allowing herself to be held for ransom with the rest of the company. Bianca Jagger refused, but the significance of the episode lay in the implication that someone had been assuming that she *might* have agreed. The theme of 'the enemy within the gates' had become one of the favourite morsels of Managua gossip, and at least one rich family was keeping one of its younger members on an extended European 'vacation' to avoid arrest on a charge of collaboration with the Frente Sandinista.

With this 'December 27th psychosis' heavy in the air, I had expected to walk straight into a country with all the overt trappings of a police state. In the consommé-like atmosphere of Las Mercedes airport, however, control was cursory, as if unworthy of any great effort; uniforms and armed guards there were, but hardly as ubiquitous or as bothersome as in most other Latin American capitals.

After the devasting earthquake of 1972, the site of downtown Managua was little more than an incongruous plain : block after flattened block overgrown with recent vegetation, it could have looked like the first stage of some new urban development had it not been for the ruinous hulks of the Palacio Nacional, the twin-towered Cathedral, the Post Office, and the two incredibly intact survivors of the quake, the towering Bank of America building and the grotesque bunker which housed the Rubén Darío National Theatre. The people of Managua no longer lived there. The many had migrated to León or Granada, or were resettled 'provisionally' in makeshift peripheral *barrios*. The few remained in their residential districts and country houses on the outskirts, where it was hard to detect any sign of the earthquake, but only too easy to spot the scars left by the December 27th scare.

As if re-enacting a second-rate American film set in a typical banana republic, armed guards dozed in the doorways of chalets and mansions, some toting rifles, a few with machine guns, many with revolvers or pistols. Under many a paunchy *guayabera* shirt, or hidden in glove compartments, loaded guns had become the permanent companions of the well-to-do.

In this situation, it came as something of a surprise that no-one should have even tried to interfere with my meeting Pedro Joaquín Chamorro, the gadfly editor of *La Prensa* who was the Somozas' noisiest public adversary. Nor did it seem to fit into the picture that Ernesto Cardenal, poet and revolutionary priest, an outspoken left-wing critic of the régime, should move freely between his commune on the island of Solentiname and the capital city, where he frequently addressed the students at the University.

Among Tachito's followers, friends and relatives I found frank admissions that the situation in Nicaragua was indeed rather irregular and unlike that in other countries. 'Somoza runs this place as if it were his own *finca*,' was something I would hear them say again and again. But there also seemed to be a deep respect and admiration for the President. All agreed that I would meet an intelligent, astute statesman, fully capable of 'wrapping anyone around his little finger'. There was candour and naïvety in abundance too, as was well illustrated by Somoza's eighty-year-old aunt, Margarita Debayle de Pallais (who, seventy-two years earlier, had been the little girl for whom Nicaragua's greatest poet, Rubén Darío, wrote *Margarita, está linda la mar*), when she told me,

'Tachito doesn't steal. His father did, but not this one.'

My interview with the President had been set for 12.30. Predictably, I had to spend at least half an hour cooling my heels in a waiting room packed with high government officials wielding reports and with people who had come to make petitions. The security precautions were certainly visible, but they were far from obtrusive. True, Somoza's new, bunker-like office, hurriedly set up after the great earthquake, was right in the heart of a military zone, next to the hideous, pyramid-shaped Intercontinental Hotel. But it is undeniable that approaching Somoza was far easier than, say, entering the Casa Rosada in Buenos Aires or the Edificio Diego Portales in Santiago de Chile.

When I was finally ushered into Tachito's office I found him in the classic pose of the busy executive, poring over sheaves of official documents. After pointedly ignoring me for a long time, he looked up, rose and greeted me icily . . . then, almost in the same breath, told his secretary to have his car ready to take him to lunch as soon as I had left. It could not have been made clearer that he expected only a brief conversation.

He eased himself back behind his desk, a signal that distance and formality were to be preserved. This tall, flashy, well-groomed man with his hair slicked back, eyes peering warily through thick-rimmed glasses and a very professional, polite half-smile fixed on his face, looked more like a prosperous physician than an autocrat of the tropics. Indeed my first impression of him was even more incongruously domestic : he looked so much like Carlos D'Agostino, one of Argentina's most popular TV compères, whose best-known programme was a lachrymose version of 'This is your Life'.

The conversation did not start to flow until a subject had arisen which gave Tachito something to boast about. He liked to think of himself as the man who shaped international politics in Central America, as the inaugurator of a period of 'direct diplomacy' between the Heads of State themselves. The theme that got him started was an anecdote I had picked up from a close relative : how, with a phone in each hand, Tachito had cursed and cajoled the Presidents of El Salvador and Honduras into stopping the 'football war' of 1969. The memory of this episode brought forth a satisfied chuckle and an outpouring of platitudes on the subject of international relations. But as the initial frost vanished, there appeared no sign of the cunning politician that his friends and relatives had portrayed : his conversation was careless and clumsy, his ideas barely connected, and tact was entirely absent.

'Mr President, a few days ago in Panama, General Torrijos told me that if you keep up this "direct diplomacy" business much longer, your Foreign Ministers will soon become obsolete. Would you go along with that?'

'Yes. But after the Heads of State reach an agreement, someone has to do the carpentry. That is what you need the Foreign Ministers for—for the carpentry.'

He evinced as little interest in being truthful as in being tactful. Indeed he seemed unable to resist the temptation to make wildly improbable claims about his achievements in every field of activity we mentioned. Thus he had managed to *eliminate* the critically high dropout rate in Nicaraguan schools (when far more literate Latin American nations would even be satisfied with checking its growth); for the past seven years he had based all of Nicaragua's development on *agrarian reform* (in a country in which two-thirds of a predominantly rural population are still landless, and Somoza himself is one of the biggest landholders); his own and his family's huge economic interests did not in the least affect his attitude in the conduct of public affairs.

Nicaraguan folklore has made a legendary hero out of 'Nachón' Gago, the notorious nineteenth-century liar from Masaya, who told the most unbelievable tall stories, and always ended them with a plea to his listener : 'Do believe me, *pipe*, because if you don't, I shall be condemned.' Tachito Somoza makes no such plea to his audiences, nor does he insist on people believing what he says. He simply asserts, following the tradition set by the Cuban dictator Fulgencio Batista, as if the very time of day were whatever he wished it to be (it is facetiously held in Managua that this became literally true after the 1972 earthquake, when clocks were set by decree to 'Somoza time' in a bid to save energy). A chorus has always been standing by to echo every pronouncement he makes. It is true that when they met privately and lowered their guards, his collaborators, friends and relatives would sometimes concede that certain things 'were not perfect'. But even when they did so, they had on hand dozens of justifications for these 'minor imperfections' : after all, they would say, the country is peaceful, it is progressing, there are opportunities galore, deep down inside Tachito means well, any other alternative would be worse, there is really no other way of running this sort of country. In public, the acolytes' style is unrestrained. Tachito, immaculate in his populist *guayabera*, becomes 'the most authentic leader Nicaragua has ever had', each one of his acts is 'historic', he is proclaimed 'hero', 'standard-bearer of national dignity', even

'Liberator'—one with Simón Bolívar and José de San Martín.

'This is a truly unparalleled case of corruption,' said Pedro Joaquín Chamorro as he poured out the umpteenth whisky. Four generations of Chamorro involvement in Nicaraguan politics looked down from the walls of his study: documents signed by his great-grandfather Fruto Chamorro, founder of the Conservative party and first President of the country; a huge 'Proclamation of War', one of the many issued by General Emiliano Chamorro, Nicaraguan conservatism's perennial revolutionary; old copies of *La Prensa*, the newspaper founded in 1926 by Pedro Joaquín's father and whose editorship Pedro Joaquín had inherited in 1952.

This tall man, peaceful-looking behind his horn-rimmed glasses, had been fighting the Somoza dynasty since the age of nineteen; on several occasions he had been forced to flee into exile, and at least five times had been flung into Somoza's prisons. In true Chamorro tradition, however, he had always managed to return to the fray. At the time of our conversation Chamorro was engaged in the floating of UDEL, a 'third party' which hoped to agglutinate opposition to the régime.

'Somoza likes to cast me in the role of the reactionary, right-wing Conservative who is battling for the restoration of lost privileges,' said Chamorro, 'but I have never been a Conservative in the strict sense of the word. The problem is that in Nicaragua the name Chamorro and the title "Conservative" have almost become synonymous. But it makes no sense to be a Conservative in this day and age.' Chamorro preferred to describe himself as a 'social Christian', and had adopted a political language which lay somewhere between John F. Kennedy and Pope John XXIII.

Energetic as his anti-Somoza efforts were, he did not sound too optimistic about the prospects of his new political alliance, or indeed about his own chances of success. He had already stated publicly 'Somoza is out to get me,' and now he added, 'It is an easy matter for anyone to kill me. I have no bodyguards, and I drive around alone and unarmed.' The way things were evolving in Nicaragua, he felt, the country would soon split into two bands, 'armed *sandinistas* and armed *somocistas*'.

Sitting at his desk, surrounded by electronic security devices, fiddling with the pile of pictures of himself he keeps handy to autograph for his visitors, Tachito was not getting any friendlier as I attempted to steer the conversation towards the December 27th guerrilla coup. I pointed out a brand-new book lying on a shelf behind him. A garish dust-jacket proclaimed the title as *Terror and Urban Guerrillas.*

'Ahhh! Just a little present from some friends . . .'

'General, everybody here seems to be suffering from this *December 27th psychosis . . .*'

'That's hardly surprising!'

'Is the guerrilla organisation any larger than what surfaced on December 27th?'

'Yes, that is what our investigations have proved.'

'And what about its political significance?'

'None whatsoever! This is a small group of youngsters who have been indoctrinated . . . I could do exactly the same to Castro. I could do it in the Soviet Union, if I were willing to spend the money, to seek out the dissidents and so on. But I know that they will die. There is more than crust to this little pie.'

Tachito rejected out of hand Chamorro's estimate that about two-thirds of Nicaragua's university students were Marxists, as well as the suggestion that the *sandinistas* were attracting the younger members of the bourgeoisie to their ranks. The only 'middle-class' guerrillas he had spotted, said the President, came from broken homes, or were 'illegitimate children rejected by the Church'. A couple of days earlier, a friend of Tachito had told me : 'Nobody here can trust his own sons, or even his daughters.' I mentioned it to Somoza.

'Yes,' he replied. 'Ha, ha. Well, uh . . . that is where the reign of terror begins.'

Reign of terror it was. Repression was unusually harsh and vindictive. Scores of people were arrested and indicted for 'crimes against internal security', hundreds more were taken away to detention centres in the departments of Zelaya and Matagalpa, never to be seen again, and there were a number of cold-blooded massacres in rural areas (including the annihilation of everyone living in the hamlet of Varilla).

On three occasions in the following three years, when successive leaders of the Frente Sandinista were killed by the Guardia Nacional, subversion was pronounced to be dead in Nicaragua. Yet each time it reared its head again, apparently strengthened by the blows it had received. By the end of that three-year period, the *sandinistas* were no longer alone in openly challenging Somoza's authority. 'Traditional' politicians, including Tachito's Conservative allies, had granted the Frente Sandinista recognition as a peer. The Church publicly denounced the injustices of the Somoza régime and called on Tachito to resign. Even the Somoza dynasty's staunchest ally and supporter, the United States, turned its back on the strongman.

Managua in 1978 is not the same place I visited in 1975. Pedro Joaquín Chamorro is dead, killed as he himself had forecast, as he was driving alone in his car. Ernesto Cardenal no longer commutes between Solentiname and the University; his island commune was overrun by the Guardia Nacional and he is in exile. As Tachito had announced, many of the December 27th raiders have indeed died.

Somoza, however, is still in power. But he is no longer the plump, confident man of earlier times; his face shows the ravages of a heart condition which almost killed him in 1977. He also survived a general strike and considerable international pressure in early 1978 and a series of pitched battles in the autumn. But hanging on to the Presidency is becoming an uphill task : the opposition shows no sign of weakening and is indeed spreading to the ranks of Somoza's own party and to the officer corps of the Guardia Nacional. A series of purges has thus far averted the possibility of a coup from within the régime, but many Nicaraguans feel it is only a matter of time before the men in power decide to cut their losses and jettison Tachito in order to save their own positions.

Tachito's 'formal' term of office expires in 1981, and even if he manages to hold on till then, it is hard to imagine any manoeuvre whereby the Nicaraguans could be persuaded, or even forced into suffering him, in person, or by proxy, any longer. And yet. . . .

We shall briefly go back in time, to September 21st, 1956, when a shot was fired in the crowded Casa del Obrero in the city of León. The target was far too bulky to miss at short range, and the bodyguards, lulled by the heat and the sluggish gaiety of the official reception, were slow to react. By the time they shook off their surprise and gunned down the assailant, the victim, President Anastasio Somoza García, ruler of Nicaragua for twenty years, lay motionless on the floor.

Rigoberto López Pérez was no professional hit-man, nor did he belong to any high-powered and well-trained terrorist group. But he had planned his coup well. He had followed Somoza around from afar, studied his habits, mapped his itinerary. Well in advance he had made out a life insurance policy which, he hoped, would support his mother when he was gone, and had written her a letter announcing : 'Though my comrades disagree, I have decided to try to be the person who will begin the end of this tyranny.' He had posted the letter as he left his exile in San Salvador only ten days before the date chosen for his attempt on Somoza's life. His original purpose had been to shoot the President during a ceremony López Pérez considered most fitting—the anniversary of Nicaragua's victory over William Walker, a nineteenth-century North American adventurer who had usurped the Presidency of the country. López Pérez was under no illusion that he would survive the attempt, but he abandoned that first choice because security was so tight that he did not feel confident of actually hitting his target. The date was moved back a week, to September 21st, 1956, when Somoza was scheduled to announce his 'candidacy' for yet another term of office at an official reception in León, the second-oldest of Nicaragua's cities. In León López Pérez was successful.

The action of this lone assassin, a twenty-six-year-old journalist born 'on the wrong side of the tracks' in León, was acclaimed throughout the continent. At the time, Latin America's liberal intelligentsia was embarked on a holy war against all dictators, a full fifty-six of whom had seized power in different republics since 1947. The powerhouse of this crusade was the Caribbean Legion, an organisation with headquarters in San José, Costa Rica, where the revolutionary régime of José Figueres had taken the unprecedented step of disbanding the armed forces. Among the members of this motley, romantic crowd were personalities of the stature of the Dominican Juan Bosch and the Venezuelans Rómulo Betancourt and Raúl Leoni, all three of whom were to become Presidents of their countries in later years. This 'Democratic International' also included the early survivors of the attack on the Moncada barracks in Havana, and attracted the passing interest of a young Argentine exile, Ernesto Guevara, not yet known to the world as 'Che'. International support for their campaign came from Mexico's governing party, from the pages of the Colombian newspaper *El Tiempo,* and from Juan José Arévalo, the Guatemalan teacher who had become President when Ubico, doyen of Latin America's dictators, was ousted in 1944. The entire hemisphere was on fire with the notion that History itself was speaking, that the end was finally at hand for the paternalistic autocrats in uniform.

It was not simply wild, hopeful idealism—not in the glorious 1950s. It was actually happening : Perón toppled in Argentina, Pérez Jiménez in Venezuela, Rojas Pinilla in Colombia. Even the hardy Dominican *Benefactor,* Rafael Leónidas Trujillo, was blasted into oblivion. And the Cuban Fulgencio Batista was chased into exile by the bearded guerrillas led down from the sierras by Fidel Castro and 'Che' Guevara.

But Anastasio Somoza did not die that day in Rivas. Critically wounded, he was flown to a military hospital in the US-controlled Panama Canal Zone. The man who, of all his peers, looked most like a fictional prototype of the Latin American dictator seemed bent on enacting one of its most hallucinatory myths : that the Dictator is immortal. He cannot be killed or overthrown; he will not even lie down and die a natural death. Plots against him may be hatched and nurtured to maturity, public opinion on his home ground and abroad may rise to paroxysms of indignation, peaceful and violent demonstrations may flare up, strikes may paralyse the country, bombs may explode, sabres rattle and armed uprisings become more and more frequent—but the Dictator will survive. He is the master of the eleventh-hour counter-coup, the last-minute reprieve, the most unexpected political *legerdemain*.

This nightmare is deeply embedded in Hispanic tradition on both sides of the Atlantic and fatalistically rejects the evidence of history. Time and again, as in the good old 1950s, it has been proclaimed that the Age of Dictators is at an end. Time and again, facts have seemed to go along with this gospel of deliverance : there really *was* a successful coup which terminated Ubico's thirty-year reign in Guatemala, an unexpected volley of gunfire which tore Trujillo apart, a final gasp through the tangle of plastic tubes which kept Franco classified as a living organism. But popular wisdom has doggedly scorned this sort of proof. There has always remained the sneaking suspicion of a masterly fraud : somehow, it is feared, the Old Man, the eternal Patriarch, will find his way back from the dead, or from exile. Did not an octogenarian Perón return in triumph after an exile of eighteen years? Did not a decrepit Franco rise again and again from his deathbed?

Anastasio Somoza did not find a way back from his hospital bed in Panamá. For Nicaragua, however, it was as if he had done so. When he died on September 29th, 1956, his eldest son Luis was already sitting at the Presidential desk. And a full two decades after Rigoberto López Pérez fired his pistol in Rivas, Nicaragua is still ruled by a Somoza, the third in a dynasty hardly touched by the 'winds of change' that have swept the continent for forty years.

CHAPTER I

THE EMERALD COLONY

Seen from far above, Nicaragua looks like a slipped disc in the mountainous backbone of the Americas. But that is no more than an optical illusion for U-2 pilots or astronauts : the country started out, long before the ocean poured into the Gulf of Mexico, as a kink in the sweeping arc of rock that dips into the Caribbean and emerges here and there in the Antilles. It was the southernmost vertebra of North America, from which in the course of several thousands of years a thin hammock of land was to be slung, the other end hanging precariously from the huge mass of South America. An uneasy link still swaying and rocking with every heave of the continents, often torn apart by earthquakes and moulded anew by outflows of lava.

The mountains troop down from Honduras, cutting close to the Pacific, scarcely allowing room for a narrow plain and the string of volcanos that stretches southward, past the lake once called Xolotlán and on to the island perch of Ometepe in the inland sea known centuries ago as Cocibolca. The higher mountains stop short of this point and swerve away toward the Caribbean, descending into steamy, luxuriant lowlands streaked by erratic rivers. Cocibolca, the third largest lake in Latin America, was renamed Lake Nicaragua by the Spaniards. Before anyone had given it any name at all it had been a gulf on the Pacific, and when a convulsion of the isthmus closed it in, it also entrapped sharks, swordfish and seahorses, forcing them to choose between extinction and a painful adaptation to freshwater life. They survived. A river, the San Juan, found its way from Lake Nicaragua to the Caribbean, a natural route for future vessels wishing to sail to within a few miles of the Pacific.

It is an impermanent geography, given to unforeseeable antics; deadly, but also bountiful. It has cool hillsides and sweltering plains covered in cedar and pockwood, mahogany and laurel, rosewood and ebony, granadilla and logwood, God-tree and arbutus, oak and gigantic guanacaste, persimmon and calabash, mangrove and almond-tree, sweet-gum and purple-heart, tamarind and indigo, cochineal-bearing nopal and coconut palm, coyol and corozo, agave and cabrilla—and maize. Below, above and between them move monkeys, jaguars and ocelots, boas and rattlesnakes, macaws, toucans and loriots, pelicans and herons, storks and cranes, peccaries, deer, coyotes, pumas. And, at some point in time, man.

10

Mariano Picón-Salas, the Venezuelan essayist, writes of the feeling of *strangeness* which overcame the first Spaniards who wrote about the America they found. 'Not ever in the most colourful of the histories told by Herodotus, confined as they were to the narrow causeways of the classical world,' he claims, 'could the tale have been told of such an ambitious experience, such an extraordinary convergence of differing elements—that mixture of marvel and panic which drove Bernal Díaz to say, next to the walls of Tenochtitlán, "that it resembled those enchanted things they tell about in the Book of Amadís".' This feeling of strangeness, akin both to philosophical awe and simple bewilderment, surely did not affect the Spaniards alone. Time and again before them it must have struck the many nations and indigenous people who had to cope with the daily surprises of their beautiful but wrathful landscape.

The peopling of present-day Nicaragua took place beyond the boundaries of the best-known pre-Columbian civilizations. Records of the early times are scarce—either they never existed in great quantities or they are still waiting to be found, or decoded. In their absence, piecing together the mosaic of archaeological and linguistic remains is an excruciatingly slow task. Nothing much can be said about the time, perhaps four thousand years ago, when an ancestor of the Nicaraguans stepped across the soft soil of Acahualinca, leaving behind no more than his fossilized footprints. Nor about the later days, when other inhabitants of this land sculpted large rocks into lifesize figures of men bearing alligators on their backs, then vanished without a trace.

Even in the relatively short period for which records are available, the history of Nicaragua is mainly confined to the slender strip of land that separates Lakes Managua and Nicaragua from the Pacific, and the avenues linking this isthmus-within-an-isthmus to the rest of the world. It was on this natural bridge that the first known meeting took place between North and South America, between the Nahua-speaking mountain tribes who built the Aztec commonwealth and the Chibcha-speaking hillsmen from beyond Darién. As far as we can tell, it was on this spot that Nicaragua first became a colony.

The arrival of strangers from the north must have been a wonderful sight for the lakeside dwellers. Out of the shimmering blue came this long column of men bent under the weight of the loads they carried in net bags, preceded by a regal personage in a multicoloured feather cape, and a small escort of soldiers clad in quilted armour, bearing circular, leather-covered shields and menacing short swords with obsidian blades, said to be sharp enough to sever a human head with one blow.

It was the first time the foreigners had been seen in these parts, but the lakeside people were in no doubt about their identity. Their fame, inflated to mythical proportions in the marketplace gossip of many lands, had arrived long before them. They were Tenochas, or Aztecs, members of the most fearsome war-machine the continent had ever known.

Yet the northerners were not greeted with hostility, or with fear. The presence of that long train of human carriers made it quite clear that this was not the usual military embassy of the Aztecs, which always heralded the establishment of yet another tributary state of Tenochtitlán. The group's lordly leader was a Pochteca, a member of the privileged caste of merchant-princes whose mission it was to satisfy their wealthy capital's increasing demand for exotic luxuries. Not, however, through conquest and plunder : in exchange for their acquisitions the Pochtecatl delivered the finely-crafted manufactures of Mexico.

The Pochteca who arrived in Cocibolca was not just passing through. Even before he had started assembling his caravan in the Aztec capital, scouts had been there and beyond, studying the lay of the land. The place we now call the isthmus of Rivas was the site they had chosen to establish the commonwealth's southernmost trading post. This hot, humid, low-lying locality had not been picked for comfort, or for its own natural riches. The one product for which the merchant-prince had ventured so far came from even more distant lands. No, the primary considerations were strategic : it was quite evident that the Aztecs could not march any further south without running the risk of being cut off from the 'safe' regions where Tenochtitlán's might was feared; where instant, savage reprisal could be meted out to anyone daring to interfere with the sacred activity of trade.

As it was, the route to the south had already been overstretched beyond both the comfort of Aztec roads and the vigilance of the outer garrison-towns. It had woven its way from southern Mexico along the Pacific seabord, bypassing the territories once controlled by the Maya as well as the homelands of countless unknown tribes on the Caribbean side of the isthmus. What had brought the Pochteca all that long way from home was the lure of the emeralds which had found their way through the complex network of marketplaces to the Mexican capital, where their beauty had captivated warrior-lords and nobles. The guild of Pochtecatl had lost no time in tracing their origin, and their search had led them down, past Yucatán, into the isthmus and even beyond.

In those days, the only known source of emeralds was Muzo, in the highlands of Colombia, well inside Chibcha country. Nicaragua was as far south as the Pochtecatl were willing to go, but it was good enough, since Chibcha traders often brought the gems down from the hills, across the Darién and into Panamá, in their own quest for goods in exchange.

That first anonymous Pochteca to arrive in Nicaragua followed usual Aztec colonial policy. He began to negotiate immediately with a local chieftain, offering him the support of Aztec military technology and training (easily translatable into dominance over neighbouring tribes) and constant access to the manufactures of Tenochtitlán. In exchange, he asked only for a secure marketplace. Awesome as the sharp blades of the Aztec swords may have been, it could not have escaped the lakeside Nicaraguans that the trade mission's military accompaniment was more of a bluff than a threat. But it was a bluff they did not wish to call—the bargain was altogether too good.

Over the following few years, life for the lakeside Niquiranos was to undergo a momentous change. They learnt to speak a broken version of the Aztecs' Nahuatl, to fight as the Aztecs did, even to ape their manner of dress. As increasing amounts of emeralds passed northwards for the Aztec lapidaries to labour into exquisite patterns, more and more goods became available for barter, and much of the hardship was removed from mere subsistence in Cocibolca.

The exact date when the Aztec trading colony was established in Nicaragua is not known; the Aztecs themselves are rather hazy about their chronology. Their records state that commerce in Tenochtitlán began in the year 1504, but it is almost impossible to take this as the literal truth. It was in 1503 that Moctecuzoma Xocoyotsin (Montezuma II) was elected Chief Speaker in Mexico. One of his first reported acts on that occasion was 'to pierce the gristle of his nostrils, hanging thereat a rich emerald' from his own impressive collection. Quite clearly, the far-reaching traffic in these gems, one of the later developments of Aztec trade, had already started by then. And by then, too, Christopher Columbus had recorded his first sighting of Nicaragua's eastern coast, adding it to the targets of the Spanish *conquista*.

But a full decade and a half of Moctecuzoma's ministry was to pass placidly before the Niquiranos heard anything but wild rumours about this last development. True enough, strange goings-

on in the Caribbean were reported, but hopelessly mixed up with
a lot of mystical gabble about predictions of the return of a long-
departed Aztec god, Quetzalcoatl. During those years it was business as usual in Nicaragua. When the first hint of trouble came,
in 1518, it was to be followed almost instantly by disaster. No
sooner had the Niquiranos heard on the commercial grapevine
that some fantastic strangers had come out of the sea and into
Mexico, than couriers were turning up at Cocibolca to announce
that the caravans from Tenochtitlán would not be arriving on
schedule. The tributary states, they said, were in revolt; the Aztec
garrisons had fled back to the capital and the southern trade route
had been interrupted. Almost overnight Nicaragua was left without the flow of supplies from the north upon which it had grown
so dependent, and without purchasers for the gemstones and other
goods that poured in from the south.

Then, before the Niquiranos had had time to adjust to this
calamity, problems arose from the other direction. Again without
warning, as suddenly as the earthquakes which often ploughed
through the isthmus, the traders from the Chibcha country stopped
coming : they too had clashed with the white-skinned centaurs
who arrived from the sea.

The lakeside dwellers still held sway over their neighbours, but
the purpose of their overlordship was gone. Gone were the supporters of their new life-style, the colonial masters under whose
loose reins they had adopted a new language and new customs.
Gone also was the prosperity of the last few decades. All that
remained was bewilderment at being left alone, a colony abandoned without a word of farewell.

CHAPTER II

FROM HERNAN CORTES TO
HENRY MORGAN

The forsaken Niquirano colony was not to remain alone for long. Up in Mexico, the victorious Spanish conqueror Hernán Cortés was soon casting his eyes towards the south. One of Mexico's treasures had caught his fancy. Like Moctecuzoma before him, he had fallen in love with the magnificence of America's emeralds. His collection became famous on both sides of the Atlantic, and so fond was Cortés of his sparkling green stones that he is said to have risked the Spanish Queen's displeasure by refusing to part with some pieces coveted by the monarch. His fiancée, Juana de Zúñiga, was presented with several of these fabulous gems during his courtship, 'one in the form of a rose, one like a fish, one like a trumpet, one like a cup'.

Eagerly Cortés sought the source of the Aztec emeralds, but the only information he managed to prise out of the Mexicans was that they came from somewhere 'down south'. The captains Cortés sent out into the isthmus were given strict orders to report whatever news about the emeralds they should happen to stumble across. They marched through Guatemala and El Salvador. They reached Honduras. New lands they found, tribe after tribe they conquered. But they found no emeralds. What they did run into, to their great astonishment, was another group of Spaniards, charging up the isthmus and poaching on 'their' villages and Indians as they came. Surprised as they were, Cortés' men had enough of their wits about them to swoop on the intruders and arrest them.

Far more than straightforward looting, landgrabbing was the name of the *conquistadores'* game. Claiming new territories for the Crown also meant receiving 'in custody' the natives who inhabited them, ostensibly to coax their souls away from paganism, but practically as a plentiful source of unpaid labour. And Hernán Cortés was not the only landgrabber abroad. Pedrarias de Avila had landed in the Darién and set up his headquarters in Panamá, commanding the land route to the South Sea. Then he had started spreading his domains towards the north and west, into Veragua, into Costa Rica, along the southern shore of the isthmus. Apart from land and riches, he was searching, as were all Spanish explorers, for *the straits*; the passageway between the oceans. In 1522 Pedrarias ordered one of his captains, Gil González Dávila, further up into the isthmus. On his arrival at Cocibolca, after proving Spanish superiority in battle, González had been well received by the Niquiranos, whose headman embraced Christianity with the same alacrity shown by his forebears in the adoption of Aztec customs and beliefs. Once again the Niquiranos were in business as the middlemen of the colonization, and their warriors soon set out to convert their neighbours to the cause of their new overlords.

Enthused by González's first reports, Pedrarias despatched captain Francisco Hernández de Córdoba with a host of riders and cross-bowmen to settle this promising territory of the Nicarao, or Niquiranos—Nicaragua, as it was always to be known thereafter. Close to where the Aztecs had established their trading post, Hernández founded the city of Granada. Further north, passing lake Managua into the highlands, he planted the foundation stake of León. 'Modern' Nicaragua was being called into being. As he traversed the valleys and hills of western Nicaragua, collecting the left-over baubles of Aztec commerce and carefully counting the numbers of aborigines and leagues of land just waiting to be ruled, Hernández hatched the first Nicaraguan *coup d'état*. Instead of reporting back to Pedrarias in Panamá, he ordered his lieutenant Pedro de Garro to head north to Mexico, to send a message to the King demanding the creation of a new governorship in the land of the Niquiranos.

It was Garro's troop which was intercepted by Cortés' men. The soldier-chronicler Bernal Díaz del Castillo described the scene : 'We took the captive captain, a man called Pedro de Garro, and his soldiers as prisoners, and marched them to Naco. We walked by their side; they brought Indian women from Nicaragua, many of them beautiful, and had native mistresses in their service, and they all had horses. As we were worn and torn from our journeys, and had no Indian women to bake our bread (except a few), our poverty made them look like nobles.' Garro was taken hastily to Cortés. True to form, the conqueror of Mexico lent a sympathetic ear to Garro's story and promised to intercede before the King on behalf of Hernández. As proof of goodwill, he sent one of his own soldiers to Nicaragua with a trainload of ironware, mining tools, clothes, silverware and gold, and a reassuring letter to Don Francisco. Then he privately summoned another of his captains, Luis Marín, and ordered him to prepare a march on Nicaragua so that he might claim the governorship for himself.

Marín dallied far too long. When Cortés' gifts arrived in Nicaragua, not everyone was overjoyed. In fact, a soldier named

Garabito was particularly incensed by this reminder of a past humiliation: as a youth he had been knifed by Cortés in Santo Domingo, in a quarrel over a girl. Garabito and three comrades slipped away at night and galloped to Panamá to warn Pedrarias of the conspiracy. The governor reacted instantly. He had Francisco Hernández de Córdoba arrested, summarily tried him for treason, and ordered his decapitation. The governorship of Nicaragua was officially entrusted to Pedrarias' son-in-law, Rodrigo de Contreras. But peace did not follow. Squabbles and petty rivalries continued for some time before Nicaragua was allowed to settle down to what many historians consider a long, dull, uneventful colonial siesta. Power changed hands all too frequently. From his retirement as a civil servant in Guatemala, Bernal Díaz del Castillo would write in disgust: 'And there have been other governors there, whose names I do not declare; because that is a province with very few Indians and worth less every day, it would be a better thing if it did not have so many governors.'

If the Niquiranos thought that the Spanish conquest meant a restoration of the good old days, events soon made it clear that they had made a sad mistake. The new invaders were not looking for amenable local administrators, nor were they planning to be absentee overlords, like the Aztecs. They had come to stay. And with a vengeance too, as soon as they realized that Nicaragua was not the source of all the finery that had caught their eye in the first encounters with the natives. Once the land was 'pacified', the Niquiranos were disarmed (a couple of attempts at using them as soldiers, especially on the South American campaigns, convinced the Spaniards that they were far too mutinous to be worth the risk). The Niquiranos had done their job: twice in less than a century they had put all their strength into destroying indigenous patterns of life for the sake of friendship with powerful foreigners. Thanks to them, Nicaragua was not to inherit the colourful diversity of dress, tongue and mores one can find, say, in Guatemala. Now they too were deprived of whatever they had thought was their due.

Pedrarias of Panamá won the first jurisdictional skirmish with Cortés, but was swiftly cheated of his victory. One of the Mexican conqueror's most distinguished lieutenants, Pedro de Alvarado, made the mandatory pilgrimage to the court in Madrid and returned with the title of Governor and Captain-General of Guatemala, with the provinces of Nicaragua and León firmly under his control. Alvarado was more often away from his palace than not: trouble-shooting in Honduras, heading an expedition to

wrest at least a piece of fabulous Perú away from Pizarro, organizing an armada to sail to China. Consequently, the government of
his Nicaraguan domains was entrusted to local authorities in León,
who pursued their task practically on their own. One of the few
things in which Alvarado took a personal interest was the opening
of a water route from Granada to the Caribbean, along the San
Juan river. Thus, Granada came to replace the former Aztec
colony as the local seat of trade, a position which, under the strict
rules of Spanish colonial monopoly, implied wielding as much power
as the *politicos* did at León. And having as many ambitions too :
the merchants who set up shop in lakeside Granada expected their
city to replace Panamá, a hope that grew in strength as it became
clear that there was no natural passage between the oceans. Lake
Nicaragua's western bank was just a few miles away from the
Pacific, and the San Juan river linked it to the major Atlantic sea-
routes. For an overland crossing, they argued, this made much
more sense than malarial Panamá. Furthermore, they added, one
could easily build a canal across the Isthmus of Rivas and sail
straight through from one ocean to the other.

It was an exciting notion. Philip II ordered his engineer,
Batista Antonelli, to study the technical aspects of such a canal.
This he did, but Spain was not willing to act upon his recommenda-
tions. The Spaniards' reluctance could be explained, not in the
language of twentieth-century ecologists, but in terms of their
strangely similar respect for the divinely-ordained balance of
nature. In the words of Father José de Acosta : 'Some people have
talked of breaking open this seven-league road and joining one
sea to the other in order to render more comfortable the passage
to Perú, in which more toil and trouble are given by the eighteen
leagues of land between Nombre de Dios and Panamá than by
the two thousand and three hundred leagues of sea. But I hold
this project to be vanity, even though there should be no problem
in carrying it out, and I maintain that no human power will
suffice to topple the strong, impenetrable mount placed by God
between the two seas, of very hard rocks and crags that can with-
stand the fury of both seas. And even if man were able to do this,
it would be just to fear punishment from Heaven for pretending
to modify the works that our Maker, with greatest accord and
providence, ordered in the fabric of this Universe.'

This was no more than a reprieve. Nicaragua's strategic position
had already attracted Aztecs and Spaniards; in years to follow it
would draw the attention of other seekers of power, making the
country the target of one invasion after another.

Once the warlike labours of conquest were over, the Spaniards set themselves to changing the face of Nicaragua. Where previously the Indians had had small, movable cornfields, the new colons established vast *fincas* to graze the animals they had brought from the islands, to cultivate corn and beans and cacao somewhat more regularly. In Nicaragua, most of what they produced was for their own consumption, though cacao, indigo and cochineal were exploited for export. The first ranchers were the soldiers of the *conquista* who had claimed the land, and the Indians on it, as prizes. Dispossessed commoners in their own country, here they became landed gentry and as such were directly represented in the local government they set up at León.

The ranchers also handled most of the local commerce in 'fruits of the land', but Spanish colonial regulations did not allow them to engage in import-export trade. This was reserved to the few people with the right sort of connections back in Spain : the monopolists who were granted the right to supply American provinces with manufactures, to handle the trade between different colonial jurisdictions, and to act as bankers. Just as the plains around León made that city the logical centre for the ranchers, the great lake and the port created by Alvarado made Granada the obvious choice for the merchants.

As Spain rushed inland to consolidate its new empires in Mexico and Perú, and set itself to the task of organizing the mammoth trading fleets which provided a twice-yearly lifeline to the metropolis, it began to ease its grip on the Caribbean islands that had earlier served as stepping-stones to the Americas. Others started moving in. Small settlements began to appear here and there, of individualistic outcasts from France and England who befriended ostracised Indians and runaway slaves, and kept themselves alive mainly by hunting the animals the Spaniards had let run wild. Spanish coastguards would occasionally pounce on them and cast them in irons for trespassing on domains they considered their own by virtue of a Papal bull. Occasionally, too, these eaters of *boucan* —buccaneers—would rally to the call of an impromptu leader and sally forth to capture a well-laden stray Spanish galleon or even plunder one of the small Spanish coastal towns.

Their ranks were swollen by the arrival of enterprising traders who felt that business on the American coasts was profitable enough to risk violating the Spanish ban on dealings with outsiders. Smugglers were welcomed by the creole population, as Spanish mercantilism deprived them of access to cheap manufac-

tures (the story has been told many times of the pennyworth of
American cotton that returned to the Americas in the form of a
two-dollar handkerchief from Ghent), and Spain's lack of footholds
on the West African coast made black slaves a very scarce commodity. The *peninsulares* who handled Spain's monopoly trade, on
the contrary, were violently opposed to any tolerance of such
goings-on, and the local Inquisition officials did not want any
contact at all with heretics. Hence Spain's implacable persecution
of the newcomers. Smugglers, logwood-cutters or *bona fide* buccaneers were treated as potential raiders; inevitably, more and
more of them did become raiders. The Hawkinses and Frobishers
and Drakes, the big names of piracy, appeared on the scene, treat-
ing the Spaniards to the spectacle of a 'friendly' monarch eagerly
snatching up her share of the booty and regaling the pirates with
official appointments and knighthoods. Commercial and religious
repression evolved into political enmity. And then it was war, a
disastrous war that destroyed the best of King Philip's proud
Armada.

The roguish community of Caribbean outcasts soon became
more than the ill-equipped coastguards could handle—a force to be
respected and feared. In their wake followed the flags. A hundred
years after Gil González marched into Nicaragua, England had
acquired its first Antillean colony, on the tiny island of St Kitts.
A few years later, in 1633, a Dutch buccaneer known to his peers
as Blewfields settled on the eastern coast of Nicaragua and struck
the first alliance with local Indians, a new breed, formed by the
mixture of native Ramas and Sumus, warlike Caribs and a sprink-
ling of Africans who had not taken well to slavery. These were the
'Miskito' people, who had carved themselves a homeland out of
the district the Spaniards called Tologalpa : the low-lying, forest-
covered coastal region stretching from present-day Trujillo in
Honduras to the mouth of the San Juan river on the southern
boundary of Nicaragua; the 'Mosquito Coast', in buccaneer par-
lance. Hated by the Spaniards, and hating them in turn, the
Miskito became the eyes, ears and even arms of the buccaneers;
pilots, lookouts, foot soldiers. Their daughters became buccaneers'
mates, adding another bellicose strain to their ethnic composition.
They led the buccaneers to the best hunting grounds, supplied
canoes for river raids, and perching on the masts guided their ships
through the Caribbean maze of coves and bays to the best places to
ambush unsuspecting Spanish galleons.

Spain tried hard to stem the tide. Edicts were issued banning
the *corsarios luteranos* from landing at any Spanish settlement

or engaging in any sort of commerce with them. Year in, year
out, a game of Antillean hopscotch was played with the buccaneers,
evicting them from one island only to find them reappearing somewhere else. They moved from Española to Tortuga to Old Providence to Curaçao to Jamaica, and back again; and every time
round an island or two would be withdrawn from the game, lost
to Spain forever. Then the buccaneers, to the delight of the English,
turned their attention to the mainland.

In the early 1660s a young man not yet in his thirties, born in
Llanrhymney, Glamorganshire, turned up in Barbados seeking a
place among the sea-raiders. Opportunities there were not quite
up to his expectations, so he moved on to Jamaica. A few minor
forays helped him make a name for himself, and when the buccaneer captains Jackman and Morris started planning a major
assault on the mainland, he was invited to join them. In 1664 they
sailed for the Gulf of Campeche and put ashore near Villa de Mosa.
Their first town fell easily and they pushed on to capture Trujillo,
then into Miskito territory, where they rounded up extra support
for the most important part of their plan : a major drive across
the isthmus to strike at the undefended cities far from the Caribbean. Avoiding contact with the Spaniards whenever they could,
guided by their Miskito friends through forest and river, in a
matter of days they were poised on Lake Nicaragua for a swoop
on Granada. There was not much of a battle : the buccaneers
rushed in and swiftly but thoroughly looted the warehouses, the
cathedral, all seven churches, even the colleges and monasteries.
Their return to Jamaica, aided by Miskito stealth and rapid down-
stream currents, was virtually unimpeded. The young Welshman
now was not only wealthier; his prowess on the Nicaraguan raid
had made him someone to be reckoned with. His name began to
be mentioned with respect that would soon turn to awe : it was
Henry Morgan, *el pirata*.

Back in Port Royal, Morgan was invited to become Vice-
Admiral of a fleet which was preparing to set off for the South
Sea, under the orders of Edward Mansvelt, a Dutchman from
Curaçao. The expedition never really got going : sponsors were
scarce and sceptical, provisions were far from sufficient, and the
force was not strong enough to attempt any major town on the
way. But Mansvelt and Morgan were not to be put off. They set
their sights on the island of Santa Catalina, which the Spaniards
had recaptured from Blewfields, the first buccaneer settler of the
Mosquito coast, and had fortified in order to protect their fleets
on the Panamanian and Nicaraguan routes. The Spanish fort was

besieged and taken. A buccaneer called Le Sieur Simon was left in charge, it being Mansvelt and Morgan's intention to convince the governor of Jamaica that it made sense to hold the island as a British possession.

But they had another more immediate prospect on their minds too : the amount of plunder to be obtained on the mainland. Morgan talked Mansvelt into a second raid on Nicaragua, even bolder than the Jackman-Morris invasion of 1664. They recruited Miskito guides and soldiers, then audaciously rowed up the San Juan river in a fleet of canoes, traversed Lake Nicaragua and fell for a second time upon Granada. Loot was not as plentiful as on the previous occasion, but the cost for Granada was higher— before leaving, the buccaneers set fire to the city.

Morgan never returned again to Nicaragua : greater exploits, even a knighthood awaited him elsewhere. But the Spaniards were thrown into a defensive frenzy. Santa Catalina was recaptured, new fortifications were built, garrisons were posted throughout the coastal settlements, patrols on land and sea were multiplied. When the sadistic Jean David Nau, 'L'Olonnais', landed on the Nica-raguan coast in 1667 after sacking Maracaibo, he ran into fierce resistance. The Spaniards pursued him all the way to the Darién, where he was captured and sentenced to a horrible death : first he was dismembered, then pieced together again for burning at the stake. The mouth of the San Juan river was fortified, guns were emplaced fifty miles upstream, and a formidable 'castle' was built further up. At long last, Granada began to feel safe. A couple of decades would come and go in relative peace, allowing Granada and León to resume their struggle for domestic supremacy.

But disaster struck again in 1685. A huge buccaneer force had assembled under the command of de Graaf, Grognier, Townley and other veterans for an assault on Panama. The Spaniards had been waiting for them and repulsed their onslaught. Unwilling to return emptyhanded, the buccaneers retreated northwards and sought out an easier target. They found it in the Costa Rican town of Pueblo Viejo, which they carried with great ease. They then marched inland, sidestepping the chain of fortifications, and attacked Granada. There too opposition was stiff : the battle was long and losses were heavy on both sides. But Granada fell once more. Le Sieur Raveneau de Lussan, a French buccaneer who felt that God had been on their side, led a party of religiously-inclined comrades to the Cathedral to sing a *Te Deum*. Then came the anticlimax. In de Lussan's own words, 'we went to visit the houses, wherein we found nothing but a few goods, and some provisions.'

This was the last time buccaneers would venture anywhere near the major cities of Nicaragua. De Lussan and about three hundred men did visit the country once again a few years later, but they were fleeing an irate Spanish fleet bent on recovering the 20,000 pieces of eight the buccaneers had extorted from Guayaquil, and were in no mood for further plunder. They abandoned their ships on the Pacific coast and fought their way inland to the mountainous Segovias in the north, then sailed on makeshift rafts down the Coco river—the longest in Central America—to the safety of Cape Gracias a Dios on the Mosquito coast.

The Mosquito country had changed a good deal in the twenty-odd years since Henry Morgan had first visited it. Representatives of the British crown had encouraged the establishment of a Miskito kingdom and helped to instal Old Man I on the throne. The Miskito 'prince' who would later become Old Man II was whisked away to England for a proper education under the sponsorship of Charles II. A year before de Lussan's battered survivors passed through the Mosquito coast, Jeremy I had ascended to the throne (or rather descended : he had to be coaxed off a tree to attend his own coronation). This man, with 'an aspect somewhat terrible and a harsh voice like a bear', wore a British major's uniform for the occasion.

Nicargua was in for hard times. Not only were the hated British perched on their eastern coast, but their main commercial life-line to Spain was unexpectedly severed. An earthquake barricaded the lower reaches of the San Juan river with shoals and shallows, and galleons were no longer able to sail all the way to Granada. Maritime trade dropped to a mere trickle. This setback came at the worst possible time. The Dutch experiment in peaceful co-existence through trade had made an impression upon the British; Sir Henry Morgan's 'plunder' party was displaced by the merchant lobby, and British governors in the Caribbean became as repressive as the Spaniards towards the buccaneers. Spain itself had begun to have second thoughts about the rigidity of its commercial setup and was on the verge of a major change of policy.

All over Europe people were looking hard at their new, finally comprehensive maps of the world, and more than a few were casting glances at the narrowest part of the Americas.

CHAPTER III

ENTER HORATIO NELSON :
INDEPENDENT NICARAGUA

By the beginning of the eighteenth century, it seemed that America had managed to drown Spain in gold and silver. Inflation was rampant in the mother-country, industry was in ruins and the old monopolistic system no longer made any sense—Spain had no manufactures available with which to supply the Americas, and cargo tonnage on the colonial routes had dropped to less than that of two centuries earlier. The last, politically inept Habsburg king died in 1700, and the throne of Spain went to the reform-minded Bourbons. Change was soon on its way. The Treaty of Utrecht (1713) granted Britain the right to send one trading ship a year to Spanish America, and a new breed of colonial administrators began to take full advantage of the new opportunities.

Spurred on by their commercial success, British traders began to cut corners : 'secret' fleets of small craft followed the single authorised merchantman on its rounds, replenishing its holds between ports of call. By the time the last Spanish galleon fleet sailed in 1737, there were no markets left for the goods it carried : warehouses were full to the brim with merchandise bought from the British.

This was much further than Spain had planned to go, so a repressive backlash was only to be expected. British ships began to be stopped and searched on the high seas, and often their captains were arrested. When one, Captain Jenkins, claimed that his ear had been ripped off by the savage Spaniards, British traders and politicians had the excuse to force a reluctant government to go to war. For the rest of the eighteenth century war would be a way of life, broken only by three brief, fitful periods of peace. Yet the economies of the Americas—including Nicaragua's—boomed. Spain had authorised the various colonies to trade with each other. A new administrative structure, copied from the French model, placed each province under the authority of an *intendente,* who was especially entrusted, among other things, with assisting economic development. This innovation had an unexpected political side-effect : the awakening of the creoles to the latent possibilities of local economies, and an urge to take the management of their affairs into their own hands. As trade figures shot up to four and five times the previous levels, the conflict of interests between creoles and *peninsulares* became clearer for all to see. The town assemblies, or *cabildos*, became stronger and more outspoken in their criticism of Spanish officialdom. New ideas began to run wild. The seeds of liberalism sown by a couple of Jesuits in Charcas and fed across the Atlantic and back again, the examples of *comuneros* rebelling in Spain and Paraguay, the ideas of Jovellanos, the smuggled tracts of Paine and Rousseau, Adam Smith and Montesquieu, all made for a heady intellectual climate.

As the rift between 'creole' León and 'peninsular' Granada grew wider, thousands of miles away in Paris, an excited Academy of Sciences listened to La Condamine, surveyor of the Amazon, explain how a transoceanic canal could be built in Nicaragua, radically changing patterns of trade (and power) throughout the world. But France was at war at the time, and its intellectuals were left to fret about yet another great opportunity lost. Nicaragua never got around to hearing about the project.

A few years later in Jamaica, a British governor, General Dalling, hatched another scheme which the Nicaraguans came close to never hearing about. Dalling wrote to Lord George Germain, secretary of State for the American department in London, drawing his attention to Lake Nicaragua, 'which for the present may in some degree be looked upon as the inland Gibraltar of Spanish America'.

He emphasised that widespread discontent was reported in the Spanish provinces, and proposed sending in a British force to capture the cities of Granada and León and march on to the Pacific, 'thus cutting off all communication between the north and the south'. Germain approved the plan, and on February 3rd, 1780, an expeditionary force sailed from Port Royal. Commanding the convoy was a young captain called Horatio Nelson. On seeing his orders, his curt comment was : 'How it will turn out, God knows.' Subsequent events were to justify Nelson's lack of enthusiasm.

Everything went wrong with the operation. The force first called at Cape Gracias a Dios, on the Mosquito coast, to await reinforcements and pick up some Miskito allies, who were expected to provide river craft and act as guides. When the reinforcements arrived, they proved to be a bunch of tired, weak, fever-wracked men. And the Miskitos were nowhere to be seen—they had fled the English, fearing that they had come to carry them off to Jamaica as slaves. This came as a nasty shock : the British had been led to believe that the Miskitos thought of themselves as loyal subjects of the Crown. (A few years earlier, an emissary had been sent to the Miskito king for the purpose of securing his allegiance. An eyewitness reported that after explaining the advantages of becoming subjects of the Crown, the emissary 'asked them if anyone had any objections; when they said no, he ordered the Union Jack to be raised.') The problem was dealt with in typical Nelson fashion : political finesse was ignored, and what Miskitos were found were coaxed, bribed or pressed into service.

And that was only the beginning. On his arrival at the mouth of the San Juan river, Nelson discovered that none of his Army counterparts knew the exact location of the Spanish fortifications up the river, nor had anyone any experience of river sailing. To make matters worse, it was at once clear that someone had failed to do his homework on local meteorology. They had arrived at the wrong time of the year : it was the end of the dry season, and only a trickle of water meandered across the sandbars and shoals of the estuary, while the banks were covered in thick, foul-smelling mud.

Once again Nelson disregarded his brief, and instead of returning to Jamaica, he decided to lead the expedition upstream. Had it not been for his sailors and the unwilling Miskitos he had dragged along, it is hardly likely that the invading force would have advanced much further. Apart from the legendary quota of indiscipline, Nelson also provided the only moment of comic relief in this tragic story. Some fifty-odd miles from the mouth of the river, the British came across the first Spanish fortification. The Spaniards, amazed at the sight of these lunatics working their way up a nearly dry river, retreated cautiously upstream. But the attackers did not know this. Nelson convinced his Army peers that an assault was better than a classic siege, and went on to prove it by leading the attack himself. Sword in hand, he cut a dashing figure as he leapt from the bow of his boat—only to get stuck shin-deep in the mud. In Southey's account, 'he had some difficulty in extricating himself, and lost his shoes : barefooted, however, he advanced, and in his own phrase, boarded the battery.'

The rest is not a military tale, but one of diseases and hostile elements getting the better of men. So much so that the best-known account of this British colonial adventure was the one written by the surgeon-general of Jamaica, Dr Benjamin Moseley, in his *Treatise on Tropical Diseases, and on the Climate of the West Indies*. Snake-bites and the dreaded 'yellow jack' had taken such a heavy toll by the time the troop reached the Castle of San Juan (only sixteen miles further upriver), that the Army commander decided to play safe and lay siege to the bastion. Nelson, seriously ill, was called away before the Castle fell, but those who remained found little to celebrate in their victory. The rainy season had set in, and no medical supplies were forthcoming upstream to meet the needs of a force that was succumbing to 'the fever' at a rate of scores per day. There came a time when there were not enough able-bodied men to bury the dead—who were either thrown into the fast-flowing river or left to the carrion-birds, the sinister *gallinazos*.

Even if they had had the strength to attempt it, the swollen river would still have prevented them from rowing up the San Juan to their ultimate targets on Lake Nicaragua, a mere 32 miles away. The British held the Castle for five long months, battling not against Spain, but against nature. Then they pulled out, leaving behind a skeleton garrison to hand the fort back to the Spaniards. Out of the 1,800 men sent to different posts on this expedition, only 380 returned.

It was not to be Britain's last attempt at offsetting her losses in North America (two similarly ill-fated invasions were to be carried out in the early 1800s, but much further south, in the River Plate), but for the time being, with Spain aiding the rebels in North America, 'tactical retreat' seemed convenient. In 1786, on the understanding that the Miskito kingdom was to be granted a certain degree of autonomy, Britain agreed to withdraw from the Mosquito coast of Nicaragua.

Politicians in Spain had warned against supporting rebellion in Britain's North American colonies. They were convinced that such an attitude would inevitably fan the flames of revolt in their own American provinces. The nightmare of revolution seemed to draw closer when the French overthrew their monarchy, but it was not until an imperial Napoleon marched into Spain that conditions became ripe for an independence movement in Spanish America. It is a common error to identify the liberation movement in the South as no more than an offspring of North American and French liberalism. True, there were liberals in Spanish America, and some of them were as bent on republicanism as their North American and French predecessors. But many other rebels were obeying the purest Spanish tradition of strong local governments reacting first against encroachment by the central authorities, and later against a foreign usurper on the throne.

And there was yet another influential party, not at all liberal or republican, which agreed with the other two only on the issue of rebellion against a French-controlled crown. These were the erstwhile monopolistic traders, the merchants and bankers of the New World who were to become the nucleus of Latin American conservatism. In small Nicaragua, with a mere 180,000 inhabitants at the beginning of the nineteenth century, a broad rule of thumb identified the ranchers with liberalism and the traders with conservatism; applied to the background of traditional inter-city rivalry, this made León liberal and Granada conservative.

But the first uprising in Nicaragua did not take place in either of these major cities; it was the tiny village of Rivas, on the narrow causeway between Lake Nicaragua and the Pacific, which rose in arms in 1811. Repression was swift and cruel; troops from Costa Rica were ordered in by the captain-general of Guatemala, José Bustamante y Guerra, and the dissidents were wiped out in a brutal manner, clearly intended to be exemplary. Yet the lesson was not taken. Before the year was out, Colonel Miguel Lacayo led another revolt in Granada. The captain-general reacted even more violently than before, putting down the rebellion and imposing a seven-year-long reign of fear known as *el terror Bustamante,* during which Nicaraguans were deprived even of Spain's half-hearted liberal reforms of 1812. The brunt of the punishment was borne by Granada, as León had seemed to remain staunchly loyal to the crown.

The ranchers' city leapt to life in 1821, when the captaincy-general of Guatemala declared itself (and all its provinces) independent of Spain. In a matter of days, León declared itself independent of Guatemala, while Granada remained within the fold. Times were turbulent; as soon as positions had been adopted, change was under way. In 1822 both Granada and León accepted union with Mexico, but continued to vie for supremacy in their own part of the world. A year later, when the union broke up, Granada proclaimed the establishment of a republic and managed to hold its own against a 1,000-man army sent by León to bring it to heel.

Immersed as they were in their domestic squabbles, Nicaraguans were hardly aware of the much larger power struggle taking place beyond their borders. Britain feared that the French takeover of Spain would lead, sooner or later, to a French invasion of Spanish America. George Canning, the Prime Minister, was fearful too lest the United States might be tempted to move in as Spain lost its grip on its American provinces. On the diplomatic front, secret British efforts had been afoot for some time, aiming not only at 'calling the New World into being in order to redress the balance of the old', as Canning put it, but also at dividing and fragmenting the new Spanish-speaking republics so that the new balance would not be upset by the appearance of another, U.S.-type power on the other side of the Atlantic.

With his forces hopelessly tied up in Europe, Canning

approached the U.S. with a proposal for a common Latin American policy. John Quincy Adams, President Monroe's Secretary of State, was not convinced. In his view, Canning was asking the Americans to make a substantial promise, probably an inconvenient one (he was toying already with the idea of annexing Texas and Cuba to the Union), in return for which they would get nothing. Adams's reply was a policy statement which came to be known as the 'Monroe doctrine' : the U.S. would not intervene in European affairs; would respect the existing colonies or dependencies of any European power; could not admit that the recognised republics be considered 'as subjects to future colonisation by any European power'; and could not view 'any interposition [in those republics] for the purpose of oppressing them or controlling their destiny by any European Power in any other light than as a manifestation of an unfriendly disposition towards the United States'.

'America for the Americans' was the motto chosen by Washington to summarise the new policy, but Latin Americans were later to point out that a more precise rendering would have been 'America for the North Americans'. In that year of 1823, however, the U.S. was still far from having the necessary force to back up its high-sounding proclamation. For the better part of the century it was forced to sit back and watch while the British invaded the Malvinas (Falkland) islands; while a French fleet bombarded San Juan de Ulúa; while Admiral Leblanc blockaded the ports of the River Plate; while Spain reconquered Santo Domingo; while Napoleon III established in Mexico the puppet empire of Maximilian of Austria; while Spain blockaded the ports of the Pacific.

Nicaragua was oblivious to all this. In the following nineteen years local violence erupted into major battles at least seventeen times, killing more than one thousand people. Executive authority changed hands eighteen times; the country joined the Central American Federation and left it again. Outside, in the meantime, the two great contenders for Latin American influence were on the move : North Americans crossed the Louisiana border into Mexico, defeated Santa Anna's army and declared the independence of Texas, while nearer home the British superintendent of Belize began to move back into the Mosquito coast, appointing a British resident in Bluefields. The U.S. were expanding at an alarming rate : war with the Mexicans led to the absorption of about half of Mexico's original territory (California, New Mexico, Arizona, Nevada, Utah and part of Colorado). The British were edging in more slowly : in 1847 the territory of the Miskito kings was again granted official British 'protection'.

Far away in France, Louis Napoleon was putting the finishing touches to a project for the construction of an inter-oceanic canal through Nicaragua.

And still local political unrest did not abate. The Conservatives called on allies in El Salvador and Honduras to help them wrest power away from the Liberals in León and set up a new capital in the town of Masaya, near Granada. The Liberals turned to organising revolution. Lawlessness spread across the land, and bandits sprang up everywhere.

The most notorious outlaw of the time was a young man called Bernabé Somoza, widely known as *Siete Pañuelos* (Seven Kerchiefs). Daring, charming but inclined to acts of ferocious cruelty, Somoza was drawn into politics when a British naval squadron captured San Juan, which it renamed Greytown, and sailed up the river to 'show the flag' on Lake Nicaragua. United for a while in face of a common enemy, a party of 130 Nicaraguans was dispatched to evict the British from San Juan, but they were no match for the well-trained, 300-man invading force. Bernabé Somoza (who, according to his critics, 'had nothing else to do') tried to capitalise on anti-British sentiment and organised a *coup d'état,* hoping that he would be able to call on the North Americans to help him rule Nicaragua. The attempt was shortlived, but it set the pattern for several similar ventures in the future, one of which would lead Bernabé Somoza's great nephew, Anastasio Somoza García, to the Presidency and the establishment of a Somoza dynasty which would last for more than forty years.

The outside world had again burst in upon Nicaragua. The British intruders were not to be evicted by local military efforts, but by the growing interests of the U.S. in this part of the world. Gold had been discovered in California, and an enterprising railwayman who had studied his geography, Cornelius Vanderbilt, turned up in Nicaragua to obtain a charter for a new concern he had dreamed up : the Accessory Transit Company. His idea was to avoid the long, dangerous overland trek to California by steaming down to Nicaragua, up the San Juan river, across Lake Nicaragua to where coaches could carry passengers swiftly to a port on the Pacific for re-embarkation on a last, short lap to the Californian coast. Almost simultaneously the State Department ordered its diplomats to start negotiating with the Nicaraguan authorities for exclusive canal rights.

Britain, ever watchful of the 'balance of power', decided that the time had come for some horse-trading. The Clayton-Bulwer treaty was signed in 1850, forbidding either Britain or the U.S. to 'occupy or fortify or colonise or exercise any dominion over Nicaragua, Costa Rica, the Mosquito coast or any part of Central America', or to obtain or maintain *exclusive* control over a canal in the region. The British did not pull out entirely from the Miskito kingdom, and public opinion was, on the whole, hostile to the treaty—after the Mexican conquests, the North Americans were beginning to feel capable of injecting some substance in the 'Monroe doctrine'. And they did not have to wait too long to prove that capability.

In 1851 the Conservative Nicaraguan ruler, Laureano Pineda, resolved to move the capital city to Managua. This sparked off a Liberal revolt, led by General José Trinidad Muñoz. The Liberals were initially successful and succeeded in returning the capital to León, but Pineda appealed for help to the Conservative president of Honduras—and with a Honduran army behind him, Pineda marched on León and crushed the insurrection. Four years later, with another Conservative president in power, the Liberals again rose in arms under Máximo Jerez. The pieces on the Central American political chessboard had changed places in the meantime; there was now a Liberal president in Honduras, and it was not President Fruto Chamorro, but the rebel Jerez who was supported by Honduran arms as he marched on León. His advance was halted before he reached the Conservative stronghold of Granada; Chamorro too had enlisted foreign aid, albeit indirectly, from the Conservative régime in Guatemala. The Guatemalans invaded Honduras; the Hondurans were forced to pull their forces out of Nicaragua; and the revolution was defeated.

The Liberals began to search further afield for a reliable ally. They found him in the United States, seated at the editor's desk at the *Democratic State Journal* in Sacramento. His name was William Walker.

CHAPTER IV

FROM WILLIAM WALKER TO JOSE SANTOS ZELAYA

Aged thirty, William Walker was a man wholly devoted to the southward expansion of the United States. He was born in Nashville, Tennessee, and pursued studies in medicine and law before migrating to San Francisco at the age of twenty-six. Very much the intellectual who felt the need for personal action, he not only wrote about North America's 'Manifest Destiny'—he set out to forge it himself. In 1853 he gathered a band of adventurers and sailed from San Francisco to La Paz, in Mexico. On landing, he declared the territories of Baja California and Sonora an independent republic. Not surprisingly, the Mexicans counter-attacked in force. Walker put up a fight, but with supplies running out fast and no support from home, he was soon defeated and thrown into a Mexican prison. Seven months after setting out on his expedition he was back in the U.S. That was when the Nicaraguan Liberals turned up, offering him land and gold if he would lead an armed band to their aid. Walker did not hesitate.

In May 1855 he sailed for Nicaragua with a party of fifty-eight men, the 'American Phalanx of Immortals'. Seizing one of Vanderbilt's lake steamers, he made for Granada and overran it. Appointing himself commander-in-chief of the Nicaraguan army, he routed the Conservatives and placed a Liberal, Patricio Aivas, in the Presidency. The new régime was recognised immediately by the U.S. A successful Walker was able to rely on reinforcements from the States, and a number of allies with different things on their minds. Two officers of Vanderbilt's Accessory Transit Company, Cornelius Garrison and Charles Morgan, talked him into confiscating the company on the grounds that it was violating its charter. Naturally enough, the company was then handed over to them. Representatives of the Southern states of the U.S. pressed Walker into going even further; they were aiming at the acquisition of yet another slave-trading state for the Union.

Just over a year after his arrival, Walker had himself 'elected' President of Nicaragua. The very day he took office he issued four remarkable decrees : the first one contracting a loan abroad, with the territory of Nicaragua as collateral; the second ordering the confiscation of Nicaraguan landholdings (starting with those of his Conservative adversaries) for delivery to U.S. citizens; the third established English as the official language of the country; and the fourth reinstating slavery.

With the motto 'Five or None', Walker launched his 'Phalanx' to the conquest of the other four Central American republics. The motto was aptly chosen. Costa Rica, supported by the British (who believed the whole thing to be an American manoeuvre) and by an angry Cornelius Vanderbilt, managed to hold Walker at bay. El Salvador, Honduras and Guatemala joined in the fray, and Walker began to lose his battles. It was a ferocious little war, with Walker vowing to make 'every town a tomb and every march a holocaust', and destroying and looting everything whenever he was forced to retreat. Granada was devastated, and so was much of the surrounding countryside. In May 1857, exactly four years after he had embarked upon the invasion, Walker found himself cornered in Rivas, the little town which had witnessed the first battle for Nicaragua's independence. But Walker did not surrender to the Central American allies : he turned in his arms to Commander C. H. Davis of the U.S. Navy, who escorted him safely back to New Orleans, where a hero's welcome awaited him.

The episode had revealed Britain as being still far too active in the region for North American comfort, and apparently still committed to the terms of the 1850 agreement prohibiting the establishment or maintenance of colonies by either power anywhere in Central America. The horse-trading between Washington and London continued, and the British managed to claim another diplomatic victory : the Dallas-Clarendon treaty, which recognised the *status quo* in British Honduras (Belize) and exempted it from the provisions of the Clayton-Bulwer accord.

In Nicaragua, with the Liberals completely discredited by the Walker incident, the government went to the Conservatives. President Tomás Martínez established the capital definitively in Managua and set about creating a strong, stable (but hardly democratic) government. He himself was to wield power for ten years; his Conservative successors for another twenty. Challenges from within and threats from abroad, however, did not disappear overnight. William Walker organised another invasion in November 1857, but was rapidly overcome and yet again shipped back safely to the States. Three years later he made a new attempt, but when he landed on the Honduran coast a British frigate swooped in on him. By this time British patience seems to have worn thin, for Walker was promptly handed over to the Honduran authorities. And the Hondurans pre-empted any repetition of the previous North American interventions by putting him in front of a firing squad.

This was the last overt British intervention in the region. Thereafter an orderly withdrawal began, first with the handing over of
coastal possessions to Honduras, then with the transfer of the Bay
islands, on the condition that they were not to be ceded to any
other power. Finally, an agreement was reached with Tomás
Martínez over the Miskito kingdom. Nicaraguan sovereignty over
the territory was recognised, the kingdom became an autonomous
'Indian reservation', and the Miskito monarchs were demoted to
mere chiefs. The hold over Belize, however, was not relinquished.

A peace of sorts descended at long last on Nicaragua. The Conservatives built the first railroads, got the gold mines working more
regularly, and succeeded in attracting to the country a number of
European immigrants. They also carried out the country's first
agrarian reform : by expanding coffee production and introducing
the banana, they made the plantation system the norm for Nicaraguan agriculture. Huge tracts of land began to be concentrated
in the hands of the few 'legal' landowners (most of whom were,
of course, prominent Conservatives), forcing the Indian and
mestizo peasants off the flatter, more productive terrain and oblig-
ing them to choose between a more precarious subsistence off difficult, poor highlands, or becoming poorly-paid plantation hands,
practically serfs.

The plantation system was growing throughout Central America,
pushed by North American banana growers. In a matter of
decades, giant conglomerates arose in the region. Foremost among
them were the Standard Fruit and Steamship Company, and the
notorious United Fruit Company, later to be known throughout
Latin America as *El Pulpo* ('the Octopus'). U.S. interest in the old
idea of an inter-oceanic canal through Nicaragua was reviving too.
In 1862 the Dickinson-Ayón treaty was signed, granting the U.S.
the right to build a waterway, but—respecting the terms of the
agreement with the British—not an exclusive right. Ten years
later, however, President Ulysses S. Grant was appointing an Inter-
Oceanic Canal Commission and stating : 'I commend an American
canal, on American soil, to the American people.' Though the
Senate in 1884 refused to ratify the Freylinghuysen-Zavala treaty
on canal rights (again for fear of British reaction), that very same
year the Maritime Canal Company of Nicaragua began work on
the construction of the canal. The political implications of the
canal were clear to all concerned. As the U.S. minister to
Nicaragua wrote in 1890, 'The construction of the Nicaragua canal
will secure the domination of the United States over the American
continent, politically as well as commercially. The nation that with

the Nicaraguan government, on a joint agreement, controls Lake Nicaragua, will then control the destiny of the Western Hemisphere.'

Alas for the planners in Washington, these political implications were also quite clear to at least some Nicaraguans. A forty-year-old Liberal from Managua, General José Santos Zelaya, was worried not only about North American expansion (the quest for exclusive canal rights and the growth of companies like United Fruit were, in his view, two arms of the same bearhug threatening Central American sovereignty), but by any kind of foreign presence on Central American soil. Foremost in his mind were the remnants of British colonialism on the Mosquito coast, where people still spoke English, danced Highland reels and kept Union Jacks in their houses. Zelaya also bitterly regretted the break-up of the Central American federation, for he saw the unity of the five republics as the only possible means of resisting outside pressures. His formula for unity was unabashedly partisan : the Conservatives could not be trusted; it was, therefore, a job for the Liberals, *his* Liberals.

Zelaya's first task was to provoke the downfall of the thirty-year-old Conservative régime, *los treinta años* which Nicaraguan Conservatives still recall nostalgically. This he achieved by supporting the ambitions of a dissident Conservative, General Francisco Gutiérrez. Together they ousted President Roberto Sacasa, a member of a traditional merchant family that traced its ancestry back to the first days of the Spanish colony, and replaced him with another Conservative, Salvador Machado. But not for long. Two months later, before Machado had had time to finish organising his government, Zelaya was leading the Liberals in revolution. On July 25th, 1893, he stepped into the Presidency.

Zelaya believed in moving swiftly. By December of that year he had armed 1,600 Honduran Liberal exiles and sent them, backed by 3,000 Nicaraguan soldiers, into Honduras. General Policarpo Bonilla was installed as President there. The first step towards Central American unity had been taken. Then Zelaya turned his attention towards the Mosquito coast. Sensing the threat, the British landed Marines in Bluefields, but Zelaya enlisted the support of the U.S. Secretary of State, Roger Gresham, to force them out. The 'king' of the Miskitos, Robert Henry Clarence, managed to flee to Jamaica with the British consul just before Nicaraguan troops marched unhindered into Bluefields. A Union Jack was stuffed into a cannon and blown to bits. Zelaya may not have known it, but this little incident convinced the

United States that it was now strong enough to enforce the 'Monroe doctrine'.

The Maritime Canal Company of Nicaragua ground its work to a halt, even as Zelaya was publicly thanking the U.S. for its assistance on the Mosquito coast issue. Nicaragua's mood was changing rapidly. Zelaya created the country's first regular army, governed by the *Ordenanza Militar,* and founded the first military academy, the Escuela Politécnica. He expanded the railways, launched new steamship lines on the lake, boosted coffee production, built public schools. But Zelaya was no democrat or model of civic virtues : his leading Conservative opponents were thrown into prison, exiled, or ruined by confiscation of their properties. He ran government operations as if they were private business deals, handed out concessions to his friends, and contracted dozens of irresponsible loans and obligations abroad.

The United States began to find Nicaragua a difficult country to deal with. A commission set up by the U.S. government had come up with a decision favouring the construction of a canal through Nicaragua, and the British had come round finally to signing the Hay-Pauncefoot treaty, which granted to the U.S. the right to build and run a canal under its exclusive control. But Zelaya turned down two successive North American canal proposals, and basked in the anti-American intellectual climate he had fostered. The great Nicaraguan poet Rubén Darío lambasted U.S. imperialism, as did Salvador Mendieta, a Nicaraguan proponent of Central American unity who wrote some of the best analyses of the region's problems at the time.

Not far from Managua, in the tiny village of Niquinohomo, department of Masaya, on May 18th, 1895, a young domestic servant called Margarita Calderón gave birth to a son, whom she called Augusto. His father was Margarita's employer, Gregorio Sandino, a local farmer and businessman. Little could either Don Gregorio or Margarita have suspected that their illegitimate offspring would in time, as one of the leaders of a future Liberal army, become the embodiment of the anti-imperialistic mood which prevailed at the time of his birth. Three years later, in San Marcos, another boy was born. He too would attain prominence in the Liberal party, and would come to embody another of the traits of the Zelaya régime : its autocratic, corrupt and cruel streak. This boy's father was an undistinguished coffee planter; his great-uncle had been the famous bandit-cum-revolutionary of the 1840s, *Siete Pañuelos.* His name was Anastasio Somoza García.

For the Americans there seemed to be no hope of Zelaya being toppled from within. A Conservative uprising was crushed in 1896, and another in 1899, an eventful year in which Zelaya clashed with the Church (he deported a bishop and several lesser clerics) and had himself re-elected as President. In this latter year, some desperate French businessmen turned up in Washington offering to sell their stake in the canal they were trying to build through the northernmost province of Colombia. The Americans, driven almost to despair by Zelaya's refusal to entertain their own canal projects, were interested.

In 1903, when Zelaya was putting down yet another Conservative rebellion, led by Emiliano Chamorro (and an eight-year-old Augusto Calderón had joined the ranks of the Nicaraguan working poor, assisting his mother with the coffee harvest) the U.S. President, Theodore Roosevelt, was busy trying to coax the Colombian government into leasing the strip of territory needed to build the transoceanic canal. When the Colombian Congress refused to acquiesce in his demands, Roosevelt funded an uprising in Panama, urged the revolutionaries on to a proclamation of independence, recognised the new republic and obtained virtually sovereign rights to a coast-to-coast corridor, all in a matter of three weeks. Said Roosevelt: 'The people of the United States and the people of the Isthmus and the rest of mankind will all be better because we dig the Panama Canal and keep order in the neighbourhood. And the politicians and revolutionists at Bogotá are entitled to precisely the amount of sympathy we extend to other inefficient bandits.'

Strong language indeed, but there was more to come. Roosevelt took it upon himself to extend the 'Monroe doctrine' until it read like the charter for a self-appointed continental police force. 'Chronic wrongdoings' he said, 'or an impotence which results in a general loosening of the ties of civilised society, may in America as elsewhere, ultimately require intervention by some civilised nation.' This 'Roosevelt corollary' to the Monroe doctrine was the sign that the United States was embarking upon a new phase of expansion, far wider in scope than the invasion of Mexico a century earlier.

'Speak softly and carry a big stick' was the odd way in which Roosevelt chose to describe his policy. The stick was wielded soon enough : in 1905 the U.S. took over the collection of customs duties in the Dominican Republic (later the Marines would occupy the country and set up a local National Guard, whose commander, Rafael Leónidas Trujillo, would seize power and hold it for thirty years).

The year 1905 was an important one in the life of young Augusto Calderón. He went to live with his father, Don Gregorio, and began to call himself Augusto C. Sandino (later he turned the initial C into César, and later still he switched his names around and styled himself César Augusto Sandino). Zelaya had returned to his plans for imposing his own brand of regional unity upon Central America. Honduras again had a hostile government, and Zelaya again supported an invasion which placed his own candidate, Miguel Dávila, in power there. The Salvadorean government sent troops into Honduras in a half-hearted attempt at stopping Zelaya's advance, and in so doing earned itself the privilege of becoming Zelaya's next target. At this point Roosevelt intervened, summoning the Central American leaders to a conference in Washington. There they agreed to a flimsy truce : Honduras was declared neutral, the governments pledged themselves to refuse recognition to any government which arose from a *coup d'état*, and a Central American court was created to deal with regional disputes.

Though he did tone down his efforts to spread revolution to the neighbouring countries, Zelaya did not buckle under U.S. pressure. Instead he did the one thing that was bound to provoke Washington's ire : he sent emissaries to Britain and Japan to seek finance for an independent inter-oceanic canal project, and negociated a huge loan with the Ethelburga Syndicate of London.

Conservative plans to unseat Zelaya began to circulate, with quite open support from the United States and (in spite of the 1907 Washington treaty) from Guatemala's Conservative president, Estrada Cabrera. In October 1909 Juan J. Estrada, the man Zelaya had appointed as military commander of Bluefields on the Mosquito coast, led 400 armed Conservatives into revolt. Among the leaders of the rebellion were General Emiliano Chamorro (already on his way to becoming Nicaragua's perennial right-wing revolutionary) and a young employee of the U.S.-owned La Luz y Los Angeles Mining Company, Adolfo Díaz. Zelaya immediately ordered a 4,000-strong force to suppress the uprising. Advancing in a pincer movement along the San Juan and Escondido rivers, the government troops easily routed Estrada's men and forced them to flee back to Bluefields. The action seemed to be over.

However, on the pretext of protecting the lives and properties of U.S. citizens in Bluefields, 400 Marines led by Major Smedley Butler entered the city. Under U.S. protection, the insurrection continued. Estrada hired two North American adventurers, Leonard Grace and Lee Roy Cannon, to blow up Zelaya's troopships. This they did, but without inflicting casualties on the troops, and got themselves arrested in the process. Zelaya had the two men summarily tried and executed.

The U.S. Secretary of State, Philander Knox, worked himself up into a hypocritical rage over the incident, expelling the Nicaraguan minister from Washington and calling Zelaya 'a blot on the history of his country'. When the U.S. broke off diplomatic relations, Zelaya decided to cut his losses by resigning and exiling himself to Mexico. Another Liberal, Dr José Madriz, was appointed to succeed him. The U.S., however, refused to recognise the Madriz administration, and fighting was resumed. Once more Estrada's revolutionary force suffered defeat after defeat; once more the rebels retreated to Bluefields. But when Madriz launched a final land and sea assault on the insurgents' stronghold, the U.S. cruiser *Paducah* intercepted his ships and prevented them from either bombarding the town or cutting its supply lines. In desperation, Madriz turned to the British for help, promising to cede the Great Corn Island in exchange for their aid. He was turned down. On August 20th, 1910, José Madriz resigned and General Estrada took over a country with empty coffers, a host of foreign creditors clamouring for payment, and a large number of adversaries who felt they had been cheated of victory by foreign intervention.

CHAPTER V

THE BROWN BROTHERS' REPUBLIC

The President of the United States, William Howard Taft, proceeded swiftly to make Estrada's takeover 'legal'. Thomas Dawson, the man who had just finished 'reorganising' the Dominican Republic's political and financial affairs, was appointed as special agent to work out a programme for Nicaragua. He brought together the various anti-Zelaya factions and engineered the calling of a constituent assembly for the establishment of a coalition government headed by Estrada. The Vice-Presidency was entrusted to Adolfo Díaz, the young former employee of the La Luz y Los Angeles Mining Company. Estrada's cabinet reflected the precarious balance of forces which had in common only their opposition to Zelaya : three centres of power were created, each under a strong contender for the Presidency. The Ministry of War, which implied at least nominal control of the country's armed forces, was entrusted to the ambitious Conservative General Luis Mena; the Interior Ministry, responsible for conducting Nicaragua's internal political affairs, went to José María Moncada, leader of the Liberals who had broken away from Zelaya; and the leadership of the Assembly was held by General Emiliano Chamorro, Conservatism's most revolution-minded *caudillo*. Estrada's power was made even more fragile by the Assembly's stipulation that he would not be allowed to run for office in the 'regular' Presidential elections scheduled for 1912.

But the formal aspects of the solution were sufficient to justify U.S. recognition of the new government, a necessary requisite for the negotiation of an agreement which would put Nicaragua's financial affairs in order. The newly-appointed U.S. minister, Elliot Northcott, arrived in Managua with the outline of such an agreement : a loan would be floated by New York bankers to cancel the country's existing obligations to British and European creditors (the 'financial corollary' to the Monroe doctrine) and to provide the Nicaraguan government with some working capital; the U.S. would appoint a collector of customs, who would act as virtual controller of Nicaraguan finances, setting aside the sums needed to repay this debt and handing over to the local authorities, in monthly instalments, only the agreed budget allocations.

Discussion of this deal gave General Mena his first opportunity to bid for the Presidency. He threatened to veto the agreement unless the U.S. backed the removal of Estrada and his own eleva-

40

tion to presidential office. When his rivals closed ranks against him and Northcott made it clear that U.S. support would not be forthcoming, he reluctantly withdrew his opposition.

On the whole, the arrangement proposed by the U.S. was not at all unacceptable to the powerful of Nicaragua : their own incomes would be only marginally affected, and an increased American presence would help to deter the masses of none-too-satisfied peasants from any violent attempt at following the example of the Mexican revolution. By the early 1900s, coffee had become the driving force of the Nicaraguan economy. It accounted for more than half the country's exports, and was therefore the main source of fiscal revenue (through levies on foreign trade) and of income to finance imports (which were mainly of consumer goods). Not all the coffee planters were big landowners; there were also medium-sized and even quite small coffee plantations. But the big planters were the people who had the necessary links with foreign markets, and they doubled as purchasers and exporters of everybody else's produce, through a long marketing chain that stretched down to the local intermediaries who bought, classified and dried the coffee produced in each area. They also controlled a considerable share of the import trade and the local distribution and sale of consumer goods. Apart from this oligarchy of coffee planters there was a large agricultural sector which produced mainly for domestic consumption, with some small exportable surpluses of bananas, rubber, hides and wood. And there was some industry, often no more than slightly expanded artisan activity, also geared to the domestic market.

The coffee oligarchy, obviously unable to exert any influence on international prices, made sure of their profitability by keeping domestic costs as depressed as possible. Thus, they controlled the small trickle of money that wound its way down the coffee marketing chain as profits for the intermediaries and smaller planters, and as wages for the plantation workers. They ultimately controlled the amount of money available for the purchase of any goods sold on the domestic market. Only the few who managed to export other agricultural goods retained some degree of independence from the pervasive power of the big coffee planters. This economy divided Nicaraguan society into two clearly defined orbits : the higher income groups (the coffee oligarchy, some other exporters, the better-off local traders) who had access to the manufactured goods from abroad and developed a quasi-European lifestyle, and the rest of the population, who could at best aspire to a decent share of locally-crafted goods and agricultural produce, and on the whole barely kept themselves above subsistence levels.

The price paid for Juan J. Estrada's rise to power had been an uneasy political truce blessed by a U.S. President who was acting to wipe out the last vestiges of British influence in the region, and the eventual mortgaging of the country to a group of New York bankers. Estrada had accepted coalition as a matter of expediency, and soon set about implementing a strategy which, he hoped, would leave him sole master of the situation. He planned to pick off his foes one by one, slowly and carefully, making sure he did not lose American support in the process. His first move was to suppress the Assembly and drive Emiliano Chamorro into exile. This went off smoothly enough, without evoking any strong reaction from Washington.

Estrada's next target was his Minister of War, the restless General Mena. In order to curtail the General's real power, the President approached the U.S. with a plan to transform the Army into an 'apolitical' force, trained and organised by American military advisers. The scheme, in line with what the U.S. had been doing in the Dominican Republic and Haiti, was well received in Washington, but before it could be activated, the situation in Managua took an unexpected turn. Unknown saboteurs blew up the capital's main arsenal, and the word spread that Zelaya's supporters were preparing an armed uprising. This was a prospect dreaded by Estrada, who immediately placed the country under martial law —a move which gave General Mena, as Minister of War, even more power than before. When the pro-Zelaya rebellion did not materialise, Interior Minister Moncada began to whisper in Estrada's ear that the whole thing was a ruse devised by Mena in order to stage a *coup d'état*. Finally, on the night of May 8th, 1911, after plying the President with drink, Moncada got him to issue an order for Mena's arrest on grounds of conspiracy. That a plot was under way seems hardly debatable; as soon as Mena was detained, his officers in provincial garrisons ordered a march on Managua to secure his release.

Estrada panicked and hurriedly resigned in favour of Vice-President Díaz before going into exile. Mena was reinstated as Minister of War, and the new government was recognised by the U.S. The American President had, in the meantime, run into trouble with the U.S. Senate, which had refused to ratify the financial deal with Nicaragua. Nonplussed, he sidestepped the Senators by signing an executive agreement and appointing a collector-general of customs, thus unofficially providing U.S. government backing for the loan negotiated by the New York bankers.

Yet this was not guarantee enough for the moneymen : before they signed over a loan of $11 million in June 1911, they demanded —and got—a controlling interest in the Nicaraguan National Bank and the State-owned railways as additional security.

The Americans soon turned their attention towards bolstering the power of the Nicaraguan President-by-accident, Adolfo Díaz. Through the local U.S. legation, they offered Díaz a belated reply to Estrada's request for a plan to restructure the Nicaraguan army. Mena predictably opposed the initiative, and Díaz hesitantly accepted it in a watered-down version, applicable only to the Managua police force. Even this was considered too much of a threat by the Minister of War, and when, only a few months later, Greg Scull (a former member of the Rough Riders, the cavalry unit led by Theodore Roosevelt in Cuba during the Spanish-American War of 1898) was appointed Inspector General of the capital's police, Mena engineered a confrontation between police and Army which ended in Scull's resignation and the abandonment of the project. The U.S. minister in Managua, George Weitzel, wrote to his Secretary of State, Philander Knox, that 'police reorganisation, so far as our participation therein is concerned, should not be renewed until political and financial conditions are more decisively settled in Nicaragua.'

Mena was certainly bent on settling these conditions in his favour. He managed to set up a new Assembly with a majority of his own supporters, who promptly elected him President. When the U.S. decided not to recognise the validity of his nomination, he threatened to have the Assembly denounce the loan agreement. This only hardened U.S. opposition, and moved Díaz to allow General Chamorro's return from exile. With Chamorro back on the scene, Mena's influence over the Assembly declined rapidly, and his Army-based power began to lose strength as a result of severe budget cutbacks. At this point he decided that his last opportunity was a direct assault on the Presidency. With a small force of men he marched on the garrison of La Loma, in the heart of Managua, but the officers there, loyal to President Díaz, halted his advance with machine-gun fire.

The U.S. Minister, Weitzel, made an attempt at mediation, offering Mena a safeconduct out of Nicaragua in exchange for his resignation as Minister of War. Mena, who had enlisted the support of the police, replied by cutting off the capital's electricity supply and fleeing to the nearby town of Masaya, where he set up his headquarters. Almost at the same time, the Liberals decided to take advantage of the situation, and a force under General

Benjamín Zeledón moved into action, aiming at a swift takeover of Managua.

President Díaz appealed for American assistance, which was almost instantly given. First a party of sailors landed at Corinto and made its way to the capital, and a few days later they were followed by a full batallion of Marines, whose presence forced General Zeledón to call off the bombardment of Managua and fall back to Masaya (General Mena's followers had in the meantime set up their own main encampment further inland, in Granada). As the Americans built up their forces to a total strength of 2,700 men in Managua, there were differences among them as to the tactics to adopt. Minister Weitzel wanted both rebels, Mena and Zeledón, captured and hanged; Admiral Southerland, commander of the expedition, favoured a more moderate course of action. Mena was offered the opportunity to give up gracefully, and when he refused, the Marines marched on Granada and quickly forced his surrender. The General himself was escorted out of the country. It took a direct order from President Wilson to convince Admiral Southerland that he ought to march against Zeledón in Masaya, and even then the way was left open for the peaceful laying-down of arms. Zeledón, however, was even more stubborn than Mena, and it took an all-out attack by the Marines to rout his entrenched but ill-equipped troops; he himself was pounced upon by a group of pro-government Nicaraguan soldiers as he tried to escape. Relieved at not having any direct responsibility for the outcome, Marine Major Smedley Butler reported to his commander, Admiral Southerland : 'I personally would suggest that through some inaction on our part someone might hang him.' The following morning a government communiqué reported that Benjamín Zeledón had died in battle.

Pax Americana descended upon Nicaragua. The expeditionary force was withdrawn, but a 100-man 'Legation Guard' remained in Managua to discourage any of the rebel factions from attempting to upset the *status quo*. Back in Washington, President Wilson proclaimed : 'We hold that just government rests always upon the consent of the governed, and that there can be no freedom without order based upon law and upon public conscience and approval.' In Managua, all pretence of unrestricted democracy was abandoned, and a Conservative-dominated Assembly dutifully elected Adolfo Díaz President for a four-year term. General Emiliano Chamorro was appointed minister to the United States.

In 1914, the year in which the first ship sailed through the Panama Canal, the U.S. decided to take full advantage of its dominant position in Nicaragua and secure its long-postponed objective of obtaining rights to a canal route through the river San Juan and Lake Nicaragua. A willing Nicaraguan minister helped draft the agreement which came to be known as the Chamorro-Bryan treaty, whereby Nicaragua granted to the U.S., in exchange for US$3 million in gold, exclusive rights *in perpetuity* in such land as was deemed necessary for a trans-isthmian canal, a renewable ninety-nine-year lease on the Great and Little Corn islands, and the right to establish a naval base on the Gulf of Fonseca.

The treaty caused an uproar in Central America. Costa Rica protested that Nicaragua could not dispose freely of the rights to the San Juan river, which forms part of the boundary between the two nations. El Salvador claimed that the establishment of a naval base on the Gulf of Fonseca represented a threat to Salvadorean security. Both governments proceeded to take their case to the Central American Court of Justice, that institution created at Washington's insistence during the troublesome days of Zelaya. The Court returned a verdict in favour of Costa Rica and El Salvador, but Nicaragua and the U.S. both refused to abide by the decision. Times had obviously changed : no longer was there a blanket U.S. refusal to recognise revolutionary governments, and the criteria of international law came a poor second to the dictates of U.S. national interests. In 1916—the year in which the fiery 'anti-*yanqui*' poet Rubén Darío returned to his native land to die and a twenty-one-year-old César Augusto Sandino, still untroubled by political thoughts, got himself a job as a mechanic's assistant on a *finca* near the Costa Rican border (his more affluent contemporary Anastasio Somoza had been packed off to the U.S. for an appropriate education and was now aimlessly doing odd jobs)—the U.S. Senate ratified the Chamorro-Bryan treaty. The three million dollars were paid, but U.S.-appointed commissioners allocated a huge portion of this sum for the repayment of foreign loans before letting a meagre balance find its way to the Nicaraguan treasury.

It came as a surprise to no one when Emiliano Chamorro, with the blessings of the U.S. State Department, was elected President of Nicaragua for the four-year term beginning in 1917. Nor was anyone surprised when the Chamorro administration approved the 'Lansing Plan', perfecting the previous financial arrangements between Nicaragua and the U.S. Under the new scheme, Nicaragua acquired all the trappings of an American protectorate. A High Commission was established in Managua; its members were two Americans (a Resident Commissioner and a representative of the

State Department) and the Nicaraguan Minister of Finance. The Commission took over from the old collector-general of customs the task of handling the country's fiscal revenue. General Chamorro was gracefully conceded a sum of just under 96,000 dollars to cover the expenses of his administration, and the rest was apportioned to Nicaragua's foreign creditors, namely the U.S. bankers who found this Central American country an increasingly attractive credit risk. New York wags soon began to call Nicaragua the 'Brown Brothers' Republic', a reference to the fact that most of the loans forced on Nicaragua by the State Department had been subscribed by Brown Brothers and Seligman, a New York banking corporation.

Under the protective wing of the U.S. 'Legation Guard' stationed in Managua, General Chamorro enjoyed a relatively peaceful four-year term of office. As its end drew near, however, he began to look for ways to overcome the constitutional ban on re-election. The formula he hit upon was not exactly imaginative or subtle : in 1920 he manoeuvred his uncle, Diego Manuel Chamorro, into the Presidency. Hardly anyone in Nicaragua, except the police, paid attention to a brawl which took place at this time in the small town of Niquinohomo. The actors were César Augusto Sandino and another youth, Dagoberto Rivas, who is only remembered because the serious wounds he sustained led Sandino to flee into the long exile that was to turn him into a political man. Accompanied by his cousin Santiago, Sandino escaped to the northern coast of Honduras, where he took employment as a warehouse watchman in one of the mills of the Honduras Sugar and Distilling Company.

Political life in Managua, though considerably less violent than in the preceding years, was as full of plots and counterplots as ever. Within the ruling Conservative party there arose a faction bent on preventing Emiliano Chamorro from returning to power when his uncle's term expired. Prominent among the anti-Chamorro group, but not very hopeful of success, was Vice-President Bartolomé Martínez. It is highly doubtful whether this faction would have stood the slightest chance of succeeding in its bid, had not Diego Manuel Chamorro suddenly died in 1923, a year before elections were due. Bartolomé Martínez stepped up and immediately set about organising a political force capable of matching Chamorro's. Together with willing elements of the opposition Liberal party, he marshalled his dissident Conservatives into a new Conservative Republican Party. Conservative Carlos Solórzano was nominated for the Presidency, and Liberal Juan Bautista Sacasa for the Vice-Presidency. Active in Sacasa's faction of Liberal collaborators was an engaging thirty-eight-year-old rogue who had married his niece, Salvadora Debayle, after drifting around the United States working as an automobile salesman, a toilet inspector and allegedly even as a counterfeiter : Anastasio Somoza García, the descendant of the bandit *Siete Pañuelos*. Tacho Somoza, as he was known to friends and family, claimed that he had been converted to Liberalism in the States. About the same time, that other young Nicaraguan expatriate, César Augusto Sandino, was undergoing a political conversion of his own, albeit a much slower and more anarchic one. He had left Honduras for Guatemala, where he worked for a time on a plantation owned by United Fruit, then moved on to Mexico, where he found employment first with the South Pennsylvania Oil Company, and later with the Huasteca Petroleum Company, in Veracruz. Somewhere along the way he picked up a strong dose of Spiritualism, which was to colour much of his later political prose, and in Mexico he made contact with Communists and with 'anti-imperialists' of every plumage.

'In those days,' he wrote later, 'I used to get together with a group of Spiritualist friends, and we commented daily on the submission of our Latin American peoples to the hypocritical or forceful advances of the murderous *yanki* empire. On one occasion I told my friends that if there were in Nicaragua a hundred men who loved their country as much as I, our nation would recover its sovereignty, threatened as it was by that selfsame *yanki* empire. My friends replied that there surely must be that many men in Nicaragua, but that the difficulty lay in identifying them.'

Back in Managua, the announcement that the U.S. were determined to pull out the 'Legation Guard' as soon as a new constitutional government was elected to office, was causing considerable concern among the Martínez-Solórzano-Sacasa factions. They had no doubt that, with the machinery of government working in their favour, and with recourse to the time-honoured tradition of fraudulent vote-counting by the ruling party, they would defeat Emiliano Chamorro at the polls. But they had even less doubts that, with the American 'Legation Guard' gone, it would only be a matter of time before Chamorro organised an armed rebellion, which they were not at all sure of being able to suppress.

The U.S. had already pressured Central American governments into signing a new 'Peace and Friendship' treaty, whereby each country undertook to set up 'National Guards', using 'suitable instructors' (which meant U.S. instructors) with 'experience gained in other countries' (namely, the Dominican Republic and Haiti where the U.S. had established similar National Guards). Although the governments signed the treaty, they were in no hurry to put it into operation. Armies throughout the region were strictly partisan forces, on which the ruling party could normally rely to suppress opposition. The proposed new National Guards were viewed as a threat, not so much out of fear of American dominance as because of their proposed 'non-partisan' nature. Parties in power were afraid they would no longer be able to use the Army to keep the opposition in check; opposition parties were worried about the effect which a permanent, professional force would have on their capacity to resort to armed rebellion. As a Chamorro supporter put it while discussing the issue with an American official, 'It is only by revolution that a party opposed to the government might hope to gain proper recognition.'

In the case of Nicaragua, the announced removal of the 'Legation Guard' was expected to shock local politicians into a greater acceptance of the need for a well-trained National Guard. But none of the actors was willing to follow the State Department's script. The stage was set for a drama which would plunge Nicaragua into a seven-year-long civil war.

CHAPTER VI

ENTER THE U.S. MARINES

Electoral fraud worked as efficiently as ever, but it was an uneasy Carlos Solórzano who took office on the first day of 1925. The President did not delay what Nicaraguan rulers had come to consider the first, elementary step towards consolidating their power : securing military control of the capital city. One of his brothers-in-law, General Alfredo Rivas, was appointed commander of La Loma, the hill-fort overlooking Managua which was itself protected from a rear attack by a steep drop down to a lake formed in the crater of an extinct volcano. Popular wisdom had it that whoever controlled La Loma was master of Nicaragua. Another brother-in-law, Colonel Luis Rivas, was put in charge of the other Managua garrison, at the Campo de Marte arsenal. And an official request by Solórzano was soon on the way to Washington, begging for reconsideration of the plan to withdraw the protective 'Legation Guard'.

The U.S. replied by insisting that Nicaragua should honour its 1923 commitment to set up an American-trained National Guard. In exchange for a promise to postpone the Marine pullout, Solórzano agreed to submit the project to the Assembly. Although Emiliano Chamorro did his best to block the initiative, before five months had gone by the Assembly passed a law creating the new 'Constabulary'. As in the days of Adolfo Díaz, it was a watered-down version of what the Americans had envisaged. The new force would not actually replace the old army, but it would act as an 'urban, rural and judicial police force' under the overall authority of the Minister of War. A retired U.S. Army major, Calvin Carter, was brought in to command and train a rag-tag band of 200 recruits, ill-equipped, underpaid and poorly housed in a wing of the Campo de Marte arsenal, under the watchful eye of the President's brother-in-law.

Once Major Carter was installed in his new job, the Marine 'Legation Guard' marched to the port of Corinto and sailed for home. The time had come to see if Solórzano's prediction of an 'inevitable' Liberal uprising would come true. In the short term at least, the President was wrong. Trouble had already begun to brew in another, unexpected quarter. Emiliano Chamorro, the irrepressible Conservative plotter, had been working hard at gaining the ear of Solórzano's eldest brother-in-law, General Alfredo Rivas, commander of La Loma. Twenty-one days after the Marines had departed, as the U.S. minister and most of the Nicaraguan cabinet were enjoying themselves at a party in the International Club, Rivas acted. A party of soldiers burst in on the gathering and arrested all the Liberals present, including the Minister of War, General José María Moncada, and the Minister of Finance, Víctor Román y Reyes. A few days later the President consented formally to being 'liberated' from Liberal pressure and purged his cabinet of all the remaining members of that political persuasion.

At that point, Chamorro surfaced in Managua as the leader of a movement of Conservative restoration. Within a matter of weeks he felt strong enough to make a more direct bid for power. He moved into La Loma and started mustering military support. When almost all the country's garrisons had assured him of their allegiance, he issued an ultimatum to the President : Liberals were to be purged from government posts throughout the nation and he, Emiliano Chamorro, was to be appointed Minister of War. Major Carter's Constabulary made its one attempt to stand up for constitutionality, and lost thirteen men in an exchange of gunfire with Chamorro's troops. The President capitulated.

As Minister of War, far from dismantling the Constabulary, the creation of which he had so violently opposed, Chamorro reversed his attitude completely and recommended an increase in its strength and continuation of the training programme started by Major Carter. But Chamorro had already damaged his old special relationship with the Americans beyond repair. Washington resented what it saw as an attempt by Chamorro to politicise the Constabulary; the U.S. minister, Charles Eberhardt, reported that 'hopes for an efficient organisation under American ideas and ideals are fastly disappearing'. And when Chamorro bullied the Assembly into appointing him first-in-line for the Presidential succession (in place of the Liberal Vice-President Juan Bautista Sacasa, who had fled the country and had later been formally banned from returning), the U.S. Secretary of State announced that he would not recognise any future takeover of the Presidency by the Conservative general.

This did not in the least deter Chamorro. In January 1926 he forced Solórzano to request an indefinite leave of absence and stepped into his place. A few months later the ouster was formalised by Solórzano's resignation. And the long-awaited Liberal revolt, which Solórzano—had he but known the truth—had no cause to fear as long as he had Liberal ministers in his cabinet, began to take shape. In May a group of Liberal exiles landed at Bluefields and captured it, but were rapidly crushed, thanks mainly to the efficiency with which the new Constabulary had been built up into a fighting force.

Washington, determined by now to get rid of Chamorro, reacted by informing Major Carter that he would cease to have the support of the State Department if the Constabulary continued to 'take an active part in the political affairs of Nicaragua'. For the time being, however, that (and a dose of personal harassment of Chamorro by the American chargé d'affaires, Lawrence Dennis) was the full extent of what Washington was prepared to do. The obvious expedient of cutting off Nicaragua's fiscal revenue, a simple enough proposition for the U.S.-controlled Nicaraguan Customs, was discarded because America could not stomach the idea of the Liberals returning to power.

The exiled Vice-President Sacasa had enlisted the support of the Mexican President, Plutarco Elías Calles, a man who was decidedly out of favour in Washington as an active promoter of 'bolshevism' in Latin America. Mexico had entered the 1920s as the world's second-largest oil producer (it accounted for a full quarter of world production of petroleum), and Calles' 'bolshevism' had consisted in having the nerve to insist on the long-delayed application of Article 27 in Mexico's 1917 Constitution, which vested all underground mineral rights, inalienably, in the State. In 1925 Calles succeeded in passing a law ordering American and British owners of oil fields to exchange their titles for fifty-year leases. Washington was very angry indeed, and considered that a return to power of Mexican-backed Nicaraguan rebels would be an insufferable blow to the prestige of the United States. As far as it was concerned, neither Sacasa nor Moncada would ever make it to the Presidency of Nicaragua.

The Liberals were not daunted by their first defeat. Soon a second rebel force appeared in the north-western province of Chinandega, severed the railway link with the capital and rushed to the coast for a rendezvous with a shipload of arms from Mexico. It too was crushed by superior government forces. Then a third uprising took place, led by Sacasa's young relative, Anastasio Somoza García, who had become a general overnight in the base he set up at his home town of San Marcos. Here again Chamorro's forces were successful : Somoza was driven underground until an official pardon was granted to all those who promised not to engage in any further subversive activities. Almost instantly, a major Liberal army landed on the opposite side of the country, and after gaining a foothold in Rio Grande, marched rapidly towards Bluefields. Their advance was halted, not by government troops, but by the surprise appearance of a detachment of U.S. Marines, which moved in and declared Bluefields neutral. Unfazed, the Liberal army, now under the command of General José María Moncada, pushed inland along the Escondido river to Rama, and northwards along the Atlantic coast to Puerto Cabezas.

The cost of this little war, plus the U.S. State Department's refusal to countenance any form of financial support for Chamorro (he tried, unsuccessfully, to sell the National Bank and the railways to raise funds) dragged the government to the brink of bankruptcy. The Americans, having found a suitable Presidential candidate of their own in the person of their old trusty, Adolfo Díaz, decided the time had come for a negotiated settlement of the conflict. The *U.S.S. Denver* sailed into Corinto, a truce was declared, and both sides were called to a conference aboard the warship. In fifteen days they only managed to agree on one point: Chamorro had to go. The Liberals were not prepared to accept Díaz as President, and neither the Americans nor the Conservatives were prepared to recognise Sacasa's claim to the Presidency.

Chamorro resigned, and in less than a month U.S. diplomats had engineered the appointment by the Assembly for Adolfo Díaz as President of Nicaragua. The Liberals countered by landing Juan Bautista Sacasa at Puerto Cabezas and setting up a rival, 'Constitutional' government. The scene was set for full-scale U.S. intervention. 'There are certain geographical considerations,' wrote Henry L. Stimson, a former Secretary of War who was soon to become heavily involved in the future of Nicaragua, 'which impose upon us a very special interest as to how certain Latin American nations fulfil the responsibilities which go with sovereignty and independence. I refer to those nations whose territory lies adjacent to and in a naval sense commands the great sea route from our eastern to our western states via the Caribbean sea and the Panama Canal. The situation does not arise out of the Monroe doctrine but from certain broad principles of self-defence which govern the policy of all nations which are in any way dependent upon the sea'.

The then Under-Secretary of State, Robert Olds, put the case even more bluntly as Washington promptly granted Adolfo Díaz's request for the return of a 'Legation Guard' to Managua. 'The action of Mexico in the Nicaraguan crisis,' he wrote in a confidential memorandum, 'is a direct challenge to the United States.' And he added: 'Until now Central America has always understood that governments which we recognise and support stay in power, while those which we do not recognise and support fall.

Nicaragua has become a test case. It is difficult to see how we can afford to be defeated.'

When the Liberal army moved into Chinandega, U.S. air support helped government troops drive them out, pounding most of the city to pieces in the process. 'Neutral' zones manned by American troops were created in the Pacific port of Corinto and in the cities of Chinandega and León, along the railway line to the capital. Yet another was set up in the city of Matagalpa, in the mountainous centre of the country. The detachment stationed at Bluefields was reinforced, and the Liberal strongholds on the Caribbean coast were occupied. Sacasa's 'capital' at Puerto Cabezas was taken; the local Liberal troops were disarmed and their weapons and ammunition were cast into the sea. In a matter of weeks the U.S. built up its forces in Nicaragua to more than 2,000; even the fort of La Loma, in Managua, was placed under American control.

From Washington it seemed that *Pax Americana* had returned once more to Nicaragua. Henry Stimson was sent to Managua to wrap up the situation legally. His proposed peace plan was quite straightforward. Adolfo Díaz would remain in the Presidency until U.S.-supervised elections were held in 1928, but some prominent Liberals would be included in his cabinet. Both armies, Liberal and Conservative, would be disarmed and a new National Guard, commanded by U.S. officers, would be created—the old one, Major Carter's Constabulary, having collapsed some time before. American forces would of course remain in Nicaragua until the National Guard was fit to take care of itself. Díaz agreed to the plan instantly. In order to bring the Liberals to heel, Stimson preferred to ignore Sacasa and his political entourage and to concentrate on General Moncada and the military leaders. His message was quite clear : the U.S. forces would prevent the Liberal army from defeating Díaz on the field. In his meetings with Moncada's officers, the man Stimson kept constantly at his side as interpreter and advisor was that 'very frank, friendly, likeable young Liberal', General Anastasio Somoza García.

Moncada did not take long to see the forcefulness of Stimson's argument, and in May 1927 he ordered his troops to surrender their arms to the Americans. Only one of his generals refused to obey : César Augusto Sandino, who had silently pulled out with his 300 men and as many guns as they could find, and was now riding with them towards San Rafael del Norte, in the northern province of Jinotega.

Somoza, as we have seen, became a general overnight to lead that shortlived uprising he staged in his home town of San Marcos. Sandino took somewhat longer to reach the same rank, which in Nicaragua depended not so much on an official appointment or on any special training, as on the concrete reality of being followed by enough armed men to justify one's claim to the title. Not long after the beginning of the Liberal revolution in May 1926, Sandino gave up his job with the Huasteca Petroleum Company in Mexico, and with 3,000 dollars of his savings in his pocket, set course for home. A brief visit to his parents at Niquinohomo, then on to the northern department of Nueva Segovia, where he got a job as assistant paymaster at the San Albino mine. There he set himself to finding those 'hundred men who love their country as much as I'. For all the revolutionary atmosphere, the task did not prove easy ; the ardent young rebel found only twenty-nine men willing to take up arms with him, most of them fellow-workers at the mine. He crossed the border to buy the necessary weapons from Honduran gunrunners and, without more ado, was ready for battle. His first, indecisive clash with government troops took place on November 2nd, 1926, in the small northern hamlet of El Jícaro. But Sandino had grander schemes on his mind, all of which called for his recognition as a full-fledged General of the Liberal Armies by the revolutionary leaders. So away he led his tiny band on a 200-mile trek across mountains and jungle to the Liberal bastion of Puerto Cabezas, on the Caribbean coast.

The liberal authorities were far too deeply engrossed in their politicking to pay any attention to this enthusiastic and presumptuous young man who wanted to be a general, with his ridiculous requests for men, money and supplies, and his crazy plans for opening a new battlefront in the mountainous Segovias region. Sandino was left kicking his heels for a full forty days, reduced to writing letter after unanswered letter to General Moncada, in the ever-fainter hope of getting a hearing. Then the U.S. Marines turned up. On Christmas Eve, 1926, they declared Puerto Cabezas 'neutral'; Sacasa and his entourage fled south, leaving behind a cache of arms which the invaders dumped into the sea along the beach that stretched out towards Prinzapolca. Sandino, indignant at what he considered an act of sheer cowardice on the part of his leaders, rallied his six remaining comrades, and with the help of some friendly prostitutes from a local brothel, set about recovering the abandoned weaponry. He managed to collect forty rifles and 7,000 rounds of ammunition, which he carted down to the new Liberal headquarters at Prinzapolca, hoping that this feat would finally convince the sceptic Liberal leaders that he was a fighter worthy of their trust.

He was wrong. A disdainful General Moncada thanked him perfunctorily and ordered him to hand over the weapons to one of the field commanders. If Sandino really wanted to fight for the Liberal cause, he said, the best thing he could do was to join one of the columns the Liberal army was preparing to send inland. A dejected, disarmed Sandino decided to return to the Segovias with his six faithful men. He had not travelled far, however, when he came across Liberal Minister Sandoval, on his way to confer with Moncada. Sandino was able to arouse the Minister's sympathy, and through him induced Moncada to receive him once more. The General was still not convinced that Sandino, a political nonentity, was sound enough to be trusted with a field command, but he agreed to a compromise : the young man could take back the forty rifles he had recovered from Puerto Cabezas and try to raise a fighting force of his own in the Segovias. In Moncada's view this was a highly unlikely prospect, and at best it would serve the double purpose of diverting the enemy's attention and getting Sandino well out of the way. But as he set out on the month-long canoe journey up the river Coco, Sandino was already a general in his own mind.

Sandino's small force began to operate in the Segovias when the tide seemed to be turning against the Liberals. Moncada's forces, dislodged from their bases on the Caribbean coast, were heading inland, towards the eastern bank of Lake Nicaragua, while the Conservative army was pushing across, in the opposite direction, from the Pacific coast towards Matagalpa and Jinotega. There was obviously something about the young general that attracted people; in a matter of weeks the force marching under his red and black banner grew from six to 200. Sandino's raiders began to spread out from Nueva Segovia, rapidly rolling the enemy back to beyond San Rafael. There Sandino established his base, in the house of the local telegraphist, whose eighteen-year-old sister, Blanca Arauz, attached herself to him and soon became the anchor of his communications network.

By early April, at long last, Sandino was getting the recognition Moncada had begrudged him back at Prinzapolca : the Liberal commander-in-chief, surrounded by Conservative forces in Chontales, began to send him urgent appeals for help. Together with Generals López Irías, Castro Wassmer and Parajón, Sandino mustered a force 800 strong and raced down to capture Jinotega before the U.S. Marines could move in and declare its 'neutrality', a move which would have driven a wedge between the two Liberal forces, condemning them to eventual defeat in isolation. He was too late to do the same in Matagalpa, but he sidestepped the Marines there and rushed south to Chontales, breaking through the Conservative 'iron circle' which had paralysed Moncada. The Liberal commander-in-chief lost little time in expressing his gratitude, and was soon trying to split up Sandino's army among the many loyal Liberal 'generals' who had been left without soldiers to command. The raiders from the Segovias, however, refused point-blank to part with their leader. Again they sallied forth under Sandino in an offensive aimed at the corridor between lakes Nicaragua and Managua, the gateway to the capital. They did not get far. A message from Moncada halted Sandino in his tracks : a forty-eight hour armistice had been declared. Just before it expired, the armistice was extended for another forty-eight hours. Then came another messenger with the news : 'It's all over!'

When Sandino hurried back to Moncada's headquarters to find out what had happened, he was astonished to discover that peace had been negotiated with the American invaders behind his back. Moncada spelled out the political aspects of the settlement, then added that the Americans had promised to pay 10 córdobas for each rifle handed over peacefully; he, Sandino, would be appointed political chief of Jinotega, and would be paid 10 córdobas a day for the entire period he had spent under arms. According to Sandino's later account, his only immediate reaction was 'a malicious smile'. Back in his own camp, Sandino addressed his troops, denouncing Moncada's 'treason' and declaring that he would not abide by the peace accord. The reply from his men was a thunderous '*Mueran los yanquis!*' ('death to the Yankees!'). The young general ordered his men to strike camp, load up all the weapons and munitions they could carry, and ride as fast as possible back north to Jinotega. He then returned to Moncada's bivouac, having worked out a ruse to allay any suspicions the Liberal commander might harbour. Playing on his promised appointment to the political leadership of Jinotega, he told Moncada that his men would be disarmed and disbanded there after he, Sandino, had taken a short rest to recover from the rigours of the campaign. Moncada tried to hold him back, reminding him that he would be required to sign the disarmament agreement with the Americans, to which Sandino replied, 'You're in command. You have my permission to sign in my name.' And off he rode.

On May 12th, 1927, the same day that Henry Stimson received

a telegram from the Liberal military leaders ratifying the disarmament treaty, Sandino issued a circular from the northern town of Yalí to all local government officials in the Segovias region. 'I am not willing,' he declared, 'to hand in my arms, even if the others agree to do so. I prefer to die with the few who follow me, because it is better to be killed as a rebel than to live on as a slave.' Six days later Sandino, dressed in his best boots and breeches and carrying his ten-gallon hat in his hand, celebrated his thirty-second birthday by leading Blanca Arauz to the altar. Their honeymoon lasted less than forty-eight hours; Sandino was impatient to get up into the hills and prepare his men for combat. Blanca stayed behind, in charge of the San Rafael telegraph office. In a last attempt to persuade the young general to change his mind, Moncada enlisted the support of Don Gregorio Sandino, the rebel's father. But Sandino ignored this mediation, and addressed his defiant reply directly to Moncada : 'I would like you to come and disarm me. I am at my post and waiting.' Soon the newly-appointed U.S. Marine commander of Nueva Segovia, Captain Gilbert D. Hatfield, was issuing a communiqué stating that 'Augusto C. Sandino, erstwhile General of the Liberal Armies, is now an outlaw, in rebellion against the Government of Nicaragua.' The 'General of Free Men', as Sandino was to style himself henceforth, answered with a political manifesto from his new headquarters at the San Albino mine, where he had recruited his first twenty-nine followers almost a year before. He taunted the Americans : 'Come, you bunch of morphine addicts! Come and murder us on our home ground. I shall be waiting for you, not caring how many of you there may be. But remember that when that happens, the destruction of your greatness will echo in Washington's Capitol, and your blood will redden the white dome that crowns your famous White House, that lair in which you plot your crimes.'

CHAPTER VII

A REBEL CALLED SANDINO

The Americans wasted much valuable time trying to make up their minds about what sort of a threat Sandino really posed, beyond that of being a nuisance they would have to get rid of for the sake of order. Many officers shared with prominent Nicaraguan politicians the belief that the young rebel was simply a bandit putting on a 'political' show for his own gain. Once he had collected enough loot, they surmised, he would skip across the Honduran border and vanish. Others were convinced that they were dealing with a political fanatic, but they were quite sure that Sandino was not strong enough to cause them any trouble outside his home base in the northern Segovias region. He was, they thought, effectively contained in that corner of the country by the strong Marine presence in the surrounding provinces, and it was under this last assumption that the brand-new First Company of the Guardia Nacional was ordered north to Ocotal, under the command of three American officers, to set up a base from which they would flush Sandino out and eliminate him. The Guardia force was new only in organisational terms : most of its members had been drawn from the ranks of the old Constabulary, reluctantly reinforced by the Americans with a bunch of 'provisionals', former veterans of the Conservative army who had no sympathy at all with Sandino and were therefore considered more reliable than the former Liberal soldiers for patrol duty in the Segovias. All told, they numbered less than 100 men, a clear sign that they were not expecting to confront a very formidable enemy.

Sandino hardly allowed them enough time to settle in. In the small hours of July 16th, 1927, he launched his forces, several hundred strong but on the whole armed only with pistols and machetes, to the capture of Ocotal. The attackers thought that the element of surprise would suffice to ensure a swift victory, but the first onslaught was turned back by a surprisingly determined fusillade. Sandino regrouped his men and ordered a second, better organised charge which managed to drive the defenders back and pin them down in a couple of fortified buildings. However, he was unable to cut off their communications before they called for help, and misread the defenders' decision to dig in : it was not, as he hastily assumed, a sign that he had all but achieved his purpose, but a deliberate move to prolong the siege until outside assistance arrived. Shortly after midday, eleven hours after the attack had begun, a growing rumble in the sky shocked Sandino into realising that he had made a sad mistake. A squadron of American bombers swooped down and severely mauled the rebels—and most of Ocotal as well. The toll was heavy : Sandino lost more than 200 men before he managed to organise a retreat into the hills. By then patrol units from outlying areas had been alerted to his presence, and they began to close in, keeping the battered rebel force on the run. In the following days Sandino suffered two further defeats, as he fled northward to the inaccessible mountain base he called El Chipote, just short of the border with Honduras and west of the River Coco and the jungle which stretched down to the Caribbean coast. His pursuers did not follow him all the way, partly because the risk of ambush was too great in those unfamiliar highlands and partly because they were confident that they had actually broken the back of the rebellion. After having suffered such massive losses, they thought, Sandino would never be able to regain the confidence of his supporters. Marine patrols reported that Sandino's men had fled the major towns they held in the Segovias, and military intelligence soon 'confirmed' that he was no longer in any shape to cause further annoyance. A couple of extra companies of hurriedly-recruited government troops, always commanded by U.S. officers, were moved into Chinandega and Estelí, and the region was declared 'safe'.

The Marines came close to dealing a *coup de grâce* to Sandino a short while later, when he felt secure enough to descend from El Chipote to Las Flores. They were not detected by Sandino's scouts as they crept up on his camp and, for the first and only time, they forced him into a classical set-piece battle in which he was cast in the role of disadvantaged defender. 'There came a point,' Sandino recounted, 'at which their military schooling began to show over our primitive tactics. We attempted to defend the position by digging in, but they outflanked us. Then their aviation joined in the attack, and we were forced into a disorderly retreat, losing more than sixty men.' Back up they scampered, to their craggy stronghold in the mountain.

But not for long. Ten days later a force led by Carlos Salgado, a forty-eight-year-old northerner whom Sandino had promoted to the rank of general, slipped through the ring of enemy camps below and rode south. He arrived unseen at his target, Telpaneca, a town of few more than 2,000 inhabitants garrisoned by Marines and Guardias. Just after midnight he overran the outer defence positions and charged into the town, but was unable to reach the centre : the roads were blocked by barbed wire and deep trenches.

Then once again, even before Salgado's troops had been deployed for a proper siege, the scales were tipped in favour of the defenders by the timely appearance of American fighters and bombers. However, unlike the fracas at Ocotal, Salgado was able to withdraw his men without suffering heavy losses and lead them back safely to El Chipote. This time the lesson was taken : never again would Sandino's army attempt a major assault on a fortified township.

The Americans had also arrived at a conclusion : they decided that the time had come for a major, definitive strike at Sandino's base on El Chipote, whatever the cost. Wave after wave of bombers began to pound the wooded slopes, while two heavily armed columns of Marines and Guardia marched into the area. Their advance was made excruciatingly slow by continuous, hit-and-run harassment by Sandino's forces. It seemed as if every bend in the mountain roads, every clump of trees, every nightfall hid an ambush party ready to riddle them with rifle and machinegun fire, or bombard them with deadly packs of cowhide containing sticks of dynamite and rusty scrap metal. It took the invading party the better part of a month to get into a position from which they could launch a final assault on the heights of El Chipote. Unknown to them, the incessant bombing of the mountain, though ineffectual in terms of casualties inflicted, had given them an edge over Sandino : the cattle herded uphill by the rebel leader to provide food for his men had been decimated and dispersed, as had too many of the horses they relied on for their will o' the wisp mobility. Long before the attackers resolved to rush El Chipote, Sandino had decided that he had no choice but to quit his hilltop sanctuary.

And quit it he did. All he left behind for his enemies to capture was a collection of straw dummies wearing wide-brimmed hats and the red-and-black kerchiefs that identified his 'National Sovereignty Defence Army'. No one had seen them leave; no one could quite make out how they had managed to do so. In a letter written a month later, Sandino said with satisfaction : 'They still had a lot to learn about our methods.'

The disappearing act performed by Sandino at El Chipote marks the true beginning of his guerrilla campaign, a little war which was to capture the imagination of the entire continent, and of romantics the world over. In its first stages, it was largely a propaganda war : through Froylán Turcios, who edited the literary journal *Ariel* just across the mountains in Tegucigalpa, Honduras, Sandino was built up abroad as a cult figure, the small man in the ten-gallon hat who was taking on one of the biggest war machines in the world because he just could not stomach the idea of its high-handed trampling of proud little Nicaragua's sovereignty. A 'Comité pro-Sandino' was set up in Costa Rica and Mexico, and his cause was taken up by well-known people all over Latin America : the socialist leader Alfredo Palacios in Argentina, the celebrated Chilean poet Gabriela Mistral, the renowned Mexican-teacher José Vasconcelos. Víctor Raúl Haya de la Torre, the Peruvian student who had just founded in Guatemala his 'indigenist' party, the legendary A.P.R.A., which was to influence Peru's political life for the following fifty years, acted as a courier for Sandino, and it was probably he who inspired him to define himself, and his politics, as 'Indo-American'.

Even in the United States Sandino enjoyed considerable popu-larity and a good deal of indirect support. Senator William Borah, of Idaho, was an active leader of Congressional opposition to U.S. military involvement in Nicaragua, and the journalist Carleton Beals was instrumental in elevating Sandino's public standing from that of a mere 'bandit' to the more respectable status of guerrilla leader. When Beals interviewed the rebel chief for *The Nation* in one of his hideouts in Jinotega, Sandino showed him his heavier weapons and asked : 'Where, except in Chicago, could a bandit travel around with thirty machineguns as part of his luggage?' The simile was picked up in Washington by Senator Wheeler, who taunted the Hoover administration by saying that if they wanted to fight bandits, they should send the Marines to Chicago, not to Nicaragua.

When hemisphere leaders met at Havana, Cuba, for the VI International Conference of American States, the Salvadorean delegation tabled a motion condemning U.S. intervention in Nicaragua. The initiative was supported by Argentina, Honduras, Colombia and Mexico, but did not prosper because at the last minute, under considerable pressure from the United States, El Salvador withdrew the motion.

Further afield, Sandino was becoming even more embarrassingly popular. In faraway China, when Chiang Kai-shek's victorious Kuomintang marched into Peking, one of its units, the 'Sandino Division', paraded bearing placards with the portrait of the Nicaraguan rebel. Inevitably, Sandino had also become the hero of the extreme left. In the U.S., the All-American Anti-Imperialist League organised rallies in his support; in Moscow, the VI World Congress of the Comintern took time off from its deliberations to send him a special salute; in Frankfurt-on-Main, the First International Anti-Imperialist Congress hailed him as a paragon of the struggle for national liberation.

On the field in Nicaragua, Sandino was rapidly assimilating the rudiments of practical guerrilla warfare. He had learned that he could gain the upper hand simply by not standing still long enough to offer the Marines and the Guardia a tangible target. When they were still searching for him in Nueva Segovia, he emerged in Jinotega, more than 50 miles to the south, on the other side of a mountain range. When government troops raced towards the centre of the country to cut him off, he slipped back into the mountain passes and rode off towards the eastern jungles. Sandino had also set up what amounted to an informal system of government by extortion in the northern departments of Nicaragua; he had notified businessmen and farmers that they would only be allowed to pursue their activities in peace if they applied to him for licences and paid taxes to his army. Faced with the only alternative of being executed as traitors, most of them paid up. Throughout the region Sandino counted on a willing network of spies and informers who kept him always a couple of steps ahead of the Marines and government troops and helped him select the most favourable spots for lightning ambushes. Apart from this first-class intelligence system, Sandino had an uncanny knack of detecting traps and decoy troop movements (on one occasion witnessed by outside observers, on being informed of an advancing Marine column, he puzzled his own lieutenants by disregarding the report and sending his troops away to three relatively distant positions; sure enough, each contingent was able to intercept enemy forces which were attempting to outflank the rebels).

Another factor which worked in Sandino's favour was the constant bickering among those who were conducting the campaign against him. There was no single, coherent anti-Sandino strategy. President Adolfo Díaz and General Emiliano Chamorro insisted that Sandino could only be finally defeated by Nicaraguan troops familiar with the lie of the land and able to operate at his speed, unhampered by the heavy equipment and rule-book movements of the U.S. Marines. What they had in mind, of course, was the rearming of the Conservative army, a prospect which did not go down well with the Liberal leader José María Moncada, who rejected anything which might conceivably jeopardise his chances of winning the forthcoming U.S.-supervised elections. Nor did it please the Guardia Nacional's American commander, committed as he was to the objective of organising an apolitical armed force. Nonetheless, Díaz's idea found partial acceptance in the creation of the 'provisional' Guardia units, although their numbers were kept deliberately low.

That was not all. There were also differences of opinion between the American commander of the Guardia Nacional, the commander of the Marine Brigade, the overall commander of the Navy's Special Service Squadron, and the U.S. minister in Managua, as to who was ultimately responsible for the day-to-day conduct of the war. This state of confusion was worsened by the arrival of Frank R. McCoy, an Army Brigadier General sent by the U.S. State Department to head the Electoral Commission that was supposed to ensure fair play in the election of Nicaragua's new constitutional President. McCoy not only felt that his brief included controlling everything that might have a bearing on the electoral climate—and that included the war against Sandino—but also entertained the hope that his own force, the U.S. Army, would take over the command and instruction of the Guardia Nacional from the Marines.

Most of this many-sided haggling, tugging and shoving was merely time-consuming, but it did have one important practical result : Guardia units began to be pulled out of the field to be assigned electoral police duties in the cities and towns, and the brunt of the war effort was thrust on to the Marine forces, who were badly handicapped by their ignorance of the language and of the terrain in which they were supposed to operate.

In February 1928 Sandino had managed to convince the visiting American journalist Carleton Beals that the rebel forces were capable of creating such a degree of chaos and uncertainty that the elections would never be held as scheduled. This impression, shared by many in the U.S., as well as the generally unfavourable attitude towards the very fact of American military intervention in Nicaragua, led Congress to deny the Navy the extra funds it had requested to finance the whole electoral supervision scheme. President Herbert Hoover decided to go ahead in spite of Congressional opposition, sought funds 'from other sources', and passed down the line the message that Sandino should be kept away, at any cost, from the major cities where most of the voting would be taking place. Sandino took full advantage of the Americans' determination, and of their over-eagerness to rely on their airpower to compensate for the ineffectiveness of their troops on the ground. Time and again he tricked them into believing that he had launched an Ocotal-type assault on northern villages, and on each occasion massive bombing and strafing strikes were visited by the Americans on startled civilian populations. The town of Murra was twice battered by American bombs; the hamlets of Ojoche,

Naranjo and Quiboto were reduced to rubble. A large column of Marines rushing headlong after him was cut to pieces by an ambush set up at El Bramadero by one of Sandino's generals, a twenty-three-year-old graduate of the Instituto de Occidente called Miguel Angel Ortez. Then Sandino suddenly vanished from his usual stomping grounds in the Segovias.

Unknown to the Americans, Sandino's army was winding its way eastwards, along the mountains of the Cordillera Isabelia, in the direction of the sparsely populated mining district of Pis Pis. It was a 'fund-raising' expedition with a clear political twist to it : Sandino's main target was the La Luz y Los Angeles Mining Company, the firm for which President Adolfo Díaz had once worked, and which Sandino alleged was partly owned by the former U.S. Secretary of State, Philander Knox. He took possession of the mines without having to use much force, confiscated money and goods, and left behind scrupulously detailed receipts 'on behalf of the U.S. Treasury'. He then briefly occupied the village of Bonanza before melting back into the hills.

At this point the impetus of his campaign began to falter. He carried out a couple of minor raids, enjoyed the diversion created in Managua by one Toribio Tijerino, who attempted to float an openly pro-Sandino 'Nationalist Party' and was jailed by the Marines for his pains, then sat back to await the outcome of the elections.

When the contest took place in November 1928, both Conservatives and Liberals agreed that it had been the fairest ever witnessed in Nicaragua; the undisputed winner, with about 58 per cent of the vote, was the Liberal candidate José María Moncada.

CHAPTER VIII

'NICARAGUANISATION' OF THE WAR

For a while it seemed as if the ease with which José María Moncada's elevation to the Presidency had been accomplished was going to spell complete disaster for Sandino's cause. On paper at least, the country had returned to normal : a constitutional government was in power, and the Americans would be able to proceed to the 'Nicaraguanisation' of the war, handing over operational control to the Guardia Nacional. Indeed, the authorities in Managua seem to have believed that these changed circumstances would make it easy to bring Sandino to the negotiating table. Rear Admiral David Foote Sellers, commander of the Navy's Special Service Squadron, instructed the Marine commander, General Logan Feland, to approach Sandino for peace talks, authorising Feland to accept any reasonable conditions which the rebel leader might demand. At the same time, a governmental emissary travelled to Tegucigalpa, in Honduras, to persuade Sandino's friend and propagandist Froylán Turcios to submit a peace proposal to the young General. The gist of this scheme was that on taking office, President-elect Moncada would demand a complete withdrawal of the U.S. Marines from Nicaragua, fully re-establish the rule of the Constitution and offer Sandino and his men the benefits of a general amnesty. Sandino would not even have to hand over his arms to Moncada : he would be allowed to deposit them in Costa Rica, as a guarantee that the President's promises would be kept.

But Sandino had already started moving towards a political 'solution' of his own. He had signed a secret agreement with a group of politicians for the establishment of a rival government in the Segovias, the northern departments of Nicaragua, as soon as the expected American withdrawal began. Among Sandino's new allies were Escolástico Lara, a surgeon from León who had the backing of the tiny Partido Laborista; Sofonías Salvatierra, a leader of the Grupo Solidario, a pro-Sandino organisation also based in León; and Salomón de la Selva, the prominent Nicaraguan poet who lived in exile in Mexico, where he had become an active trade unionist. The Mexican connection loomed large in Sandino's plan : his candidate for the Presidency of his revolutionary government was Dr Pedro Zepeda, another Nicaraguan exile who conducted Sandino's public relations in Mexico City, where a group of Communist leaders had formed the 'Comité Manos Fuera de

Nicaragua' (Hands off Nicaragua Committee). The very business-like propaganda churned out by Zepeda and the Committee had apparently convinced Sandino that the Mexican government itself was sympathetic to his cause, and politically naïve as he was, he began to plan a visit to the Mexican capital, where he imagined that he and his general staff would be officially welcomed as con-tinental heroes as they announced this new, decisive phase of their revolutionary campaign.

Froylán Turcios, who had only just received the government's peace proposal, had been kept in the dark about this new twist, and was shocked into awareness of the manoeuvre when it was leaked, in a doctored version, to the Honduran press. Disbelieving the press report, Turcios wrote to Sandino, urging him to dis-sociate himself from what seemed a blueprint for civil war (rather than the honourable conclusion of a just war against a foreign invader), and to accept Moncada's offer. Turcios warned Sandino that all the prestige he had gained by steadfastly refusing to compromise with the Americans would be lost if, with the U.S. forces on the verge of withdrawal, he were to turn his guns on his fellow-countrymen for the base purpose of conquering power for himself, or for some cheap local *caudillo*. Even before the letter had reached Sandino, Turcios received a message from the General with instructions that confirmed his worst fears; a disgusted and disappointed Turcios resigned his honorary post as Sandino's 'official representative'.

Meanwhile, Sandino continued to prepare the ground for his coup. For the first time since the struggle began, he answered the American peace overtures in a conciliatory vein. No longer did he demand complete U.S. withdrawal from Nicaragua, nor insist on considering the elections null and void; his conditions were an American withdrawal only from the northern departments of Nueva Segovia, Jinotega, Estelí and Matagalpa (the selfsame region in which he planned to set up his revolutionary government), and a conference with Moncada, to be held in the northern city of San Rafael. While the Americans and the Nicaraguan government were puzzling over the unexpected shift in his attitude, Sandino despatched one of his young lieutenants, a Mexican captain called José de Paredes, with a verbal proposal to be submitted to Emilio Portes Gil, President of the United Mexican States.

He was asking Portes Gil for a statesman-to-statesman interview, as well as for a very practical 'loan' of 10,000 dollars, which would pay for his own and his generals' travel expenses, with enough left over to begin purchasing arms and munitions for the last stage of the war. Sandino had no way of knowing that he was virtually placing a noose around his own neck. Portes Gil immediately contacted the U.S. minister in Mexico, informed him of Sandino's intentions, and requested a quick reaction from the U.S. State Department. The Secretary of State, Frank Kellogg, leaped at the opportunity being offered : he urged Portes Gil to play along with Sandino, enticing him into Mexico, but then confining him in some isolated corner of the country where he could be kept under surveillance. News of this development was relayed to the U.S. military command in Nicaragua and to Moncada, together with the suggestion that all negotiations with the rebel be protracted until he left the country.

Instead of playing the game diplomatically, Moncada took advantage of the situation, and of the American decision to leave military operations in Nicaraguan hands, by creating a 200-strong force of *voluntarios,* a partisan band led by the Mexican adventurer Juan Escamilla, to engage the rebel forces in an immediate offensive on their own ground. Escamilla's tactics were ruthless and radical; aware that the guerrillas' strength lay as much in the sympathy and support they received from the local population as in their armed contingents, he launched an orgy of repression in the northern departments, attacking not only anyone suspected of backing or aiding Sandino, but also all those identified as opponents of the Moncada régime. The *voluntarios* also chalked up an important military success : they routed one of Sandino's columns and captured its leader, General Manuel Jirón Ruano, a former Guatemalan career officer who had received German military training at Potsdam. Escamilla had Jirón Ruano summarily tried and executed by a firing squad.

In the meantime Sandino was busy writing letters to Latin American heads of state, in an attempt to draw them into his grand design for Nicaragua's future. He revived the inter-oceanic canal issue, and invited the Argentine President Hipólito Yrigoyen to sponsor an Inter-American conference in Honduras to debate the project. There is no record of a reply from Yrigoyen, nor of any response to the letters he sent to the Salvadorean President Romero Bosque and the U.S. President Herbert Hoover. But in May 1929 he received word from the Mexican government, approving his visit.

An excited Sandino departed hurriedly across the Honduran border, then sailed to the Salvadorean port of La Unión for the long rail trip across two republics to the Mexican border. His enthusiasm was dampened as soon as his train crossed the river

Suchiate into Mexico : government representatives were at hand with the disappointing news that he would not be allowed to proceed to the capital city. Enraged, Sandino crossed back into Guatemala. A few days later, however, he decided to accept the conditions laid down by the Mexican authorities, and made his way to Mérida, in the peninsula of Yucatán.

Although his Mexican representative, Dr Zepeda, assured him that this was only a temporary measure, dictated by the need for discretion, Sandino soon began to suspect that something was badly wrong. He spent a long month ensconced in a sleazy Mérida hotel, cut off from the outside world, and especially from Nicaragua. Presently a Mexican government official turned up to inform him that, on Presidential instructions, he was to be paid a stipend of 1,000 Mexican pesos a month for as long as he remained in Yucatán. The interview with the President, Sandino was informed, would have to be postponed, and there was no news about the loan Sandino had requested. Almost simultaneously, a telegram from Tegucigalpa brought disastrous tidings from home : the column headed by his Salvadorean lieutenant, General José León Díaz, had had to flee in confusion across the border into Honduras.

An increasingly despondent Sandino began to observe how Moncada and the Americans gleefully represented his departure from Nicaragua as a flight in defeat, while he, with his old friend Turcios now gone, had been silenced. He began to shop around for another propagandist, and luckily found one in Gustavo Alemán Bolaños, a Nicaraguan writer and journalist who was living in exile in Guatemala.

On paper, the war began again. Sandino wrote a fiery manifesto, calling on all Nicaraguans to keep their spirits high and announcing that his return was imminent—his forces were being reorganised, and the renewed struggle would soon reveal itself in its true, continent-wide proportions. His private correspondence, however, clearly betrayed the fact that he was getting nowhere in Mexico. Every other day he felt compelled to dash off a letter setting a new date for his triumphal return, and claiming new, unidentified victories for his forces. 'My plans for actions are now ready,' he repeated, 'I am not a prisoner; I am still in touch with Nicaragua and in command of operations there.' At home, though, only fifty-nine-year-old General 'Pedrón' Altamirano was managing to pull off a few successful coups against government forces, and the guerrilla war was rapidly losing its sense of purpose and degenerating into outright banditry.

Months crawled by, and still the Mexican President kept putting off the interview with Sandino. The rebel leader's sense of isolation became more and more acute. 'We do have agents,' he confided plaintively to a journalist from Veracruz, 'but regrettably many of them have been selfish; others have, quite frankly, become traitors; others again have simply been inactive. I have been left alone.' In December 1929 he made a last, hopeless appeal to Portes Gil in which, anticipating a rebuff, he begged the President 'not to place obstacles in the way of our return to the Segovias'. It was, of course, a bluff; Sandino was far from ready to go back. But another month went by in absolute silence, and a despairing Sandino wrote to his man Zepeda : 'What has happened? Why so much beating about the bush? Are we really the victims of treachery?'

At long last, on January 29th, 1930, Sandino was summoned to Mexico City to talk with the President. It was a short, sad meeting, and its result was unequivocal : no help would be forthcoming.

'Our shots of protest and warning have not ceased in the plains and mountains of the Segovias, nor shall they ever cease !' Sandino's new manifesto reached General 'Pedrón' Altamirano together with a rather pathetic gift : two 38-calibre revolvers and four boxes of bullets. But it seemed to do the trick. All of a sudden, guerrilla forces were striking at Guapinol, at Yalí, at El Bálsamo, and the government was evidently thrown off balance. The Marines had by then pulled back to the major cities; the *voluntarios* had been disbanded after their excessive zeal had led to a border incident with Honduras; and a fund-starved Guardia Nacional was completely unprepared for the onslaught.

Sandino slipped out of Mexico in April, and by mid-May (ten months after he had started out on his ill-fated journey) he was back in the field. His cause was granted an unexpected bonus by the government's precipitate approval of a Guardia scheme for the forcible resettlement of villagers in the sparsely-populated Segovias. Wide areas were declared 'no-man's-land', the people were evicted, houses were razed to the ground, crops were destroyed, and troops were instructed to shoot anyone remaining behind. Apart from the insensate brutality with which the measure was carried out, there were no plans for the re-housing, or even feeding of the stream of refugees that began to pour into the northern cities. When famine ensued, causing the death of more than 200 refugees, mainly women and children, the American minister forced Moncada to call off the programme. But the rectification came too late : in a matter of weeks, thousands had been converted to the rebel cause.

CHAPTER IX

THE AMERICANS PULL OUT

During Sandino's absence from the country, the divergence of views among his enemies had become slightly narrower. Moncada had continued to insist on the enlargement of the Nicaraguan armed forces along traditional (i.e. more partisan) lines, for the very simple reason that he felt threatened not only by Sandino, but also by his Conservative rivals. The American military leaders tended to go along with him, but not for the same reason : they thought, in spite of the problems the *voluntario* experiment had created, that native troops would greatly enhance the effectiveness of the U.S.-led Guardia Nacional. But the U.S. minister adhered firmly to the State Department's position : Nicaragua was to have only one armed force, the Guardia Nacional, and this force was to be completely apolitical. For a long while the U.S. military commanders preferred to ignore the minister, and took to working out the day-to-day conduct of the war with President Moncada. This, however, they did indirectly, through a member of Moncada's cabinet : the personable young Anastasio Somoza García, who had continued to style himself General although he had never again gone near a battlefield.

Somoza's usefulness as a go-between had been recognised by both sides as early as 1927, when Henry Stimson and Moncada were negotiating an end to the Liberal revolution. Moncada had kept him at his side, and made him Under-Secretary of Foreign Affairs with special responsibility for dealing with the Americans.

The struggle for supremacy among the American authorities in Nicaragua was presently settled by the State Department in favour of the minister, but this did nothing to heal the rift between the Americans and Moncada. The Liberal President was definitely less amenable than Adolfo Díaz had been to having his policy dictated by U.S. legation memoranda, and as the U.S. forces began to withdraw from active combat duty (leaving in the field only the Marine officers in command at Guardia units), Moncada began to take advantage of every opportunity to assert his independence. True enough, the Americans forced him to abandon the resettlement programme which had created so much anti-government feeling in the northern departments, but this was only a temporary setback.

Sandino had followed up the government's resettlement fiasco with a fierce offensive throughout the Segovias. In the remaining five months of 1930 his guerrilla forces fought eleven major battles, none of them decisive victories in a classic military sense, but all combining to create the impression that the government was in retreat. So distinct was this image of government weakness that, as Moncada had feared, the Conservatives started trying to get in on the act. A year earlier, the President had nipped a Conservative plot in the bud, and exiled eight of their most prominent leaders. And in spite of American opposition, Moncada began to use the Guardia Nacional to crack down on the least sign of dissent, usually by trumping up charges which the Liberal-controlled judiciary could use as grounds for ordering arrests. However transparent the political motivation of these actions might be, the Guardia were duty-bound to obey the judges' orders.

In August 1930, Vice-President Enoc Aguado secretly got in touch with Sandino to let him know that he was organising a revolution against Moncada, and that he would appreciate the rebel leader's support. Sandino replied very formally, laying down a series of conditions under which Aguado would be authorised to use the symbols and banners of the 'National Sovereignty Defence Army'. But, he added, 'if your plans do not coincide with all the fuss I have made in this letter, do not let that deter you. If that is the case, this Army will simply abstain from attacking your forces and will intensify the offensive against the interventionists.' Sandino went on to halt a major attack he had been planning on the Caribbean coast, and ordered the three columns under Generals 'Pedrón' Altamirano, Ismael Peralta and Pedro Blandón to stand by 'until we hear from the people who are planning to rise in arms in the interior of the Republic'.

In spite of all this subterranean unrest, the Americans managed to go ahead with their plans to hold Nicaraguan Congressional elections in November. The outcome—an impressive Liberal victory—strengthened Moncada's resolve to stamp out all remaining threats to his régime. In December, as the twenty-five-year-old rebel General Miguel Angel Ortez swooped out of the Segovias for a series of daring raids on the hitherto peaceful department of León, Moncada announced that a huge Communist conspiracy was afoot and ordered the Guardia to lock up almost every known Opposition leader in the country. The wave of repression seems to have dissuaded Aguado and his would-be insurgents, and their plans for revolution were never heard of again. Furthermore, Moncada's use of the 'Communist threat' to justify his actions successfully silenced any American misgivings about the whole affair, a precedent not lost on young Anastasio Somoza García.

But it was one thing to suppress dissent in the cities, and quite another to put an end to the war. If anything, the war was getting uglier every day. Sandino himself had changed considerably since his frustrating sojourn in Mexico. His orders to the field commanders were becoming hasher, especially when it came to prescribing the sort of treatment to be meted out to those who were less than generous in their contributions to the rebel treasury, or who protested at the confiscation of goods and supplies by rebel commanders. All of these were placed in the same category as police informers, deserters and turncoats. The sentence '*que sea pasado por las armas*' became a frequent ingredient in Sandino's circulars and letters. It means 'Execute him', but the English rendering suggests something quite different to what actually occurred to a sentenced traitor in Nicaragua. Execution was not a clean job carried out by a firing squad, or by hanging. The official instrument of death was the machete, and it was not used simply to behead the condemned man, but to perform specially devised *cortes,* ranging from minor mutilation to vile combinations which caused death after prolonged suffering. Minor offences were punished by the *corte de bloomers,* a slash across the backs of both legs which severed tendons and bared the bone behind the knees. Quick but spectacular death was achieved by the *corte de cumbo,* a single swipe that sliced off the crown of the head, baring the brain and leaving the victim to perform contorted leaps like a headless chicken. The slowest, most horrible death was caused by the *corte de chaleco* (the 'waistcoat cut'): two vertical slashes severed arms from shoulders, and a horizontal stroke disembowelled the victim. The hideous show was sometimes, but not always, ended by a blow beheading the condemned man. Sandino would write in a public manifesto: 'Freedom is not conquered with flowers, but with bullets, and that is why we have had to resort to the *cortes de chaleco, cumbo* and *bloomers.*'

This kind of savagery was not perpetrated by Sandino alone. Marine Captain 'Chesty' Puller had hit upon the novel idea of recruiting a special company of Guardia among the Indians, the pariahs of the northern departments, playing upon their age-old resentment against the white man. His thirty-strong 'Company M', constantly on patrol, played the same game as the guerrillas, and often engaged in 'black propaganda' operations, committing atrocities that were later attributed to Sandino's men. The machete was their tool too, and their anonymity allowed them to carry out reprisal raids against pro-Sandino villages which the 'formal' Guardia units were barred from doing.

Alongside his hardened, cruel self there lived another Sandino who had suddenly revived his youthful interest in Spiritualism, now expounded as the official policy of his rebel army. In October 1930 he wrote a remarkable letter to Colonel Abraham Rivera, the man in charge of rebel operations along the River Coco. In it he informed Rivera of the impending move towards the eastern coast, then added :

Keep in mind that the divine law we are subject to is only one: *the law of love.* From that law of love all others derive. The law of love only recognises *justice,* its favourite daughter, born from its womb.

In order to explain the above-mentioned ideas, I beg of you fifteen minutes of your time, whenever you are alone and in repose. . . . It is my sweet illusion that you are already alone and willing to grant me those fifteen minutes:

Just imagine that you are gazing over all the seas of the world together, and that a sparrow is ordered to come and take a sip of those waters every hundred million years. When the sparrow, in that fashion, has emptied that immense sea, a single second of eternity shall have elapsed.

However, the *time of eternity* does not suffice to traverse all of space, even at the highest imaginable speed. The first substance that existed in this immensity was *ether,* but even before ether there existed a great will, that is to say, a great desire of what was not, to be. More clearly: *eternal love. Ether* is now matter, and it is the life made evident by the electricity which is the life of men; that is to say, it is all *light* (*the spirit*). *The Spirit is consubstantial with the Father, the Creator of the Universe.*

Thus, my dear brother Rivera, you are now in possession of these ideas, so that you may always be ready to defend just causes, even though they should demand every imaginable sacrifice, because sacrifice is *love* (*the Creator, or God*). Injustice comes from ignorance of the divine laws, from the time that mankind was still in embryo form. Therefore, there is no reason for injustice, because it is against the law of *love,* the only one which will reign on Earth, when human fraternity finally prevails and men become *light,* as the Father, the Creator has ordained.

In order to reach that point we must start walking, because unless we start we shall never arrive. In order to destroy this injustice it has been necessary to attack it, which is why we have seen many appear on Earth with that mission, like Jesus. Any man who fights for the Freedom of the People is a continuer of those doctrines.

There are on Earth some men who believe that if they themselves enjoy a good life, it is madness for them to make any sacrifice for the good of others. If this is said in ignorance it is not as bad as if it is said in full cognisance of the facts, because in the latter case the individual is acting out of niggardly selfishness, which is hatred for mankind. They live their orgies at the expense of human tears and lives.

That is injustice, and sooner or later injustice will be vanquished by *divine justice*. The Earth has been a world of expiation, where for millions of centuries divine justice has imprisoned the spirits that rebel against divine law, but now the Earth has reached its point of regeneration, and those rebel spirits will be expelled to other, more backward planets. Thus, injustice shall disappear from the face of the Earth, and justice alone shall prevail.

The Earth produces everything that is needed for the joy and comfort of mankind, but, as I have said, injustice has been dominant for many millions of centuries, and all those enormous stocks of necessary things have been in the hands of a few bigwigs. The vast majority of peoples have lacked even what was most indispensable, perhaps even dying of hunger, after having produced with their own sweat what others fritter away in their sprees.

But justice shall prevail, and the war declared by the oppressors of free peoples shall be destroyed by the war of the Liberators. And later, there being justice, there shall also be peace on earth.

Dear brother Colonel Rivera: let not these explanations drive you to despair. I have always recognised your intelligence, and I wish all those who are closest to me to become wholly saturated by the greatest love for justice, because it is our standard of freedom. I shall write again soon, telling you the news of our military operations on the many fronts that our Army has opened. Receive a fraternal embrace from this brother who holds you in great esteem.

The year 1931 began with the announcement of a schedule for complete 'Nicaraguanisation' of the war. Henry Stimson, the man who had negotiated the peace with Moncada in 1927 and now U.S. Secretary of State, made public Washington's intention to scale down the strength of the Marine contingent from 1,500 to 500 men that very same year, and to complete the withdrawal of American forces as soon as new, U.S.-supervised general elections had been held in late 1932, and a new Constitutional President sworn in.

Sandino appeared to ignore this development. Indeed his mystical mood seemed to be getting stronger : at about the same time as Stimson's announcement, he issued a public manifesto under the title *Luz y Verdad* ('Light and Truth') in which he reinterpreted the prophesies about the Day of Judgement as meaning that the oppressed peoples of the earth would defeat imperialism in the twentieth century. 'Do not fear, my dear brothers,' he wrote, 'and be assured, most assured, that we shall soon achieve a definitive victory in Nicaragua, thus igniting the fuse of the "Proletarian Explosion" against world imperialism.'

His growing mysticism, however, did not impair his military judgement. As soon as it became evident that the promised civilian uprising would not materialise, he ordered his lieutenants to proceed with the eastward offensive he had postponed towards the end of 1930. A force led by General Pedro Blandón, aided by local sympathisers, including a National Deputy named Adolfo Cockburn, infiltrated the eastern region and emerged not far from Puerto Cabezas, suddenly overrunning logging camps and company towns. Almost simultaneously, a column headed by Abraham Rivera surfaced on the lower reaches of the Coco river and rushed into Cape Gracias a Dios. The Americans reacted by sending naval units and Marine landing parties to the Caribbean ports, but by the time they arrived the guerrillas had vanished.

Then disaster, though not of Sandino's making, struck in Managua. On March 31st, the city was ripped apart by a fearful earthquake, which sent big buildings tumbling, wrecked the water reservoir and badly damaged the arsenal at Campo de Marte. The earth had not ceased its rumbling and shaking when fires broke out, rapidly spreading through the splintered woodwork of the poorer houses and the dried palm roofing of the shacks on the outskirts of the town. Then came the roar of dynamite, as wide tracts of no-man's land were blasted clear in an effort to contain the spread of the flames. And then began the long, painful process of restoring some semblance of order to the battered capital.

In a circular letter to his field commanders, Sandino exulted : 'Since Divine Justice itself is taking a hand in the punishment of the enemy, we must finish the job by terrorising the terrorists once and for all.' His forces in the east unleashed a second round of raids on the Caribbean settlements, and young General Miguel Angel Ortez rode down from the northern hills towards the western extremity of Nicaragua. For a moment, it looked as if Sandino had finally bitten off more than he could chew : General Pedro Blandón was killed by government forces in Logtown, and Miguel Angel Ortez fell during a pitched battle at Palacagüina. But their forces quickly regrouped under new leaders, and the momentum of the campaign increased when yet another front was opened, as General 'Pedrón' Altamirano sallied forth from Matagalpa into Chontales, attacking Santo Domingo and then racing on to overrun the town of Rama, only a few miles from Bluefields. In the west, Ortez's old column, now commanded by Generals Juan Pablo Umanzor and Juan J. Colindres, occupied the town of Chichigalpa, on the railway line leading to Managua. Other forces were descending from the Segovias and striking deep into León.

These were still hit-and-run raids; the rebels were making no

attempt to hold on to the towns they managed to capture. But
their virulence gave the war a new twist. On the one hand, even
though Stimson had already made it clear that U.S. forces were
no longer able to protect American lives and properties in the
interior of Nicaragua, it was considered necessary to send the
Marines out of the cities again, to guard the railway which provided Managua with its lifeline to the sea. On the other hand
Moncada's long-standing demand for the revival of the *voluntario*
forces was hastily approved, now under the name of *auxiliares*.

Moncada had other things on his mind apart from the threat
posed by Sandino's countrywide offensive. Banned constitutionally
from succeeding himself in office, he began to seek ways to hold
on to the largest possible slice of power. The most obvious course of
action was to put forward his own puppet candidates for the
forthcoming elections, but the bulk of the Liberal party had
already made up its mind to back Juan Bautista Sacasa for President. Moncada's next ploy was to break away from his party with
a splinter group of Liberals, and to offer the Conservatives an
alliance. The Opposition, however, had already settled on the candidacy of Adolfo Díaz, the erstwhile favourite of the Americans.
This second failure did not dishearten Moncada; convinced as he
was that the upswing in guerrilla activity would delay the departure of the American forces, he came up with an 'emergency' plan
to extend his own term of office for two years, on the pretext of having
to hand over a completely pacified nation to his successor. But even
this last bid failed, for the American government, under increasing
political pressure at home, was determined to disengage its troops
from this situation which at the end of 1931 was, in the words of
the U.S. chargé d'affaires Willard Beaulac, 'as grave or graver than
at any time since I have been in Nicaragua'. Politicians in Washington were already promising the American nation that the
United States would never again become entangled in such a pre-
dicament.

Nicaragua's two-party system tended to leave a number of
aspirants to the Presidency in the lurch once Liberals and Conservatives had decided on their nominations, so it was hardly surprising that several politicos, gambling on the instability created by
Sandino, should start approaching the rebel leader with a view
to setting up a third alternative *fuera del sistema*. The first such
hopeful was a disgruntled Conservative from Granada, Evaristo
Carazo Hurtado, who persuaded Sandino's representative in
Guatemala, Gustavo Alemán Bolaños, to put his name forward as a
possible President of a revolutionary régime.

Sandino rejected the notion out of hand, mainly because he had already made contact with the Comité Pro-Liberación de Nicaragua in Mexico City for the proclamation of General Horacio Portocarrero as President of a revolutionary government which would include such pro-Sandino stalwarts as Escolástico Lara, Salomón de la Selva and Gustavo Alemán Bolaños himself. Though this was publicised as Sandino's final word on the subject, it did not stop a prominent Nicaraguan businessman, Manuel Balladares, from approaching the rebel General with an offer of support from a couple of Liberal veterans, Generals Carlos Castro Wassmer and José María Zelaya, in exchange for the nomination of Balladares as head of the revolutionary government. Sandino told Balladares that if he wanted to help, the best he could do was to support Portocarrero.

But Sandino was certainly not putting all his eggs in one basket. He also approached Sacasa, the Liberal candidate, offering him the guerrilla army's backing should he be elected, on the condition that the Ministry of Finance be entrusted to Escolástico Lara and the Ministry of Foreign Affairs to Salvador Calderón Ramírez, a pro-Sandino Nicaraguan journalist who lived in exile in San Salvador, and that the key garrisons of La Loma in Managua and La Pólvora in Granada should be occupied by *sandinista* troops. There was no reply to this proposal.

Sandino was, of course, very much on everyone's mind in Managua as the elections drew closer. The Conservative candidate, Adolfo Díaz, had returned to his favourite theme and was lobbying for an extension of the American military presence in Nicaragua. The U.S. military and political leaders, for their part, were worried about some very practical problems concerning the handover of the Guardia Nacional to the new Nicaraguan authorities. Their main dilemma was that, although they had achieved part of their aim in training an efficient, more or less apolitical armed force, the war against Sandino had prevented them from building up an adequate native officer corps. Field-grade commands, and of course the higher echelons of the Guardia hierarchy, were still in American hands. The new President of the United States, Franklin Delano Roosevelt, did not intend to compromise his 'Good Neighbour Policy' (the belated antithesis of his cousin Theodore Roosevelt's 'Big Stick') by leaving American officers behind after the new Nicaraguan government took office. So it was a matter of finding an adequate face-saving solution.

So keen were the Americans to pull out at this stage that they started by ditching the key feature of the Guardia as it had originally been conceived : its 'apolitical' nature. They agreed that officers for the Guardia would have to be political appointees, drawn from the ranks of veterans who had served in the Conservative or Liberal armies of yore. A lame attempt was made to soften the obvious impact of this decision, by stipulating that the appointments should be made on a strictly bi-partisan basis : there were to be as many Conservatives as Liberals in the officer corps.

The most thorny problem of all was the selection of the future commander of the Guardia, the *Jefe Director*. Long before the elections, the U.S. minister Matthew Hanna had expressed his opinion that 'the best man' for the job was that friendly and helpful chap at the Ministry of Foreign Affairs, General Anastasio Somoza García. The American commander of the Guardia, General Calvin Matthews, agreed. So did Moncada. But the crux of the matter was that the appointment would have to be approved by the incoming President.

Despite the fact that Sandino's forces had managed to advance right up to the northern bank of Lake Managua, the elections were held as scheduled on November 6th, 1932. The Liberal candidate, Juan Bautista Sacasa, the self-same man whose claim to the Presidency had led to U.S. intervention in 1926, won by a comfortable margin.

Although he was related to Somoza, whose wife Salvadora was the President-elect's niece, Juan Bautista Sacasa had his own candidate for the command of the Guardia : General Carlos Castro Wassmer. For some unknown reason, Sacasa did not insist on the nomination of the latter when it was opposed by both Moncada and the Americans; instead, he agreed to choose one of three candidates on a list submitted by Moncada, with General Matthew's approval. The three names were Anastasio Somoza García, Gustavo Abaunza and José María Zelaya.

On January 1st, 1933, just after Juan Bautista Sacasa had been sworn in, General Anastasio Somoza García took over his new post as first Nicaraguan *Jefe Director* of the Guardia Nacional. Less than twenty-four hours later, in a rather undignified scramble, the last American forces sailed away from the port of Corinto. They did not leave as victors; in Ambassador Hanna's words, Sandino was 'as strong as, if not stronger than at any time'.

CHAPTER X

THE END OF SANDINO

When the American troops pulled out of Nicaragua seven years after they had come to protect Adolfo Díaz's puppet régime against the rebel Liberal forces headed by Juan Bautista Sacasa and José María Moncada, they left the country in, if anything, a greater state of disarray than that in which they had found it. Nicaragua's constitutional ruler was the self-same Juan Bautista Sacasa whose accession to power the American intervention had been intended to prevent. A huge portion of Nicaraguan territory was controlled by some 3,000 armed men under the command of Augusto C. Sandino, the man who had resorted to guerrilla warfare in 1927 in order to defend Sacasa's constitutional rights against the foreign invaders, and who now challenged the power Sacasa had inherited from the American intervention. The Guardia Nacional, which the Americans had devised as an apolitical, stabilising force, was now commanded by Anastasio Somoza García, and an officer corps appointed on a bipartisan basis. The old *caudillos* of the 'historic' Liberal and Conservative parties, Generals José María Moncada and Emiliano Chamorro, had been outmanoeuvred in the struggle for key positions in the new power structure, but they still retained considerable influence over the legislative and local cadres of both political organisations.

Each of these began to jockey for a greater share of power even before the departing American troops had sailed out of sight. President Sacasa had a tough threefold task ahead of him if he was to be President in fact as well as in name. First, he had to neutralise the very real challenge to his authority posed by Sandino's armed men up in the northern departments. Secondly, he had to eliminate the potential threat posed by the many Conservative officers who held positions of command in the Guardia Nacional. And, last but far from least, he had to find a way to prevent Somoza from becoming the head of a state within the state as *Jefe Director* of a powerful and united Guardia.

Sacasa believed that he could draw Sandino to the negotiating table, and for this purpose he appointed the rebel leader's old crony Sofonías Salvatierra to a minor position in his cabinet, as Minister of Agriculture and Labour, and charged him with making peace overtures to the obstinate 'General of Free Men'. At the same time he began to appoint more staunch Liberals to positions within the Guardia Nacional, making sure that the key garrisons of La Loma in Managua and the Acosasco fort in León were controlled by men of proven loyalty, and to edge the Conservative officers, if not out of the force, at least into lesser, remote commands.

As to Somoza, the President was confident of keeping him in check, in the short term, by the simple expedient of cultivating the friendship of General Gustavo Abaunza, one of the three candidates for the command of the Guardia, whose hopes had been dashed by the Americans' clear preference for Somoza, but who had been rewarded by Sacasa with the subordinate yet influential position of Chief of Staff. In due time, thought the President, he would manage to move enough of his own men into the key notches of the Guardia's command structure to neutralise the *Jefe Director* completely.

Sandino responded at once to the peace feelers put out by the President, but he did so with a set of terms which were unlikely to find acceptance in Managua. The rebel demanded the creation of a huge new department in northern Nicaragua, stretching from the Segovias to the Caribbean coast along both sides of the River Coco, over which his forces would retain political and military control. He also threw in a demand for the setting-up of an inter-American conference to renegotiate the trans-oceanic canal rights ceded to the United States by the Bryan-Chamorro treaty.

Everything seems to indicate that Sandino expected these conditions to be rejected, and was putting them forward only as a basis for further negotiations, out of which the definitive terms would arise. Certainly he did not order his troops to halt their operations; indeed he continued to harass the Guardia Nacional, and even mounted a major attack on the Guardia garrison at San Isidro. But the wording of his proposal had made it clear that he was offering Sacasa the conditional support of his army should the President decide to do away with that visible remnant of foreign intervention in Nicaragua, the Guardia Nacional.

Just as Sandino identified the Guardia as his main enemy, Somoza viewed the rebel leader as the one adversary with whom coexistence would be impossible. The *Jefe Director* chose to ignore the President's quest for a negotiated settlement, and concentrated instead on building up his force in preparation for a decisive military victory. He recalled the notorious Juan Escamilla to command an enlarged force of *auxiliares*, and swelled the ranks of the Guardia to record levels. Somoza was hardly unaware of Sacasa's strategy of displacing Conservative Guardia officers and appointing men of Liberal profession who were personally loyal to the President. He actually went along with this policy, inasmuch as the Conservatives were his enemies as well as the President's, but he brought into play all his powers of persuasion and charm to redirect towards himself the allegiance of the Presidential appointees.

His first conquest was Sacasa's most important 'plant', General Abaunza, who was quick to recognise that Somoza's political ability was far greater and more promising than the President's. The *Jefe Director* also made a point of showing himself particularly sympathetic towards the career officers in the Guardia, who resented having been left in junior positions while political appointees landed all the senior commands.

Somoza's first opportunity to make a public show of his power came early in January, when he managed to avert a mutiny by the Guardia's junior officers. The discovery of the plot made two things very evident: first, that Somoza was a quick learner at the spying game that made for success as the head of an internal security apparatus; and secondly, that he personally had gained the confidence of the career men in the Guardia—the plotters had been aiming at the removal of all political appointees *except Somoza*. Though the General did not hesitate to crush the mutiny, he was equally swift to use the circumstances of the plot to push for a number of benefits for the career officers, enhancing his own position *vis-à-vis* both the President and the men who actually controlled the rough, nasty end of the Guardia's big stick.

Apart from Sandino and the subterranean rivalry with President Sacasa, the first public enemy Somoza made for himself was General Emiliano Chamorro, the Conservative *caudillo,* who was indignant at the way the *Jefe Director* was riding roughshod over the agreed bipartisan composition of the Guardia's officer corps. Every Conservative officer shunted away from an important post in the country's only official armed force naturally meant further erosion of the already weak toehold Chamorro retained upon Nicaragua's power structure. The Conservative leader's first, automatic reaction was to turn to the Americans for assistance in halting this trend; when he obtained no satisfaction, he began to campaign for a curtailment of the Guardia's manpower and budget.

Yet far from the Guardia's strength being reduced, it seemed for a while that Somoza had managed to convince President Sacasa that the only way to deal with Sandino was by force, and official missions were sent abroad to purchase enormous quantities of arms and munitions.

Then, out of the blue, came a momentous announcement : Sandino was willing to travel to Managua in person to sue for peace. President Sacasa sent a plane to fetch him from San Rafael del Norte, had him rushed to the Presidential Palace, and within a few hours thrashed out a peace treaty which was endorsed by representatives of Nicaragua's two major political parties.

It was a curious, ambiguous document. Hostilities were to cease, all Sandino's men were to benefit from a general amnesty, and the rebels would hand over their arms to the government. However, Somoza and his Guardia Nacional were granted no part in these proceedings : it would not be Somoza, but Sofonías Salvatierra —the friend of Sandino who held a minor ministerial post in Sacasa's cabinet—who would supervise the disarmament of the rebels. Furthermore, disarmament would not be complete : although Sandino had not been granted his wish of a department of his own in the north, he was given control of an 'empty' area on the River Coco, and was authorised to keep there an 'emergency force' of 100 armed men.

General Somoza was furious at what he considered excessive concessions on Sacasa's part. He was not the only one who was disillusioned by the peace treaty; many of Sandino's supporters, and especially his contacts abroad, felt they had been let down too, and accused the rebel leader of having conceded too much : so much so that Sandino felt it necessary to justify his action in a long letter to Gustavo Alemán Bolaños. He wrote :

Had it been impossible to sign the peace treaty, I would have taken my own life in the Presidential Palace, so that my blood could have served my men as a new stimulus and a banner. Although you are not aware of the fact, I must tell you that now, when foreign intervention in Nicaragua has ceased, albeit in appearance alone, the people's spirits have cooled down. Political and economic intervention is suffered by the people, but they cannot see it—even worse, they do not believe in its existence. This situation placed us in a very difficult position, and in the meantime the government was negotiating a multi-million dollar loan and preparing to *blast us to hell and consolidate the political, economic and military intervention in our country*. As this government was elected mainly by the Liberals of León, our strength would have dwindled in any confrontation; our financial and military resources were exhausted, and our troops could not have sought refuge in Honduras, because the war in that country is raging intensely, and Nicaraguan refugees are being murdered there. Nor could we count on El Salvador, where the government is machinegunning the peasants, nor, as you well know, is there better hope for us in Guatemala: in the new, unionist mood prevailing in Central America, Ubico [President of Guatemala

1931-44], Moncada and Uncle Sam are three different persons and one true God.

If anyone was justified in harbouring suspicions about the peace treaty, it was Somoza—Sandino had certainly interpreted the agreement very liberally, and President Sacasa seemed willing enough to let him get away with it. When Sandino's men turned up at San Rafael del Norte to hand over their weapons to Minister Salvatierra, all that the entire force of close to 3,000 men were able to produce was, according to the official inventory, '14 Springfield rifles, 55 *Concón* rifles, 199 Krag rifles, 8 Mausers, 28 smokeless rifles, eight 22-cal. Remingtons, 2 Mausers without butts, 2 Krags without butts, 11 Springfields, 2 Lewis machineguns, 10 Thompson machineguns, 9 Browning machineguns, and 3,129 rounds of assorted ammunition'. All the ammunition and the best firing pieces were promptly returned to Sandino to arm his 100-man 'emergency force', which would be stationed at Wiwilí, on the River Coco, where the erstwhile rebels planned to establish an agricultural co-operative. The peace agreement stated that the situation of this force, which was answerable to the President alone, would be reviewed a year later.

General Somoza was convinced that Sandino had stored away the bulk of his armament for future use against the Guardia, and that the President was party to the conspiracy. But in the wake of the peace treaty he had other, more pressing problems to attend to on the political front. With the rebellion in the north formally at an end, the Liberal party joined the Conservatives in demanding substantial cutbacks in the Guardia's strength and budget, and through the party legislators, Sacasa himself began to put forward the idea that many of the Guardia's functions should be handed back to the municipal police and the Treasury guards of yore. The *Jefe Director*, playing again on the mood of the junior officers of the Guardia, who felt their livelihoods threatened by these proposals, successfully resisted the latter demands, but was forced to agree to reductions in the Guardia's salaries (including his own) and to dismiss a large number of Escamilla's *auxiliares*.

In the meantime, the General was preparing carefully for his offensive : he ordered strict surveillance of everyone who was known to have dealings with Sandino, all the way up to the President himself, and routinely opened their mail and listened in on their telephone conversations. He organised a discreet campaign of harassment of the *sandinistas* who wandered beyond the protective umbrella of their 'emergency force', trumping up charges to throw them in prison and provoking armed clashes with Guardia patrols in the interior of the country. At the same time, he began to seek American approval of a plan whereby he would arrest Sandino and disperse the force he still had under arms.

Sandino replied with a stream of telegrams to the President, denouncing Guardia abuses and calling Sacasa's attention to a clause in the peace treaty which called for the placing of the Guardia within a proper 'constitutional' framework. Publicly, Sandino denounced the Guardia as unconstitutional, illegal, and an intolerable remnant of American intervention. He began to warn anyone who would listen that the Guardia were a threat to the constitutional government, and that it was only a matter of time before Somoza would feel strong enough to overthrow Sacasa and take the Presidency into his own hands.

In August, less than eight months after the new administration came to power, Managua was shaken by a chain of explosions. Someone had blown up the main arsenal at Campo de Marte. Sacasa reacted by imposing a state of siege, handing out arms to loyal Liberals and imprisoning hundreds of his Conservative adversaries; Somoza followed suit by purging the Guardia of its Conservative officers. There was, however, no evidence that the Conservatives had had anything to do with the explosions : no uprising followed in their wake, and the few feeble protests against government repression in the Conservative press were soon silenced by the imposition of censorship.

The most interesting reaction to the incident came from Sandino's camp up in the north. The former guerrilla leader, obviously convinced that the whole affair was a prelude to a coup by Somoza, sent a telegram to Sacasa informing him that he had mobilised 600 armed men, who were standing by to protect the President against any enemy. Sandino's hidden cache of arms had been flushed out into the open, although the former rebel attempted to explain them away as 'leftovers from the recent Honduran revolution' that he had managed to collect.

With a state of siege in force, the *Jefe Director* of the Guardia was in virtual control of the entire country but, contrary to expectations, he did not make an immediate takeover bid. Instead, Somoza began to set the pattern for many of his future actions by approaching the situation obliquely. Now that Sandino had shown his hand, Somoza went to the President with a report that the Guardia personnel, especially the junior officers, were indignant, and that it would be all but impossible to hold them back unless something was done about Sandino (as proof of his allegations he pointed to the increase in clashes between Guardia patrols and sandinistas—clashes which took place with the General's knowledge and approval, if not open encouragement). Simultaneously, Somoza started injecting funds into the newspaper *La Nueva Prensa,* the editorial columns of which began to call for a military *coup d'état.*

A worried Sandino flew hurriedly to Managua for talks with Sacasa and Somoza, but his fears were allayed by the *Jefe Director,* who went to the extreme of issuing a conciliatory statement jointly with the former rebel. Yet no sooner had Sandino left Managua than the Guardia had resumed its harassment of his men, and Somoza had begun to play his definitive hand. In public and in private he delivered an indirect ultimatum to Sacasa, demanding the complete disarmament of the *sandinistas* by February 1934, when according to the peace treaty the status of the 'emergency force' was due to be reviewed.

As the deadline drew near, top-level meetings of Guardia officers became more and more frequent, and units in the interior were marched out of their barracks and into the field, reportedly in the general direction of Sandino's headquarters at Wiwilí. Alarmed at these developments, Sandino wrote to Sacasa informing him that there would be no disarmament before the issue of the Guardia's 'constitutionality' was resolved, and reassuring Sacasa that the *sandinistas* would support him in any confrontation with the Guardia. The President summoned Sandino to Managua.

After three days of conversations which alternated with Sandino's violent public denunciations of the Guardia's 'unconstitutionality', the President came up with a wholly unexpected solution which seemed to tip the balance of the situation in Sandino's favour. The political and military control of Nicaragua's northern departments was to be unified under a special Presidential delegate, and the man chosen for the job was General Horacio Portocarrero, Sandino's erstwhile candidate for the Presidency of a revolutionary government.

Somoza was enraged. Though he still protested his loyalty to Sacasa, he insisted both to the President and to the American minister, Bliss Lane, that he would be unable to control the angry reaction of his men, who felt 'insulted' by the President's decision.

His warning went unheeded, and on February 21st the President held a celebratory farewell dinner party for Sandino, which was attended by Sandino's father, the Agriculture Minister Sofonías Salvatierra, and the former rebel Generals Francisco Estrada and

Juan Pablo Umanzor (two other members of Sandino's entourage, his half-brother Sócrates Sandino and the former General Santos López, stayed behind at Salvatierra's house). That same evening, Somoza had ordered the officers of the Managua garrison to attend a poetry recital and had convened an emergency meeting of his General Staff for a discussion of a delicate operation : the assassination of Augusto C. Sandino.

It was almost ten o'clock when Salvatierra drove the President's guests away from the Palace towards his own house, which lay beyond the Campo de Marte in central Managua. As they drew up to the barracks, they found the road blocked by a Guardia patrol. All five occupants were forced out of the car at gunpoint; Minister Salvatierra and Don Gregorio Sandino were led away into the military compound, and the other three were bundled into a truck and driven off into the night. A few minutes later the vehicle stopped. Sandino, Umanzor and Estrada were pushed out, unceremoniously lined up and shot. Their bodies were buried nearby, under the runway of Managua's airport.

At about the same time, another Guardia patrol surrounded Salvatierra's residence and ordered Sócrates Sandino and General Santos López to give themselves up. They resisted, and in the ensuing fight Sandino's half-brother and Salvatierra's son-in-law were killed. López escaped.

The clandestine operation had not passed unnoticed. Sacasa's daughter had witnessed the arrest and the American minister had heard the shooting, but when the President and Bliss Lane each tried to contact Somoza for an explanation, they discovered that their telephone lines had been cut. The *Jefe Director* did not emerge from his heavily fortified residence until well into the next day, and then only to claim that he had no knowledge of what had happened to Sandino (though he admitted that the Guardia were holding Salvatierra and Sandino's father, and ordered their release into the custody of the American minister).

A few days later the Guardia troops which had been massed quietly around Wiwilí advanced on the *sandinista* camp and massacred its occupants. Only General 'Pedrón' Altamirano and a handful of men managed to escape. Away in Guatemala, a saddened Gustavo Alemán Bolaños recalled one of Sandino's last few letters, in which he wrote : 'I shall not live much longer. But here are these lads who will continue with the struggle; they might manage to do great things. . . .'

CHAPTER XI

THE RISE OF SOMOZA I

The Sandino threat had disappeared, but in the aftermath of the rebel leader's assassination it began to seem as if Somoza had gone a little too far. In a rare display of determination, President Sacasa launched a counter-offensive. His first act was to issue a mysterious summons to the diplomatic corps, calling them to an unscheduled meeting at the Presidential Palace. When the envoys arrived, they found that Somoza and his General Staff had been compelled to attend as well. Then, without warning, Sacasa treated the diplomats to the embarrassing spectacle of the country's highest-ranking military officers being forced to renew their oath of allegiance to the President. Somoza's public humiliation was compounded when he was obliged, following a scathing Presidential denunciation of Sandino's murder, to give a formal pledge to discover and punish those responsible.

Sacasa streamrolled on, ordering the replacement of a number of leading Guardia commanders by his own appointees. The President's brother Antioco became Chief of Staff, and their cousin Ramón was placed in command of the key Acosasco garrison at León. Sacasa's personal guard at La Loma was reinforced by party stalwarts from León, and the hilltop fort was strengthened as if to resist a siege.

For a while, Somoza continued to deny in public any responsibility for or knowledge of Sandino's assassination, and even performed the charade of an investigation which produced a culprit : Captain Policarpo Gutiérrez, the only participant whom witnesses had been able to identify. Covertly, however, he began to spread by word of mouth and through his press organ *La Nueva Prensa,* an entirely different story : the assassination had been approved by Washington and obediently carried out by 'their man' Somoza.

Flaunting this alleged American patronage none too discreetly, Somoza began to lobby for support among the Liberal Congressmen, and was soon testing his strength against Sacasa's by ordering them to block the Administration's legislative proposals. Within three months he felt confident enough to tackle Sacasa head-on. He provocatively admitted that he had issued the order to kill Sandino and commended those who had committed the deed, and called upon Congress to decree an amnesty for everyone involved in the assassination. The bill was passed. An irate Sacasa vetoed it, only to see Congress pass it again with an overwhelming majority.

Delighted, Somoza abandoned all restraint and began to speak openly of his plans to run for the Presidency in 1936 at the expiry of Sacasa's term. He knew full well that, unless he were to resign the command of the Guardia (the one thing he never dreamed of doing) and retire from active duty six months before the elections, he would be banned by the Constitution from running for office, and on two counts : because he was related to the President by reason of his marriage to Sacasa's niece (the Constitutional ban affected everyone within four degrees of blood relationship to the incumbent), and because he was a serving officer. Quite unabashedly, the *Jefe Director* started sounding out his friends and acquaintances, including the American minister, on the relative merits of three solutions which did not involve his relinquishing any power at all. The first two were drastic but only went part of the way : he could either force Sacasa to resign six months before the elections, or divorce his wife Salvadorita, but that still left unsolved the problem of his military commission and command. The third solution was comprehensive enough, but far more complex and risky : to engineer a constituent assembly which could amend Nicaragua's charter so as to remove the obstacles to his candidacy.

Before 'Tacho' Somoza had actually made up his mind to pick this last alternative, an unexpected incident shook him into the realisation that he was still far from having achieved full control of his main power base, the Guardia Nacional. His friend Rigoberto Reyes, Colonel in charge of the Jinotega garrison, sent him a confidential report warning him against an assassination plot, apparently hatched by junior Guardia officers, the very career men Somoza believed he had firmly behind him. The ringleader, a young captain, was arrested, court-martialled and sentenced to prison, while twenty other captains and lieutenants were forced to resign their commissions. Although Somoza was unable to prove it, he was convinced that the plot had originated in the Presidential Palace, a suspicion that became even more firmly rooted when Sacasa seized upon the occasion to assert that the Guardia's officer corps were manifestly opposed to their *Jefe Director*'s Presidential aspirations.

On September 12th the capital city was once again rocked by an explosion at the Campo de Marte arsenal. Both Sacasa and Somoza believed at first that the bombing signalled the beginning of an entirely unexpected open confrontation, and they rapidly drew up their defence lines. However, the tension subsided as soon as the truth emerged : the explosion was the work of a young lieutenant, Juan López, who had chosen this unorthodox procedure as a means of settling a personal vendetta against the Campo de Marte's quartermaster.

Unsettled by this second successive instance of mutinous behaviour in the Guardia, Somoza had López sentenced to death. An equally rattled Sacasa, anxious to show that he was still in command, promptly issued a decree commuting the sentence to life imprisonment.

However much of an anti-climax this outcome of the incident may have been, it awakened both parties to their relative vulnerability in face of an eventual surprise coup. From that moment on, neither Sacasa nor Somoza would move from their fortified residences without a heavy armed escort, and Somoza took to having his food tasted in his presence for fear of being poisoned. The exaggerated precautions adopted on each side ended up by creating more conspiratorial tension, enhancing the position of the hardliners in either camp. Advocates of a military *coup d'état,* and particularly a group of young Fascist-leaning hotheads, flocked to Somoza's side and began to urge him on to an immediate takeover of the government.

Advisers to the President, with the encouragement of Sacasa's strongminded wife María, started urging the indecisive Sacasa to dismiss the ambitious *Jefe Director* before it was too late. But Sacasa procrastinated, on the grounds that he had to build up enough bipartisan political support before he could even contemplate such a drastic move. Somoza, on the other hand, was rash enough to heed the advice of his new Fascist supporters, and in November, taking advantage of the President's temporary absence from the capital, provided them with funds to organise a pro-Somoza rally in Managua. It was a total failure, and many of those who attended it or read the later press reports were not too excited by the organisers' portrayal of Somoza as Nicaragua's Hitler or Mussolini.

Somoza rapidly changed tack and launched another, more intense lobbying campaign among Liberal Congressmen, clearly aiming at mustering enough support to summon a constituent assembly which would clear his path to the Presidency. Although he seemed to be making some headway in this direction, a few months later a surprise government initiative gave him a nasty shock. Acting as a block, pro-Sacasa legislators and Conservative Congressmen passed a bill granting an amnesty to the cashiered Lieutenant Juan López, the man who was serving a life sentence for blowing up the Campo de Marte arsenal. The intention was evidently to slight the *Jefe Director,* who had originally wanted López shot.

Tacho reacted instantly. On the spur of the moment he rushed out his troops, fully armed, for a menacing parade in front of the Palacio Nacional. The legislators took the hint : they returned docilely to the Chamber and repealed the amnesty bill.

A few weeks later, Somoza received another danger signal. A disgruntled lieutenant, apparently inspired by Sergeant Fulgencio Batista's revolt in Cuba, was organising a mutiny among the Guardia's rank and file. The plot was nipped in the bud, a few score men were imprisoned or discharged, and the lieutenant, like Juan López before him, was sentenced to death.

Again President Sacasa intervened, commuting the sentence to life imprisonment. But this time, in open defiance of the President's decision, Somoza announced that he would proceed with the execution. It took a direct intercession by the American minister to make him change his mind.

Sacasa attempted to pursue the slight advantage he had gained in this prestige contest by announcing the imminent creation of a separate police force, which he would control himself through the Interior Ministry, but he withdrew the project as soon as Somoza threatened him with an 'uncontrollable reaction' on the part of the Guardia. Then Somoza turned the tables on him completely by confronting him with the issue of his candidacy—Sacasa buckled under, and agreed to Tacho's suggestion of calling an assembly to amend the Constitution. The President was abject enough to hint that such a constituent assembly could designate Somoza directly, dispensing with elections altogether.

If the President was easily cowed by Somoza, his wife María, who commanded the respect and obedience of most of Sacasa's advisors and Ministers, certainly was not. Exasperated by her husband's spineless behaviour, she took it upon herself to organise Somoza's downfall. Her efforts, however, were continually thwarted by a formidable obstacle : the new Rooseveltian United States, with its 'Good Neighbour' policy which at least made a pretence of not interfering overtly in the internal affairs of Latin America nations. It was true that the Americans had created the Guardia Nacional and virtually imposed it upon Nicaragua's last two elected governments. Through Arthur Bliss Lane, the U.S. minister, they had also been a decisive factor in the appointment of General Anastasio Somoza García as *Jefe Director,* and most of Nicaragua was convinced that Lane had at least tacitly agreed to Sandino's assassination. Furthermore, Lane always seemed to be on the scene whenever a major crisis was brewing.

But when *la Señora* approached Washington for assistance in restraining Somoza, she was rebuffed with the reminder that the United States were no longer responsible for the Guardia. Señora Sacasa was not daunted by this, and turned to engineering a solution nearer home. Calling on her extensive array of personal contacts, she managed to obtain assurances of military support from the neighbouring governments of Honduras and El Salvador in an attempt to dislodge Somoza by force. Yet again she was cut short by the State Department, which instructed Lane to make it clear that the United States would not tolerate any such action.

Shortly afterwards, however, the American minister did approach Somoza, and talked him into withdrawing his candidacy to the Presidency. Lane, Somoza and Sacasa met at the Presidential Palace to hammer out an agreement, which turned out to be a postponement rather than a complete renunciation of Somoza's ambitions. The General was to be guaranteed his position as head of the Guardia under the new administration, and the Presidential candidate, to be nominated jointly by the Liberal and Conservative parties, would have to meet with the Guardia's (i.e. Somoza's) approval. The formula looked neater in abstract than it was going to prove in practice. Almost as soon as it had been announced, the Liberal party leaders declared that while they agreed in principle, they would never accept a candidate of Conservative complexion; the Conservatives riposted that there was only one Liberal whose candidacy they were willing to espouse—General Anastasio Somoza García.

Tacho, having made his public show of statesmanlike selflessness, proceeded to exploit by proxy the unexpected boost which the Conservatives had given to his aspirations. 'Spontaneous' demonstrations of support for the General were orchestrated throughout the country, reaching a peak when Managua was hit by a mini-crisis which, if not actually caused by the *Jefe Director,* was certainly magnified and manipulated by his followers. Petrol began to run short in the capital city, and the anxiety of the country's growing sector of independent chauffeurs was deftly played upon by pro-Somoza activists and agitators. A chauffeurs' strike evolved into a series of anti-government demonstrations and riots; the coup-haunted President, losing his nerve once again, instructed the Guardia to restore order, adding the specific proviso that the Guardsmen were to use their firearms if necessary.

Somoza made sure that the President's harsh orders were leaked to the public at large, then deliberately ignored them. He called a meeting with the strikers, and in a rousing, populist speech, promised to defend them from exploitation by placing petrol distribution under direct Guardia control. The response was delirious : not only did the rioting and the strike cease forthwith, but Somoza emerged as a considerate conciliator, sympathetic to the plight of the downtrodden, in clear contrast to the insensitive President who had thought only of ordering violent repression. Even many of his erstwhile opponents began now publicly to extol his virtues, while among his supporters the call for a military coup surfaced again.

Floating on this wave of popularity, Somoza set himself the task of consolidating his hold over the Guardia by removing the pro-Sacasa officers, often in open defiance of the President's counter-manding orders, from all command posts in the interior of the country. The only two *sacasista* bastions he left untouched were the Presidential guard, which Sacasa had staffed with loyal men, and the Acosasco fort at León, commanded by the President's cousin Ramón, which had also been reinforced by a contingent of armed party members. But they could wait. Somoza's immediate objective was to keep his opponents off the streets while he effected a quiet takeover of most of the country. For this he needed, first, a Guardia which would obey him unquestioningly, and secondly, an independent shock force, capable of acting without even the minor restraints imposed upon his army-cum-police force. The latter he found in the earnest group of young Fascists, whom he supplied with the arms and funds they needed to set up a corps of *camisas azules* (blueshirts), a Nicaraguan version of Hitler's brownshirts and Mussolini's blackshirts.

Somoza's favourite tactic was to stage a riot in a town or city (at which the *camisas azules* excelled), then move in with the Guardia and, on the pretext of guaranteeing law and order, place the local government under military control. One locality after another fell under his grip in this fashion, and by April, with most of Nicaragua being effectively ruled from the *Jefe Director*'s residence, Tacho was feeling strong enough to renege on his agreement with Lane and Sacasa, and to proclaim that he was the only 'acceptable' candidate for both parties' nominations.

But time was running out for Tacho. Sacasa was still in power, he himself was still both married to the President's niece and serving as a military officer, and there was no sign of a call for the constituent assembly which would remove the legal obstacles to his candidacy in time for the scheduled 1936 elections. The Con-servative and Liberal leaderships had formally agreed to unite behind a single ticket, knowing full well that Somoza was ineligible to head it. The Sacasa faction believed that this gave them an edge over the General, whom they considered incapable, in the last instance, of running the risk of non-recognition by Washington through staging a *coup d'etat*.

Then, albeit indirectly, the United States intervened again to tip the scales in Tacho's favour.

In South America, Washington had long since abandoned the policy of non-recognition of revolutionary governments; since 1931 it had found it convenient to extend recognition to *de facto* régimes in Bolivia, Peru, Argentina, Brazil and Panama. In Central America, however, the rule was still the 1907 Washington agreement forced upon the region to stop Nicaragua's President Zelaya from overthrowing neighbouring governments. This inconsistency in the hemispheric policy of the United States was finally removed in early 1936, when Washington recognised Maximiliano Hernández Martínez's *de facto* régime in El Salvador. At the end of April, as Nicaragua was warming up for the nomination of a candidate to the Presidency, it was formally announced that the United States would apply to Central America the same criterion used in the rest of the continent—governments would be recognised if they were in full control of the country.

The first person to realise that this new situation called for negotiating with Somoza was the Conservative *caudillo* Emiliano Chamorro. In exchange for the General's approval of a candidate other than himself for the 1936 elections, Chamorro promised that two years later a constituent assembly would be convened to clear Somoza's way to the Presidency. Chamorro's old rival, the Liberal *caudillo* José María Moncada, advised Somoza instead that the best course of action in these changed circumstances would be to go ahead and topple Sacasa without bothering about elections at all.

Tacho decided to steer a middle course. Once again he withdrew his candidacy and declared his willingness to back the bipartisan agreement, but on two conditions : that he himself should nominate the candidate, and that he be given full control of the Guardia (which meant removing Ramón Sacasa, the President's cousin, from the command of the Acosasco fort). Sacasa rejected the latter condition, then went on to veto three successive candidates put forward by Somoza. Instead of insisting on the acceptance of his nominees, Tacho broke off the negotiations and shifted his attention to Sacasa's main bastion, the Acosasco fort at León.

He ordered Major Ramón Sacasa to dismiss his contingent of armed civilians and replace them with a supplement of handpicked Guardia soldiers from Managua. When the Major refused, Somoza left his friend Rigoberto Reyes in charge of the Managua garrison and rushed out to León at the head of a 2,000-strong Guardia force to quell the 'rebellion'. President Sacasa, inexplicably emboldened, ordered his cousin to resist and speedily convened a meeting with the Conservative leadership, out of which there emerged an agreement to nominate Leonardo Argüello (Sacasa's Foreign Minister) and Rodolfo Espinosa (his Vice-President) as joint Liberal-Conservative candidates to the Presidency and Vice-Presidency respectively.

The *Jefe Director* did not bother to argue. He replied by ordering a simultaneous attack on the Acosasco fort at León and the Presidential Palace at Managua. Fighting continued for three days, until on June 2nd, 1936, Sacasa ordered his cousin to surrender.

A triumphant Somoza offered to see Sacasa through to the end of his term, but four days later the President resigned and, leaving the government in the hands of his Interior Minister, scampered off to exile in El Salvador. Rodolfo Espinosa and Emiliano Chamorro, who had taken part in the proclamation of the Argüello-Espinosa ticket, also sought sanctuary abroad.

On June 9th, Somoza railroaded a submissive Congress into appointing his friend Carlos Brenes Jarquín as head of a caretaker government. All power of any consequence was now firmly in the *Jefe Director*'s hands.

CHAPTER XII

'OUR SON OF A BITCH'

Now that Sacasa had resigned 'of his own free will' and his main adversaries had chosen to leave the country, Tacho Somoza had nothing to lose by being punctiliously legalistic about the circumstances surrounding his entry to the Presidential Palace. There being already in existence a joint Liberal-Conservative ticket, he got the Liberal party to change its name to Partido Liberal Nacionalista, and persuaded a Conservative faction to set up a breakaway Partido Conservador Nacionalista, both of which dutifully nominated him as their Presidential candidate. His puppet interim President, Dr Brenes Jarquín, obliged by putting the date for the elections back to December, so that a six-month spell might elapse since his relative Juan Bautista Sacasa had held the highest office in the land. Also in keeping with the rules laid down by the Constitution, Somoza resigned his post as *Jefe Director* of the Guardia and doffed his uniform (though he continued to turn up at his office in mufti to issue the orders which his successor, his loyal friend Colonel Rigoberto Reyes, would formally impart).

No one was ever in any doubt as to what the election results would be, but to keep up appearances Somoza cavalierly allowed the first returns to show 1,200 votes for the Opposition (who had announced that they were boycotting the elections) against 79,000 for himself. However, by the time the final results were published, seven days later, these totals had changed to 107,000 for Somoza and only 169 for the Opposition—perhaps a needless addition to his margin of superiority, but certainly indicative of the fact that the General felt it would look better if he showed a much higher voter turnout.

In terms of Nicaraguan political tradition, it was not really the size of Somoza's 'landslide' victory that mattered most, but the fact that no President had ever before taken office wielding so much power of his own. Tacho made this abundantly clear by reassuming command of the Guardia as soon as he was inaugurated, Colonel Reyes being packed off to the War Ministry. His government was not the product of a shaky political entente, as were so many of those which had preceded his, nor had his victory depended on the electoral machinery of either of the major parties. His constituency, his real electorate, had been that Guardia Nacional which he had built up and moulded in his own image through a combination of guile, demagogy, opportunism and ruthlessness.

He now controlled, without having to tolerate any imposed rival power centres, the entire administrative apparatus of the country and the only armed force in the land. And a formidable force this was, by Nicaraguan standards at least. Not at all like the rag-tag bunch of ill-equipped, poorly trained and worse paid men who had formed the Nicaraguan Army of pre-1927 days, his was a corps 3,000 strong, of well-organised, reasonably remunerated soldiers led by a hard core of highly trained officers.

The Guardia Nacional was not only Nicaragua's army, but it was also its police force. It ran the prisons too, and through the rural magistrates (*Jueces de Mesta*) it administered justice. It granted business licences and controlled the trade in arms, explosives, liquor, tobacco and prostitution. It ran the national health service and the only countrywide radio network. And since it took over the functions of the *Guardias de Hacienda,* it also policed the collection of revenue for the government.

On reaching the Presidency, Somoza actually enlarged the scope of the machine. Into its hands went the national railroad, the postal and telegraphic services and the control of all border traffic, be it of persons or goods. And of course, he increased the Guardsmen's salaries. After all, if one took into consideration their families as well, some 15,000 or more people (close to 2 per cent of Nicaragua's population at the time) owed their livelihood to the Guardia payroll. If they were satisfied, the General could rest easy, so Tacho made doubly sure that they were happy, by turning a blind eye to the alacrity with which the Guardsmen took advantage of the almost limitless opportunities for graft and outright extortion that their pervasive influence conferred on them.

For himself, he perfected the kickback system that was already an institution with Nicaraguan administrations, making it more systematic and all-embracing. At a time when the country's small industrial and services sectors were expanding, it soon became the rule that the best, indeed often the only way of opening a business or even staying in business was to make a 'contribution' to the General's personal funds.

There was, however, a rather large area of Nicaragua's economic life over which Somoza held little sway: the landowning, coffee-planting oligarchy. With their own strong interests in financial institutions, their long-established contacts with overseas purchasers, and their widespread marketing network at home, they could afford to do without the government to a considerable extent. The key to their autonomy lay in their possession of Nicaragua's best lands and of a commodity for which the market seemed to be inexhaustible. True, they had their ups and downs, and at the time of Somoza's inauguration they, and in consequence the whole of the Nicaraguan economy, were being dogged by a seemingly everlasting worldwide depression. Yet one of Tacho's first acts of government, a strong devaluation of the *córdoba,* was a welcome boost both to their competitive standing abroad and to their wealth in domestic terms.

This, however, was not to be for much longer. The coffee planters' heyday was almost over, and Tacho Somoza was to be instrumental in hastening their demise as the dominant factor in Nicaragua's economy. He first set about becoming a landowner in his own right : people were 'persuaded' to part with choice lands which the President coveted, often at half their market value, and at times even as straightforward gifts. Somoza's control of the administrative apparatus enabled him, moreover, to pick the best and the cheapest of the unoccupied lands, and then to 'stimulate progress' by using the nation's public works budget to build roads to them and to lay telegraph and telephone lines. Labour for clearing those lands and preparing them for cultivation was often not even cheap, but actually gratis—the Guardia soldiers performed the necessary tasks.

Somoza was not satisfied with merely purchasing the lands and speculating with artfully increased real estate values; it was what he did with them that made the big difference. Very much in the spirit of showing his people how to better themselves by setting a personal example—one of his favourite maxims—he plunged into business by planting coffee (of course), but also by becoming a pioneer in cattle ranching and in the commercial crop which would soon take over from coffee as Nicaragua's most profitable export : cotton. The success of his cattle ranching ventures was assured by the precaution he took of charging a personal levy of 1.5 cents per lb. on everyone else's exports of beef.

As if all this were not enough to guarantee Somoza a more than comfortable income during his term of office, he reinsured himself by slapping on all civil servants a forcible contribution of 5 per cent of their salaries, to be paid into the central fund of the Partido Liberal Nacionalista, an account of which he disposed as if it were his own.

Pax somociana was underwritten, on the 'carrot' side, by a cunning application of the National Bank's credit lines to buying over potential rivals, such as the old Liberal *caudillo* José María Moncada and Somoza's adversary in the 1936 elections, Leonardo Argüello, both of whom became outspoken propagandists of his cause. On the 'stick' side, its guarantors were an informal system of press censorship, which operated mainly through fear of savage Guardia reprisals, and an all-embracing extension of the Guardia's network of *orejas* (ears, or informers) which ensured that even the most harmless gathering of known members of the Opposition would end up in a short spell of preventive incarceration. More obdurate opponents—and there were soon none too many of them—were rewarded with exile or never-to-be-investigated fatal accidents.

Apart from a number of quickly muted grumbles, the peace and quiet of Somoza's presidency was only marred by the fleeting appearance of a ghost from the past. A band of guerrillas emerged from a period of minor banditry to sack a plantation and a township in the River Coco area. Its leader was General 'Pedrón' Altamirano, the only one of Sandino's lieutenants to survive the Wiwilí massacre.

It was Somoza's first opportunity to test the capability of his security forces to handle subversive threats. The task was almost too easy. Five undercover agents (two of them prostitutes) infiltrated Altamirano's guerrilla group. Less than six months after the River Coco raid, 'Pedrón' was lured away for a night-long assignation. When he fell asleep, the three Guardia agents pounced upon him and severed his head with a machete blow. They returned to Managua to report to their commander, carrying Altamirano's head with them as proof of their deed.

Three years of Anastasio Somoza García's first term of office passed in relative calm. In 1939, he called a constituent assembly to give his country a better, more modern Constitution. The Guardia Nacional's powers and jurisdictions were again extended, and the President's term of office was extended from four to six years. The traditional constitutional injunctions against re-election and the candidacy of the incumbent's blood relations or of serving officers were firmly reiterated, but there was one exception to whom they would not apply : the current officeholder, Tacho.

In a remarkable show of political frugality, Somoza decided to dispense with the unnecessary bother of elections. He got the constituent assembly to transform itself into the nation's Congress for an eight-year spell, and once it was so metamorphosed, 'induced' the Congressmen to appoint him as President for the same term.

The very next year, Somoza received a reward for which he had always yearned : an official invitation to visit President Franklin D. Roosevelt at the White House. At long last the much-deserved recognition that he was the best friend of the United States in

Central America! Friends and foes alike have never tired since then of telling the following anecdote. It is said that when Secretary of State Cordell Hull showed Roosevelt the list of Heads of State to be invited to Washington, the President picked out Somoza's name and asked, 'Isn't that man supposed to be a son of a bitch?'

'He sure is,' replied Cordell Hull, 'but he is *our* son of a bitch!'

Tacho returned to Nicaragua from Washington with the renewed aura of being the Americans' chosen man, and never let anyone, least of all his opponents, forget it for an instant. Managua's Central Avenue, leading down from the Explana de Tiscapa to the lake, became the Avenida Roosevelt. Nicaragua's oldest aspiration, the trans-oceanic canal, became the subject of new, excited conversations with the United States. The Americans, proclaimed Somoza, would invest three million dollars in the canalisation of the San Juan river as the first major step of the project (and when this proved not to be feasible, Somoza talked Washington into granting him a two-million-dollar loan to build a coast-to-coast road from the Pacific to the Caribbean, opening up new lands—many of which were by then owned by him—for cattle ranching, crop planting and logging).

Coffee had hit an all-time low on the international markets, but Tacho was not unduly worried about this. Hardships for many there would certainly be, but thanks to a timely injection of American and Canadian capital, Nicaragua had found itself a new, valuable export commodity: gold, the gold for which the Spaniards had come searching but had not discovered. The President, of course, received a percentage of the mining profits.

War had begun in Europe, but other than in business terms Somoza paid little attention to it until the Americans began to crack down on Nazi spy nets. Then he too, the self-same Somoza who had been equated with Hitler and Mussolini after his first-ever political rally, who had used his pro-Nazi *camisas azules* to destabilise President Sacasa, who had actually appointed their leader Minister of Education in his first cabinet, rushed through Congress a bill banning all 'subversive' pro-Nazi propaganda and activities, and ordered the arrest of scores of people accused of sympathising with the Axis. And when Pearl Harbour was attacked, he promptly declared war on Japan, Germany and Italy. It was to prove a sound investment, especially in terms of the American military aid which would pour into the Guardia Nacional over the next few years.

Nicaragua's Fascists were not the only ones to discover that friendship with Somoza was not something on which they could rely forever. His Minister of War, Colonel Rigoberto Reyes, was suddenly sacked when it crossed Somoza's mind that he was becoming too well-known and respected. One of the few formal reasons Tacho gave for dismissing Reyes was that he had fallen under Nazi influence.

The Guardia Nacional emerged from the Second World War without having fired a shot in anger (beyond Nicaragua's borders, that is), but richer by an air force, a small navy and almost two million dollars of modern equipment. Tacho Somoza had fared well too : long before the end of the war he had managed to round off his personal fortune to somewhere in the vicinity of five million dollars.

CHAPTER XIII

THE ARGUELLO INTERLUDE

Somoza himself may have written the ban on re-election into the 1939 Constitution, but he certainly had no intention of abiding by it. Nevertheless, he had considered it politic to inform only a few acolytes of his plans; in Tacho's view, all he really needed to guarantee success when the time came for making his projects public was a firm grip on the Guardia Nacional and skilful playing of 'the American card'. His pervasive network of *orejas* kept him abreast of most of the plots and schemes hatched both within his own party and among the various Opposition groups, so it was hardly a coincidence that he chose to bring matters to a head at the Liberal convention in early 1944.

It had come to his notice that an important Liberal faction, headed by Carlos Pasos, was taking the 1939 Constitution too literally and was actually preparing the ground to nominate a candidate of its own to succeed the General in the elections scheduled for 1947. Furthermore, his spies had warned him of increasing unrest among the Opposition, whose appetite for power had been whetted by the recent ousters of General Maximiliano Martínez in El Salvador and of Jorge Ubico in Guatemala. Agitators backed by the adventurers of the 'Caribbean Legion' were already at work in Nicaragua, stirring up trouble in the University and the budding labour unions, creating the atmosphere for the launching of a general strike, a tactic which had proved only too successful in the neighbouring republics.

Somoza's moves were planned in absolute secrecy and executed with swift, calculated ruthlessness. When dawn broke on convention day, the leaders of the Pasos faction found themselves confined to their homes by contingents of armed Guardsmen, who did not bother to offer any sort of explanation for their action. Those who did attend the party gathering, some of them genuine supporters of Somoza's aspirations, many others cowed by his arbitrary display of force, promptly approved a motion committing the party to amending the constitutional ban on re-election.

There was an immediate, angry public backlash, of such intensity that a number of Liberal leaders began to believe that Tacho had finally overstepped himself. The Pasos faction broke away from the ruling party and set itself up as the Partido Liberal Independiente, which instantly started churning out the most vitriolic abuse the General had ever had to face in his eight years in power. The other Opposition forces took their cue from the newborn P.L.I. and, as Somoza had been expecting, embarked on an all-out offensive against the régime. The students spearheaded the revolt; demonstrations and riots flared up across the country, and the call went out for workers and businessmen to join forces and bring the country to a standstill.

Somoza turned a deaf ear to the many hints from his own inner circle, and from prominent Liberals like José María Moncada, that he should forgo his plans to run again for office. Instead, he ordered the closure of the National University and the arrest of anyone engaging in 'subversive activities'.

The U.S. State Department was just as dubious as the Liberal hierarchy about Somoza's prospects, and even went to the extreme of dissociating itself, and the American embassy in Managua, from a Fourth of July parade Tacho staged in order to convince the populace that he was still 'Washington's man' in Nicaragua. This rebuff, unknown to the public at large, did not deter Somoza from waving the American banner. Indeed he went on to convey the impression that the United States were behind his every action by making the American president of Nicaragua's Price Control Board, Colonel Irving Lindberg, issue an order for the confiscation of any businesses closing their doors in support of the general strike advocated by the Oppositon. The strike did not materialise.

Having averted this immediate threat to his permanence in power, Somoza changed course abruptly, throwing the Opposition into confusion and halting the slide towards disaffection which was becoming all too noticeable within his own ranks. He cunningly allowed his obsequious Congressmen to pass an illegal constitutional amendment lifting the ban on his re-election; then, in a patronising show of righteousness, he vetoed the measure. And instead of clamping down hard on further Opposition attempts at agitation, he amnestied those who had participated in previous riots and demonstrations.

Then came the masterstroke. Taking his cue from what Colonel Juan Domingo Perón was doing in faraway Argentina, Somoza railroaded his Congress into passing an ultra-progressive Labour Code, thus robbing the Opposition leaders of their most effective banners, and simultaneously creating a smokescreen which enabled the government to organise the labour force into an assortment of new, officially-controlled unions.

The weakness of his relationship with the Americans was now the only remaining flank to take care of. Even more than their eventual support for this re-election plans, Somoza needed their

backing for a pressing practical purpose : the strengthening of his
Guardia Nacional. The General was genuinely worried by the
'Caribbean Legion's' continual harassment of his régime from
abroad, and believed that it was only a matter of time before his
domestic Opposition regrouped for a serious attempt at unseating
him. He now had a couple of hostile neighbours to the north, and
word had reached him that the Legion's anti-dictatorial gospel
was making many converts in Costa Rica to the south. He began
to be obsessed with the notion that the Legion would provide bases,
weapons and training for an invading force of Nicaraguan exiles,
and that his only long-term chances of survival depended on his
building up an army capable of delivering decisive pre-emptive
strikes beyond Nicaragua's borders. For this purpose he required
aircraft, arms and munitions. In other words, he needed American
military aid.

The U.S. State Department was becoming increasingly reluctant
to make any move which would not only be construed by the rest
of Central America as an approval of Somoza's political aims, but
which might even, in Tacho's present belligerent mood, spark off
a war in the region. So instead of approaching the politicians and
diplomats, the General concentrated his efforts on the American
military establishment, which not only considered him an old
and reliable friend, but also felt that it was strategically sound to
bring the Nicaraguan armed forces up to U.S. standards, so that
they could be incorporated into the American Army without more
ado in case of a major conflict. The military, moreover, were far
more realistic than the State Department about Somoza's future in
Nicaraguan politics.

They had paid close attention to the way in which the General
was intertwining the Guardia Nacional with his own family. His
bastard son José had only recently been brought up from the
ranks into the officer corps. His brother-in-law Luis Manuel
Debayle was a colonel. His twenty-two-year-old son Luis had been
made Captain when he returned from California with a degree in
agricultural engineering—indeed, Captain Luis Somoza was the
man the General had chosen to conduct negotiations with the
Americans for the purchase of new military hardware. His younger
son Anastasio ('Tachito') had just completed his studies at the
La Salle Military Academy and, already a First Lieutenant in the
Guardia at the age of sixteen, had entered West Point to further
his military career. It was quite clear that Somoza, whether or not
he continued in the Presidency, was not going to relinquish his
hold over an armed force he had turned into yet another of his

booming family concerns.

Yet when Harry S. Truman came to power, the United States' official attitude towards Somoza hardened into outright opposition. Nelson Rockefeller, the new Assistant Secretary of State, summoned Somoza's ambassador (and son-in-law) Guillermo Sevilla Sacasa to warn him that if Tacho's candidacy was not withdrawn, the States might even consider breaking off diplomatic relations with Nicaragua.

Always the master tactician, the General reacted instantly, in a fashion no one expected. He called U.S. ambassador Fletcher Warren and 'confided' to him that the whole issue of his re-election was simply a crafty ruse to ensure peace and quiet in the country, and especially in the Guardia Nacional, until election time came. Somoza brazenly claimed that he had never really harboured any aspirations for a third term of office; he was just pretending to do so in order to discourage the more ambitious of his Guardia officers from engaging in a mad, suicidal scramble for the Presidency. When the time was ripe, he assured Warren, he would announce his withdrawal from the race. Then, lowering his voice, he told the Ambassador that he would appreciate Washington's help in choosing the right sort of successor.

Like the shepherd who had cried 'Lamb! Lamb!' once too often, Somoza was not believed. In fact, his stubborn refusal to climb down began to foster within the Guardia the unrest he claimed to be preventing. Somoza was still very worried about the threat posed by the 'Caribbean Legion', particularly now that two of the Legion's notables, Rómulo Gallegos and Rómulo Betancourt, had been swept to power in Venezuela by a civilian-military coup. The Caribbean seemed to be getting smaller for Tacho's kind of régime, and the Americans were still steadfastly refusing him the aircraft and arms he considered vital to his survival. The Guardia officers were hardly oblivious to this. Furthermore, the American military attaché in Managua, Colonel Frederick Judson, was actively fanning discontent among the career men in the Guardia's officer corps, harping on their second-class status *vis-à-vis* Somoza's political appointees, and hinting broadly that their only real opportunity for advancement lay in purging the Guardia of its party-political elements. This, naturally, meant getting rid of Somoza.

When the General got wind of Judson's activities, he demanded his recall by Washington. This, however, did not halt the spread of the cancer. Indeed the mutinous mood grew stronger, and Somoza's immediate entourage began to lose its nerve. But Tacho himself did not cave in until his own brother-in-law, Colonel Luis Manuel Debayle, resigned his commission in the Guardia, and both Somoza's wife (Luis Debayle's sister) and his eldest son Luis pleaded for his withdrawal from the Presidential race.

On November 29th, 1945, Somoza handed the U.S. Ambassador a written pledge that he would publicly disallow his candidacy, repeal the emergency legislation that had suspended civil liberties in Nicaragua, and free all political prisoners. The decision was made public a month later.

The General kept his word. Political detainees were released, anti-Somoza rallies were authorised, the press began openly to criticise the régime.

In their elation, people paid little attention to what Tacho himself was doing. And Tacho was hard at work modifying some of the key controls of Nicaragua's power structure, in order to ensure that when he moved out of the Presidency most of his power would move with him. He had, for the time being at least, given up hopes of remaining at the Presidential desk, but he certainly had not contemplated for an instant stepping down from his command of the Guardia Nacional. On the contrary, he began to reorient many of the more important of the reins of power towards the office of the *Jefe Director*. The office itself was located in *La Curva*, a newly-built mock castle which now harboured the arsenal previously stored in the cellars of the President's mansion.

His twenty-two-year-old son Tachito, already a Major and Inspector-General of the Army (his fellow-students in the States had joked that he was the first West Point man to be given an Army as a graduation present, while Managua wags punned that Somoza had performed the miracle of 'making the Minor Major'), was given command of the Guardia's élite First Battalion, stationed at the strategic fort of La Loma. Officers whose loyalty to the *Jefe Director* was beyond doubt were shuttled to key posts throughout the country and, perhaps even more important, emissaries were sent abroad to try to find a way of circumventing the U.S. State Department's ban on arms sales to Nicaragua.

Somoza's influence on the political scene had not vanished overnight either. When the Conservatives and Independent Liberals joined forces behind the candidacy of Enoc Aguado, it was Somoza who engineered the nomination of Leonardo Argüello as candidate for the ruling Liberal party. Argüello was already an old man, who had served as Juan Bautista Sacasa's Minister for Foreign Affairs and stood against Somoza in the 1936 elections, but who had later been converted to Somoza's cause to the extent of having been instrumental in the unification of the 'historic' Liberal party behind Tacho. The General felt quite confident of his ability to manipulate the ageing politician once he took office, for take office he would—Somoza was taking no chances on that account. If he had allowed the Opposition to campaign unhindered, the press to criticise openly, it was not because of any new-found love for democratic procdures, but simply to lull them into complaisance.

Somoza did not interfere with the process until February 2nd, 1947, when the crowds began to queue up in front of the polling stations. Balloting was not exactly secret, since even before entering the stations voters were separated into two lines : on one side those in favour of Argüello, on the other side voters for the Opposition. From the outset the Opposition queues were plagued by all sorts of bureaucratic difficulties : arguments arose over identification, officials vanished for long spells of time, guards kept changing their minds about precisely where the queues should be.

Towards the end of the day there was only one long, almost motionless line of Opposition supporters waiting to cast their vote. At sunset, pointedly ignoring their existence, the Guardia closed the polling stations and sped the ballots off to the electoral headquarters at the National Palace, while armed patrols cleared the streets. Vote counting was remarkably swift : the following day Somoza announced that the Liberal candidate, Leonardo Argüello, had been elected by an overwhelming majority.

Everything seemed to be proceeding according to plan. Except that the General had grossly overestimated Argüello's loyalty and pliancy. No sooner had the election results been confirmed than the President-elect was rushing off to inform the American ambassador of the new government's intention to remove Somoza from his command. Argüello laboured silently and efficiently in the few weeks before his inauguration, and immediately after being sworn in he began to spring a series of changes designed to undercut Somoza's control of the Guardia. Most of the recognisably pro-Somoza stalwarts, including Major Tachito Somoza and the Chief of the Managua Police, were relieved of their duties and posted to less important commands in the interior. The public administration was purged of many Somoza appointees, and the new cabinet ministers were carefully chosen for their animosity towards the General.

The speed and brilliance of the manoeuvre convinced many, not least the American ambassador, that Somoza's hour had come. And when the General's visible response was a bumbling show of second-rate bravado (he ordered the Guardia's only three tanks to trundle out in front of the President's residence), they began to write him off as a bad dream from which Nicaragua was finally awaking.

But Tacho did not take long to recover from his initial surprise. Without failing to assure the U.S. Embassy that he felt no ill-will towards President Argüello, the General speedily rearranged his pawns. When Congress went through the routine procedure of nominating the men who would succeed the President in case of his death or disability, it was Somoza who actually picked out the 'designates'. In a matter of days, 300 of the best men in the First Battalion of the Guardia, control of which had been wrested by Argüello from Tachito Somoza, were posted to new duties in the *Jefe Director's* personal guard and in the Campo de Marte. Orders were sent out to the provinces, instructing garrison commanders to disregard orders that did not come from Somoza himself, and especially those issued by the President. Then came a series of telephone calls to the Opposition leaders whom Somoza had cheated of victory at the polls by blatant fraud, offering them participation in a new, revolutionary government. They refused, but instead of warning Argüello they began to prepare for a revolt of their own taking advantage of this obvious split in the ruling party.

Twenty-five days after Argüello had entered the Casa Presidencial, Somoza made his move. The President's telephone lines were cut before dawn, and as troop carriers from the provinces rumbled into Managua, officers loyal to Argüello were dragged from their beds and placed under arrest. In less than twenty-four hours it was all over for Leonardo Argüello; he had barely made good his escape to the Mexican Embassy when, down at the Palacio Nacional, bleary-eyed Congressmen, surrounded by Guardia troops, heard him accused of nothing less than plotting to establish a dictatorship. They promptly decreed his formal removal from office, and in his place they appointed Benjamín Lacayo Sacasa, the General's first 'designate'.

Up in Washington, Truman reacted by denying recognition to the new government and pressuring the rest of Central America to follow suit. All U.S. military personnel stationed in Nicaragua were recalled, and the few military aid programmes that remained in force were frozen.

Somoza was completely unfazed by all this. He seemed to know, better than the State Department itself, which way American international policies were heading, and proceeded to play his cards with extraordinary skill. A constituent assembly was convened and

Nicaragua was given a new charter, one of the first in the hemisphere to anticipate the cold war by including specific anti-Communist provisions (as well as an enticing piece of bait: an open invitation to the United States to set up military bases of its own on Nicaraguan soil). In the process, the interim President, Lacayo Sacasa, was shunted aside, and Somoza's uncle, his former Foreign Minister Victor Román y Reyes, was appointed in his stead.

Far too late, the irrepressible Emiliano Chamorro led the Conservatives into revolt. Somoza hurled at them everything the Guardia had, and in a matter of days had forced Chamorro into yet another exile, and had imprisoned every Opposition leader who was likely to cause any trouble.

The Washington-inspired boycott of Tacho's new escapade was a flop. The President of the Dominican Republic, Rafael Trujillo (himself an erstwhile commander of a Guardia Nacional created by the Americans in the good old days of 'big stick' diplomacy), and the Costa Rican President Teodoro Picado (a partner of Somoza's in some *sub rosa* livestock business deals) extended their recognition to the new 'Constitutional' Nicaraguan administration. Through them Somoza had already found a way around Washington's arms embargo, and had even managed to buy some old B-24 bombers from Brazil. By early 1948 a menacing, belligerent Nicaragua again enjoyed diplomatic relations with all of Latin America, and with the United States as well.

CHAPTER XIV

THREE LITTLE WARS

Tacho Somoza was not allowed to sit back and enjoy his diplomatic victory for long. Events in neighbouring Costa Rica soon renewed his fear of becoming encircled by anti-dictatorial governments. His good friend and business partner Teodoro Picado had called elections, confident that power would return into the hands of his patron and mentor Rafael Angel Calderón Guardia, who had preceded him in the Presidency. But the Costa Rican electorate refused to go along with his plans, and lent their support instead to the Opposition candidate, Otilio Ulate. Picado, backed by an unholy alliance of extreme right- and left-wing groups, promptly annulled the election results and prevented Ulate from taking office.

In March 1948, with the enthusiastic endorsement of the 'Caribbean Legion', Colonel 'Pepe' Figueres launched a civilian uprising against the *calderonista* régime. Sensing the gravity of the threat, Somoza ordered Guardia units to cross the border and engage the rebels, and offered to airlift 1,000 Guardsmen into the capital, San José. Picado demurred—a fatal error; within a few weeks, only minimally affected by the Nicaraguan offensive in the distant border region, the insurgents were charging into San José and setting up a revolutionary junta.

Picado and Calderón, and a number of their followers, sought refuge in Nicaragua. Somoza refused to let them accept their defeat as final, and immediately set about planning a counter-revolution. The *calderonistas* were taken into Guardia camps for crash military training, and a select group of Guardsmen was secretly drawn from the élite units to join them in a special, 1,000-strong strike force. Emissaries were sent into Costa Rica to organise the scattered *calderonistas* into clandestine support groups, and a scathing propaganda campaign was launched against Figueres, accusing him, in order to curry favour with the U.S. State Department, of attempting to set up a Communist bridgehead in Central America (a particularly hypocritical allegation, given the fact that the Costa Rican Communist Party was a firm ally of the *calderonistas*).

Planning, plotting and training were still far from complete when 'Pepe' Figueres himself signalled the opportunity for a coup. On December 1st, 1948, on the grounds that a peace-loving nation like Costa Rica had no need for an army, Figueres disbanded the armed forces. Internal security was entrusted to an enlarged

109

national police force, and the Bella Vista barracks, which had formerly housed the Army headquarters, were handed over to the Ministry of Education for transformation into a museum.

Only ten days later, the strike force of exiled *calderonistas* and Nicaraguan Guardsmen in civilian clothing slipped across the border to occupy the village of La Cruz, in north-west Costa Rica. An amphibious unit landed further down the Pacific coast and made for Liberia, the main city in the province of Guanacaste.

Figueres declared martial law, issued a call for volunteers to repel the invasion, and launched a diplomatic offensive to isolate the Nicaraguans. The U.N. Security Council was alerted, the Rio de Janeiro reciprocal defence treaty was invoked, and the Organisation of American States was called upon to put an end to the hostilities. The instant response of the Costa Rican people, plus the immediate aid offered by Guatemala's President Juan José Arévalo allowed Figueres to halt the invading force in its tracks. A series of air strikes pushed the last of the attackers back across the Nicaraguan border only a week after the invasion had begun.

Rather belatedly, an investigating committee appointed by the Organisation of American States turned up on the scene, only to turn Somoza's military defeat into a diplomatic gain. The Nicaraguan government was absolved from any guilt, getting away with a mild rebuke for not having prevented the incident, while Costa Rica was severely criticised for harbouring on its soil 'the so-called Caribbean Legion'.

Tacho was far from satisfied with this outcome, but deferred further immediate action for the sake of consolidating his domestic situation. He invited the Conservative *caudillo* Emiliano Chamorro to return from exile, with an enticing bait : a deal which would allow the Conservatives to share power with him, in exchange for a pact of non-aggression. The agreement was formalised through yet another constituent assembly, which transformed Nicaragua into a political duopoly. The party of the majority (and there was no real doubt as to what this euphemism meant) would take two-thirds of the seats in Congress, and a majority in each and every one of the nation's collegiate bodies, while the other third (which included a seat on the Supreme Court) was reserved for the runners-up, to the exclusion, by means of a deviously concocted electoral code, of anyone else. The adoption of a new Constitution also had the virtue of enabling Tacho to run for another term of office, from which he would have been barred by reason of family ties with the incumbent, his uncle Víctor Román y Reyes. There were two attentive learners next to Tacho throughout this particular Constitution-bending exercise : his sons Luis, aged twenty-seven, and Tachito, twenty-four.

As it turned out, Somoza did not have to wait for the elections to take over the Presidency again. Román y Reyes died of a heart attack a couple of weeks before the nation went to the polls, and Congress duly appointed Tacho to complete his uncle's term of office. The usual dose of electoral fraud, compounded on this occasion by the Conservatives' satisfaction with their part of the power-sharing agreement, ensured Somoza of a comfortable majority when the votes were cast.

'Dictatorship!' sneered Tacho at the time; 'the Opposition knows how kind I am. I pardon them; we have no political prisoners here. I am beginning to believe that the word is just an honorific title.'

As Somoza began his fourth term as President of Nicaragua, things were changing too in neighbouring Guatemala. Juan José Arévalo was succeeded in the Presidency by Colonel Jacobo Arbenz, a man committed to deepening Arévalo's already radical social reforms. Arbenz had become the darling of the Latin American left, and by the same token, was soon Washington's *bête noire,* particularly when the first entity to be affected by Guatemala's revolutionary agrarian reform law was the United Fruit Company. More than 300,000 acres of *El Pulpo*'s holdings were expropriated, and compensation was set at about one-eighth of the value set on the lands by the company itself. Then the American-owned power utility, and the railways came under fire. 'Communism!' cried the business lobby up in Washington. 'Communism indeed! I warned you!' chimed in Somoza, and soon his country and neighbouring Honduras were crawling with C.I.A. agents and recruiters, led by a certain 'Colonel Carl Studer', bent on finding a way to stem the Red tide.

'*Gringos*! *Gringos* everywhere! What do you think they are doing here? Are they F.B.I. agents, or spies?' The query came from a young, as yet uncommitted 'Che' Guevara, who had arrived from Costa Rica, via Nicaragua and El Salvador, to take a close look at the Guatemalan experiment.

A force of 200 exiled Guatemalans headed by Colonel Carlos Castillo Armas was pooled by the C.I.A. with an assortment of some 600 'volunteers' seconded from the Nicaraguan and Dominican National Guards, the Honduran army, and the reserve of Colombian veterans who had fought in Korea. Clandestine training camps were set up, and some 600,000 dollars' worth of American military equipment was flown down in two Globemasters on the pretext of redressing the regional balance, which had allegedly been upset by Guatemala's importation of armaments from the Soviet bloc. When the Tenth Pan-American Conference convened in Caracas and agreed on the outlawing of Communist parties throughout Latin America, and on mutual solidarity in case of Communist aggression against any country in the hemisphere, the stage was finally set for intervention.

In early June unmarked aircraft flew over Guatemala's cities releasing thousands of pamphlets summoning the population to arms, and powerful radio transmitters set up just beyond Guatemala's borders started beaming Castillo's seditious communiqués. A week later, four armed columns entered the country from different staging points in Honduras. Surprisingly they encountered little opposition. Arbenz seemed wholly unable to organise the forces that rallied to his support, and refused to arm the civilians, so when army morale crumbled through sheer absence of leadership, the Arbenz régime simply disintegrated. Che Guevara, who had attempted to organise some sort of resistance in the capital, was among the few who managed to escape the ensuing bloodbath.

Somoza's wholehearted support of the Americans' first battle by proxy in this not-so-cold war earned him their recognition, mainly in the form of more military aid, and considerable prestige as a leader in the hemispheric struggle against Communism. Not everyone, however, was overjoyed at his heightened international standing, as he discovered when his intelligence chief brought him reports of a conspiracy to assassinate him. Hatched by none less than the hardy Emiliano Chamorro, supported by the Costa Rican leader 'Pepe' Figueres and involving a number of Guardia officers, the plot called for a re-enactment of Sandino's murder : Tacho was to be ambushed as he left a late meeting at the American Embassy. The crackdown on the plotters and their suspected accomplices was harsh. Many were hunted down and shot without even the benefit of trial by a kangaroo court; many others, including Chamorro, had to flee abroad for their lives.

And Somoza did not stop there. He despatched troops to the Costa Rican border, regrouped the *calderonista* exiles into a new fighting force under the nominal command of young Teodoro Picado (the former Costa Rican President's son) and began to harass the San José government, which he again accused of leaning towards Communism, perhaps in the hope of stirring up the same sort of anti-Communist fever which led to the U.S.-sponsored coup in Guatemala.

In November 1954 'Pepe' Figueres announced to the world that the Costa Rican police had discovered an international conspiracy to launch a series of armed uprisings throughout the country simultaneously with an invasion from Nicaragua. But this did not deter Somoza, who was in the process of enlarging his air force with 25 P-51 planes bought in Sweden. On January 11th he struck.

Troops rolled across the northern border, landed on the Pacific coast and were air-ferried deep into Costa Rican territory; clandestine radio stations, operating from Nicaraguan soil, called upon the *calderonistas* to rise in arms, while unmarked Nicaraguan air transports dropped arms and supplies at prearranged spots, and several P-51's, also unmarked, made a series of strafing raids on major cities, including the capital, San José.

Figueres again invoked the Rio treaty, and this time he got an immediate, positive response from Washington. American fighter planes were ordered out of their Panama Canal Zone bases to prevent any further violations of Costa Rican air space, and Figueres was supplied with four P-51s and a Globemaster—an act which an enraged Somoza described as 'putting dangerous toys in the hands of a lunatic'.

American intervention, coupled with Figueres' remarkable ability at mobilising an Army-less nation, turned the tide of this little war. Deprived of air support and supplies, the invaders, who had relied on achieving a lightning victory, began to fall back towards the Nicaraguan border, relentlessly pursued by the Costa Ricans' borrowed air force. Young Picado was killed in action, and by January 18th the last of his 'rebel army' had beaten a hasty retreat into Nicaragua.

With Washington backing Figueres, Somoza did not dare to throw his formidable military machine, the largest in Central America, into a 'formal' war with Costa Rica. Instead, he attempted once again to disguise his defeat by pretending to have had nothing to do with what he described as 'an internal Costa Rican affair'. Chutzpah paid off again, for when the inevitable O.A.S. 'investigation committee' produced its report, which clearly stated that the 'rebels', the ammunition, the broadcasts and the air strikes had come from Nicaragua, the Somoza régime was not formally accused of instigating and organising the invasion, but merely of having sinned by omission. One of the committee members, the Ecuadorean José R. Chiriboga, disgustedly denounced a deliberate cover-up, but no-one took his allegations any further.

Defeated in war, Tacho found his peace bedevilled by an economic crisis which threatened to undo much of what he had

achieved in the past decade. By the early 1950's, Somoza had led
the Nicaraguan economy to the first trade surplus in anyone's living
memory, and the boost he had given to public works, even though
they tended to benefit him more than anyone else, had rubbed
off on the economy as a whole, to the extent that an enthusiastic
American academic, Hubert Herring, concluded that Tacho 'could
probably win an honest election if he ever risked such a test'.
Somoza, he said, 'had done much for his retarded land; he built
schools and hospitals, extended roads, modernised agriculture,
erected hydroelectric plants, expanded cattle raising, and spurred
mineral production . . . by 1954 Nicaragua was paying its bills,
balancing its budget, and showing a trade surplus.'

The volatility of the international markets for Nicaragua's main
exports had put all that at risk, and in July 1955 Somoza took the
drastic step of again devaluing the *córdoba* (from 5 to 7 per U.S.
dollar). It was a measure which, as usual, made many wealthy
Nicaraguans wealthier, but the changes that had been taking place
in Nicaraguan society ensured that its negative effects were felt
by many more people than before. When import prices rose, the
impact was no longer confined to a small élite which could easily
shrug aside the extra expense, but spread out to a growing middle
sector of white-collar workers and small entrepreneurs who had
risen above 'subsistence' levels of consumption. Not surprisingly,
disaffection began to spread too.

In typical, irrepressible Somoza style, Tacho's reply was to proclaim his candidacy for a fifth term as President, and to turn his
attention, with great nonchalance, to a series of diplomatic ventures aimed at improving his image abroad. His pervasive network
of *orejas* had not told him, because they had no means of knowing,
that a young poet and journalist from Léon, exiled in San Salvador, had begun to plot his assassination.

CHAPTER XV

SOMOZA IS DEAD, LONG LIVE SOMOZA!

My Dear Mother,

Though you have never known, I have always been involved in everything concerned with attacking the dismal régime which rules over our fatherland. In view of the fact that all attempts at making Nicaragua once again (or for the first time) a free country, without stain or dishonour, have failed, and even though my comrades disagree with me, I have decided to try to be the person who will begin the end of this tyranny.

If God wills me to die in the attempt, I do not want anybody to be blamed in the very least, for it has all been my own doing.

'X', who knows us all very well, has remained in charge, as have all our fellow countrymen residing here, of helping you in whatever you may need.

As I told you once before, some time ago I took a life insurance policy for 10,000 *córdobas,* with double indemnity, which is to say 20,000 *córdobas.* 'Y' will pull all the necessary strings for this money to reach your hands, as it is in your name. There is an exception to this: as you well know. I have always lived with the Andrade family, who have been so kind to me for such a long time, and I want 1,000 *córdobas* of that money to be given to Miss Dina Andrade so that she may finish her schooling, as she might be forced to abandon her studies for lack of funds. You can do this through her sister, Miriam Andrade de Rivera, since you shall have to travel to this city where, after the legal side is sorted out, the full value of the policy will be handed over to you.

As I said earlier, 'Y' and the other comrades will do everything that is needed for you to collect the money.

I hope you will take all this calmly and realise that what I have done is a duty that any Nicaraguan who loves his fatherland should have carried out long ago.

This is not a sacrifice, but a duty I hope I have been able to fulfil.

If you take things the way I wish you to, I assure you that I will be very happy.

So, no sadness, because a duty to the fatherland well carried out is the greatest satisfaction a righteous man, such as I have striven to be, can take with him.

If you take things serenely and in the absolute conviction that I have done my highest duty as a Nicaraguan, I shall be very grateful to you.

Your son who has always loved you so much,

RIGOBERTO

Rigoberto López Pérez, the budding man of letters from León, had tired of all the conspiratorial talk in which the Nicaraguan exile community indulged so readily. He kept insisting that it would only take the action of one determined man to put an end to Somoza's rule. When his friends refuted him, claiming that eliminating Somoza was not the same as destroying the dictatorial apparatus that he had created, and that the latter task demanded a slow, uphill effort of political organisation, Rigoberto replied that a successful attempt on Somoza's life would probably spark off an uprising that would finish the job of demolishing the dictatorship. As the discussion went round and round in circles, Rigoberto decided to take the matter into his own hands.

The letter to his mother shows that he had few hopes of surviving the attempt. But he planned and prepared himself carefully. He practised with his revolver until he was confident that he would not miss his target. He mentally rehearsed many of the possible scenarios, then set himself to picking an appropriate time and place. The most obvious occasion, one which appealed to Rigoberto's romantic sense of historic justice, was the centenary of the battle in which the American filibuster William Walker, who had usurped the Presidency of Nicaragua, was finally defeated. It would take place on September 14th, 1956, in Rivas. However, when Rigoberto turned up at the scene, he was unable to get close enough to Somoza to guarantee an accurate hit. Rather than risk failure, he started looking for another opportunity.

It came six days later, when Tacho travelled to Rigoberto's home town of León to attend his official nomination ceremony. An open reception had been organised for the following evening at the Casa del Obrero. Legend has it that Rigoberto spent the last hours of the afternoon refereeing a soccer game which some urchins had improvised in the street. He is said to have broken away from them saying, 'I have a little errand to run.'

It was not too difficult for him to mingle with the crowd and elbow his way to within striking distance of the beaming Tacho. Rigoberto drew his revolver and fired four times at point blank range. The President's bodyguards gunned him down almost instantly, but by then Somoza was stretched out on the floor, motionless. Though not quite dead.

A helicopter flew the stricken dictator to Managua. On President Dwight D. Eisenhower's orders, this 'great friend of the United States' was rushed to the Gorgas Hospital in the Panama Canal Zone, in a desperate attempt to save his life. Nicaraguans were not told how critical Tacho's condition really was, and by the time the news of his death was suddenly sprung on them, on September 29th, 1956, the cogs in the dictatorial machinery had been rearranged to ensure a smooth, almost uninterrupted transfer of power to his heirs, his sons Luis and Tachito. Rigoberto had been wrong.

In the ruling family's division of labour, Luis had become the 'political' animal. At an early age he had been packed off to the United States to study at the La Salle Military Academy, but he showed no inclination for a military career. He tended to see his future in terms of administering his family's extensive rural land-holdings, and persuaded his father to allow him to enter the University of California to read for a degree in agricultural engineering. On his return to Nicaragua, however, he found him-self pressed almost immediately into political service. At the time, Tacho was preparing for the 1947 elections against considerable domestic and American opposition, and was feeling threatened by the growing influence of the anti-dictatorial Caribbean Legion. He needed a trustworthy aide who was familiar with the American scene to talk the military in Washington into supplying him with arms and military aircraft (both of which were under a strict embargo), and the most obvious candidate for the job was his eldest son Luis.

Luis' sojourn at La Salle had earned him a commission in the Guardia Nacional, so it was as *Captain* Luis Somoza that he em-barked upon an unexpected career as a top-level negotiator. Luis was unsuccessful with the Americans, but skilful enough to help his father circumvent Washington's arms embargo and find else-where the hardware he needed to build up Central America's best-equipped war machine. The momentum of Tacho's belligerence dragged Luis along, through the two ill-fated invasions of Costa Rica and the intervention in Guatemala, and elevated the young agricultural engineer to the rank of full colonel before he was able to doff his uniform and start devoting his attention to more peace-ful pursuits.

Luis' talents as a negotiator came again to his father's aid during the drafting of the 1950 Constitution, when he helped Tacho work out the power-sharing agreement with the Conservatives. The eldest of the Somoza boys was granted a niche in the new power structure which rose from this agreement : he ran an uncontested race for a seat in Congress, and as befitted a Somoza, was duly elected by his 'peers' to the key office of President of the Chamber of Depu-ties, undoubtedly the best place for a man in his early thirties to learn the ropes of party-political horsetrading in the Nicaraguan style. Less than twenty-four hours after his father's death, Luis had been designated by Congress to complete Tacho's term as President of Nicaragua.

His younger brother Tachito, on the other hand, had been groomed as Tacho's successor in the Guardia, the family's military power base. His career as a soldier had been meteoric. At the age of eleven he was packed off to the United States to study, like his brother before him, at the La Salle Military Academy. Five years later he was made a Sub-Lieutenant in the Guardia and sent on to further his career at West Point. On his entry there he was promoted to Lieutenant, and while still at the Academy he moved on to Captain. The popular satirical poem which compares Tacho with God for having performed the miracle of 'making the Minor Major' celebrates Tachito's return as a West Point graduate, at the age of twenty-one, with the rank of Major, to become Inspector General of the Army.

The very next year he was designated Commander of the First Presidential Battalion, a job he held until President Leonardo Argüello shoved him aside. Tachito was packed off to León, as Commander of the Fifth Battalion, but a few months later, once Argüello had been deposed, he was back in Managua as Chief of Operations of the entire Guardia Nacional. At twenty-three he became Colonel and was entrusted, as Director of Nicaragua's Military Academy, with the formation of future Guardia officers. To this job were added, a year later, those of Chief of Staff and Commander of the Guardia's headquarters. When he turned thirty he went to the United States to qualify as a pilot, whereupon he was appointed Commander of the F.A.N., the Nicaraguan Air Force. That same year he took over as acting commander of the Guardia, and immediately after his father's assassination his brother Luis appointed him *Jefe Director*.

Seeking out and punishing those responsible for their father's murder provided the brothers Somoza with the right sort of excuse for a drastic consolidation of their grip on the country. A state of siege was declared. Guardia officers of suspect loyalty were dismissed or sent away to unimportant posts; even Colonel Francisco Gaitán, the man who as Minister of War had held the Guardia together during the brief interregnum while Tacho was dying in Panama, was forced into *de luxe* exile as ambassador to faraway Argentina.

The assassination itself was blamed on a Communist conspiracy hatched in El Salvador, but among the hundreds who were arrested or shot 'while trying to escape' there were many who had no visible connection with left-wing conspiratorial activity. They represented a threat of a different nature, that of becoming the leaders of an Opposition which might become troublesome when the time came to call elections to confirm Luis Somoza in the Presidency. At the age of eighty-five, Emiliano Chamorro was imprisoned for a short spell, then released. Other, less fortunate Opposition leaders were tried before a military court on trumped-up charges and sentenced to long prison terms. Among these was the former Presidential candidate, Enoc Aguado, and young Pedro Joaquín Chamorro, editor of *La Prensa,* who was already emerging as the visible heir to the Chamorro family's irrepressible revolutionary tradition.

Pedro Joaquín, born in 1925, a year after his father had founded *La Prensa,* had been active in the Opposition since, as a first-year student at Managua's law school, he joined an anti-Somoza university group which called itself 'The Generation of 1944'. His participation in demonstrations and riots earned him his first bout of exile. He finished his law studies in Mexico and returned to Nicaragua in 1948, shortly after his father's death. His gift for incisive political prose led him to choose the family-owned *La Prensa* as his base, and in 1952 he took over the editorship of what had already become Nicaragua's leading newspaper.

The young Chamorro was far too much of a man of action to confine his political activity to daily columns of print, and in 1954 he joined old Emiliano Chamorro in the ill-fated 'April plot' to assassinate Tacho Somoza and lead the Opposition into open rebellion. Tacho aborted the coup, and Pedro Joaquín was one of the many plotters who were arrested and sentenced to long prison terms.   He was released only a few months before Tacho's assassination by Rigoberto López Pérez, and now he found himself arrested again and sent away to the remote prison in the southern city of San Carlos. He was not, however, to remain there very long : it was a mere matter of months before he engineered an escape and crossed the Costa Rican border to join the band of Nicaraguan exiles in San José and start plotting again.

Luis Somoza demanded the extradition of a long list of Nicaraguan exiles from El Salvador, and when the neighbouring government refused, his attitude became so menacing that the Organisation of American States stepped in, despatching its Secretary General to smooth over the conflict.

The Conservative leadership decided that in this sort of atmosphere any elections would be a sham, so when Luis announced that they would be held in February 1957, the Opposition called for a boycott. Taking a leaf from his father's book, Luis Somoza exhumed the Partido Conservador Nacionalista, which dutifully nominated Edmundo Amador as a token rival to the President's candidacy. Needless to say, Luis Somoza's victory at the polls was overwhelming.

Almost as soon as the 'new' President was sworn in, he was engulfed in an international conflict. While elections were taking place in Nicaragua, the Honduran government had created the province of Gracias a Dios in a huge, roughly triangular area north of the River Coco. This territory, which had a 150-mile-long littoral on the Mosquito coast of the Caribbean, had been disputed by both countries since soon after they became independent. Spain's King Alfonso XIII had been asked to arbitrate in 1906, but when he adjudicated in favour of Honduras the Nicaraguans rejected the award. In was precisely in these 'empty' lands that Sandino had wanted to establish his own little fief, the projected *Luz y Verdad* department.

On April 18th, 1957, a party of fifty Nicaraguan Guardsmen crossed the River Coco and occupied the Honduran township of Mokorón, on the opposite bank. It was not much of an invasion, as the Nicaraguans did not seem to have any intention of penetrating deeper into Honduran-held territory, but Luis Somoza considered it an apt enough assertion of Nicaraguan sovereignty. The Honduran government reacted accordingly; two weeks after the Nicaraguan incursion a devastating bombing and strafing attack was launched on Mokorón. Thirty-five of the fifty invaders lost their lives. From Managua, President Somoza II began to issue communiqués claiming that the Guardia had begun a successful counter-attack, but when an emergency meeting of the O.A.S. council blew the whistle from Washington, Honduras was firmly in control of the area.

An incident which had begun as a bid by the young President to prove that he could be as tough as his father, on an issue with patriotic overtones that cut across party lines, ended in a resounding military and diplomatic defeat. Respect for Luis Somoza took a plunge, and before the year was out a group of Guardia officers had joined Opposition leaders in a plot to overthrow him. But old Tacho's network of *orejas* worked as well for Tachito as it had for his father, and the new *Jefe Director* cracked down on the conspirators with ferocity calculated to remind everyone that the Somozas were still in charge.

Despite the false start, the reign of Somoza II eventually got off the ground remarkably well. This was due partly to the fact that Nicaragua's economy was extricating itself from the slump of 1956. Cotton, thanks largely to the endeavours of old Tacho Somoza, had finally overtaken coffee as the country's number one export commodity. Together with cotton came an expansion of the budding textile industry, and indirectly a number of other manufacturing ventures. In the wake of this development followed the growth of Nicaragua's middle class; white-collar workers (mainly government-employed bureaucrats), small businessmen and relatively independent entrepreneurs. The State itself began to spread out its tentacles with the incorporation of 'modern' regulatory institutions.

The cotton boom and the parallel growth of the livestock industry brought with themselves an accentuation of the 'agrarian reform' produced earlier by coffee-planting. Fertile plains were at a premium, especially where large, unbroken tracts of land could be found. Land ownership began to be concentrated in fewer and fewer hands, particularly in the centre and north of Nicaragua. But the new class of landowners did not enjoy the autonomy of their coffee-planting predecessors; they depended on the government for special credit lines, for adequate tariff treatment, and for a host of minor aids to production.

Furthermore, the era of foreign aid was dawning in Nicaragua. American loans alone arose from 756,000 dollars in 1955-6 to more than 900,000 dollars two years later, and the local administrator of these loans, the agency which decided who qualified for this generous assistance, was the State. The State, in Nicaragua, was the Somoza family—the largest business concern in the land invested with the power to make or break any form of 'competition'. A whole new concept of power manipulation had come into being.

As American-inspired 'cold war thinking' spread throughout the hemisphere, it became fashionable to dwell on the many nice things that were happening in good anti-Communist countries like Nicaragua, to the exclusion of sordid little details such as the dictatorial nature of the government, and the depressing fact which even the most optimistic statistics could not conceal : that the vast majority of the population was no better off (indeed they were worse off) than before.

The 'agrarian reform' brought about by the expansion of cotton-planting and livestock raising had also dislodged many peasants from land on which they had been used to plant at least enough to feed themselves, to marginal lands on hillsides and in remoter areas. In a country where 65 per cent of the population lived off the land, this was having a catastrophic effect, and those who could not resign themselves to eking out a precarious existence from unprofitable smallholdings were forced to choose between employment as plantation hands, earning in the best of cases the rarely-enforced 'legal minimum wage' of 85 cents a day during harvest time, or migration to the cities.

The benefits of an enlarged economy certainly went to more people than before, but even if the new beneficiaries were added to those few who had enjoyed the good life previously, they would have amounted to little more than one-tenth of Nicaragua's population.

CHAPTER XVI

PLAYING THE AMERICAN CARD

On January 8th, 1959, an event took place, just 600 miles across Caribbean waters from the Nicaraguan coast, which was to have great influence on the future of Nicaragua—and on the whole hemisphere. Fidel Castro rode in triumph into Havana, his urban and rural guerrillas having put an end to Fulgencio Batista's twenty-six years of tyrannical power. Luis Somoza, and his fellow-despot Rafael Leónidas Trujillo of the Dominican Republic, had aided Batista to the bitter end, providing him with arms and munitions even after Washington had slapped an embargo on military aid to Cuba. They had been among the first to accuse the bearded men of the Sierra Maestra of being Communists (though more out of habit than due to any special gift of clairvoyance), and they figured high on the list of the Cuban Revolution's enemies.

In the first few months of euphoria following Castro's victory, the Cubans came to believe not only that their experience could be repeated anywhere else in Latin America, but that they themselves were bound by revolutionary duty to prove it. 'The Caribbean belongs to Cuba,' proclaimed Fidel, and scores of *barbudos* volunteered to accompany fellow Latin Americans in columns which set out to 'liberate' the dictator-ridden region. The targets were predictable: the Dominican Republic, Haiti, Panama. And Nicaragua. The pattern was predictable too; in a romanticised re-enactment of the *Granma* invasion which got the Cuban Revolution started, all that was deemed necessary was to land a handful of determined men and engage the enemy. The oppressed would flock to their side, and they would be invincible.

But the enemy was waiting, everywhere. In Nicaragua, the revolutionaries of the 'Columna Rigoberto López Pérez' (a group of Cuban-organised guerrillas named after Tacho's assassin, which included some young Nicaraguan exiles like Carlos Fonseca Amador, who would later become the founder of a home-bred revolutionary movement) were ambushed by the Honduran and Nicaraguan armies at El Chaparral and decimated. Their only consolation, when the survivors got back to Cuba, was that they merited Che's congratulations and the gift of one of the first, mimeographed copies of Guevara's handbook on guerrilla warfare. Other Nicaraguan revolutionaries, however, were already on the move from another quarter.

Away to the south, in San José, Costa Rica, the 'independent

123

Liberal' leader Enrique Lacayo Farfán and his young Conservative
ally, Pedro Joaquín Chamorro (in exile since his prison escape
in 1957), bundled eighty armed followers into two planes and took
to the air towards their home country. By the time they were to
touch down on Nicaraguan soil, according to their plan, another
contingent of rebels would have crossed the Costa Rican border by
land, and a call would have gone out for a general strike throughout the country. But the operation went awry almost from the start.
The planes drifted apart and lost their bearings; instead of landing
together, one landed at Santo Tomás, some 80 miles north of the
Costa Rican border, and the other at Tierra Azul, 60 miles east of
Managua. Through lack of co-ordination the strike call was never
issued, and the population in the vicinity of the two landing zones
showed great reluctance to co-operate with the rebels.

Tachito swiftly tightened the security measures in the major
cities and ordered the élite units of the Guardia into the field,
driving a wedge between the two rebel units and forcing them to
flee for the hills and the forest. He then picked them off, one at a
time. Within ten days he had dispersed one group, capturing twenty-
one of its members, and virtually cornered the others. The rebels
offered to lay down their arms if they were guaranteed safe con-
ducts out of Nicaragua, but President Luis Somoza insisted on un-
conditional surrender. They capitulated, and Tachito had them
marched through Managua in an ostentatious 'victory parade'.

Luis Somoza lost no time in accusing Castro of having master-
minded the revolt in combination with Pedro Joaquín Chamorro.
Their sinister plan, he declared, had been to recruit the scions of
wealthy Nicaraguan families and place them in the front line,
where they would certainly be killed; thus, continued the President,
they hoped to arouse hatred against the Guardia and obtain financial support from the bereaved families. That was why, he concluded smugly, he had issued strict orders to his troops to capture
the rebels alive.

Once fact is separated from fiction, what remains of Luis
Somoza's fantastic allegations is that several members of Nicaragua's
social élite had indeed taken part in the rebellion, and that repression had been softened in order to spare their lives. The pattern
was to repeat itself time and again over the next two decades.

The battle with the rebels was won not only on the battlefield,
but also abroad. As an unexpected bonus, Luis Somoza received
assurances from his Costa Rican colleague, Mario Echandi, that
the neighbouring government would prevent any further 'abuses
of political asylum'. Farther afield, the Somozas' early enmity

against Castro was beginning to pay dividends in improved relations with the United States.

The Cubans had passed their far-reaching agrarian reform law, and started to expropriate American holdings on the island. As prominent U.S. businessmen began to clamour for retaliatory action, a steady stream of Cuban refugees poured into the southern state of Florida. Castro's Air Force chief, Major Díaz Lanz, defected to the United States and announced what every anti-Castroite, Cuban or foreign, had been waiting to hear : Cuba was being taken over by the Communists. Castro-baiting became a highly respectable activity in American eyes, and Luis Somoza was way ahead of everyone else in this field.

Somoza II had sensed intuitively that the prevailing mood in Washington called for him to become something of a democrat as well as an anti-Castroite. Accordingly, he announced that his administration would become 'a bridge to democracy', and as proof of his goodwill he reinstated the constitutional bans on re-election and on the candidacy of the incumbent President's blood relatives. Political prisoners were released, press censorship was relaxed, a very moderate 'agrarian reform' law was passed, and for the first time the rural workers were granted the benefits of his father's progressive Labour Code.

As Chamorro explained many years later, 'Luis wanted to get rid of it all. Not the country or his properties, of course; he wanted to inaugurate a period of transition after which his family, while remaining the most important family in the land, would not wield power directly. What he imagined was something like Mexico's Partido Revolucionario Institucional—every so many years a new President, belonging to the same élite, to the same oligarchy, but endowed with enough power to rule on his own, always respecting the interests of the *gamonales* who preceded him in office.'

The Opposition found it exceedingly hard to believe that a Somoza could be sincere in such matters, not least because a tight lid was still kept on any attempt at political action (other than writing articles in the Opposition press), and a state of siege was declared at the slightest sign of trouble. And trouble there was bound to be, as politics in Nicaragua began to leave behind the non-ideological, personalistic approach of the *caudillos* of yore, and to adopt the ideology-laden attitudes of the 1960s.

The younger set of the Conservative party, prominent among whom was Pedro Joaquín Chamorro, was heavily influenced by the new Christian Democratic ideas which were spreading in Latin

America as a possible alternative to Castro's brand of Communism. But Nicaraguan political tradition, plus the heritage of the 'Caribbean Legion' and the frustrating experience of twenty-four years of Somoza rule, had combined to convince these young Conservatives that only a revolution could pave the way for democracy in their country.

Nor was it all theory. In spite of Costa Rica's commitment to prevent the launching of attacks against Somoza from its territory, a force of about 300 armed men was organised there. It crossed into Nicaragua early in November 1960 and marched north to capture the towns of Jinotepe and Diriamba, southwest of Masaya and not far from the capital.

Almost 1,000 Guardsmen were mobilised and rushed to the area. After a three-day siege and a number of skirmishes in which both sides suffered casualties, most of the rebel force surrendered. A group which had remained in the border area was engaged by the Costa Rican police (the commander of which was killed in the battle) and dispersed. The remaining rebels locked themselves into a schoolhouse in Diriamba, holding 260 children as hostages and demanding a safe conduct out of the country. Eventually they too surrendered, after the Bishop Coadjutor of Managua persuaded them to settle for assurances of a fair trial.

The incident had repercussions far beyond Nicaragua's borders. Following unconfirmed reports that Cubans had been spotted among the rebels, and that Cuban aircraft had been ferrying supplies to them in Nicaragua, President Eisenhower declared that the United States would take action to prevent any 'Communist-led' invasion of Central America, and ordered the 40,000-ton carrier *Shangri-La* and a flotilla of destroyers to patrol Nicaraguan waters.

But it was Eisenhower's government, not Castro's, that was planning an invasion. The C.I.A. had recruited 1,400 Cuban exiles and discreetly shipped them out, in small groups, to secret training camps obligingly provided by Guatemala and Nicaragua. The force received its name, '2506 Brigade' from the serial number of a recruit, Carlos Rodríguez, who died during a training exercise in Nicaragua.

The C.I.A. invasion plan, approved by the Pentagon, was inherited by John F. Kennedy when he took office in January 1961, and he gave it his blessing. For nine long months the C.I.A. instructors whipped the Cuban exile contingent into shape, and in the spring of 1961 it was ready to go. Luis Somoza provided an airfield, codenamed 'Happy Valley', for the invaders' small air force of fifteen B-26 bombers to sally forth, on April 15th, for the single raid on Cuban airfields that John F. Kennedy authorised. He also provided ports from which the invaders would sail.

The 2506 Brigade landed at Playa Girón and the Bay of Pigs, 140 miles south of Havana, in the early hours of the 17th. Its mission was to establish a bridgehead and hold it long enough for a Provisional Government, formed by prominent exiled politicians, to be flown in. At this point, an O.A.S. force led by the United States would respond to the call of the new 'government' for assistance with a full-fledged invasion of Cuba.

Very few things went right. The target landing area was missed, Castro's air force was not destroyed, and the clandestine support network within Cuba was disrupted by Castro's police before the arrival of the 2506 Brigade. Three days after landing, the battered invading force was being pushed back into the sea. Among the victorious defenders was a happy-go-lucky Cuban officer known to his comrades as 'Comandante Nicaragua', in memory of the good old days when he had led a column of volunteers in an ill-fated attempt to 'liberate' the land of the Somozas.

Plots, uprisings and street demonstrations continued to plague Luis Somoza's administration, but more as a nuisance than as a real threat. Co-operation with the Americans ensured that the Guardia became stronger and stronger, and the Somozas' habit of equating any form of opposition with Communism sharply reduced the Nicaraguan exiles' possibilities of operating from abroad, in a Central America where only a doomed Honduran government was described as being 'soft on the Reds'.

The continent-wide emphasis on economic and social development as an answer to Castroism highlighted the inequalities in Nicaraguan society and the immensity of the task which would face anyone who seriously wanted to pull the country out of its backwardness. Only slightly more than a tenth of Nicaragua's school-age population was actually attending schools of any sort, and only dismal Haiti had a worse level of matriculation in secondary schools (it was calculated that in this it would take Nicaragua about a quarter of a century merely to catch up with Uruguay). So even when development was noisily pursued, with the unavoidable bias in favour of the Somoza family fortune, repression remained the keystone of the dynasty's continuance in power. Only four other backward Latin American nations were devoting a bigger share of their gross domestic product to military purposes than the 3 per cent which Nicaragua was spending; ten republics were receiving more direct military aid from the United States, but only two (Guatemala and Honduras) were receiving *less* American funds for economic and social development under Kennedy's Alliance for Progress scheme.

Repression was made easier for the Somozas by the fact that the Opposition was almost hopelessly split. The traditional core of the Conservative party, whose only aspiration seemed to be to replace the Somozas at the centre of Nicaragua's power structure, still had hopes of bringing international pressure to bear on the régime, forcing it to accept a fair electoral contest. The younger Conservatives, with their newly-acquired *social-cristiano* outlook, were disgusted at the lack of ideology or even attractive policy proposals in the parent party and were convinced that the Somozas would stop at nothing in order to perpetuate their dynasty. Badly battered in their hapless attempts at starting a revolution, they hovered indecisively between taking advantage of the forthcoming elections and declaring an all-out war on the régime.

The more radical elements of the Opposition chose the Cuban Revolution as a model for their approach to politics. 'Many different circumstances conspired to delay the introduction of Marxist ideas to Nicaragua. The country never received a massive inflow of European working-class immigrants who would have brought their ideology with them. The Nicaraguan working class itself takes shape very slowly, as a result of the country's backward coffee-planting and cattle-raising economy; the introduction of the country's only modern crop, cotton, is only recent, and the sugar industry has not yet grown to significant proportions. The miners, the largest concentration of workers, suffer their plight in isolation in the distant Atlantic jungle. Add to this the fact that cultural discrimination could not be more extreme, and it will be seen clearly that all avenues were closed to the penetration of the scientific revolutionary theory. Marxist ideas begin to enter Nicaragua only as a consequence of the Cuban Revolution's victory, which is definitively defeating *yanqui* imperialism and beginning to build a socialist society, both for the first time in Latin America.'

The author of this enlightening but grossly inaccurate analysis was the young intellectual Carlos Fonseca Amador. In 1961, drawing inspiration both from the Cubans and from Sandino's guerrilla war against American intervention, Fonseca and some friends created the Frente Sandinista de Liberación Nacional and started preparing to go up into the hills of the northern departments, Sandino's hills, to wage war on the Somozas. If the President and his brother actually heard about the venture at the time, they did not rank it higher than the many minor threats which the Guardia had become quite used to aborting.

CHAPTER XVII

FROM SOMOZA II TO SOMOZA III

Luis Somoza had actually meant what he said when he announced that his administration was a 'bridge', although what lay at the other end was not exactly democracy, but a continuation of the Somoza rule by proxy, under the guise of democracy. Those among his followers who had been naïve enough to take him too literally were staking their bets on the succession going to Julio Quintana, the President's very able and reasonably popular Interior Minister. Yet when the Partido Liberal Nacionalista held the convention which was to nominate the Presidential candidate, delegates were instructed to vote for a man whom no one, except the Somozas, deemed worthy of the job. René Schick, a quiet lawyer, had decided long ago that the best way to further his political career was to become an unquestioning yes-man. His faithful services as Tacho's personal secretary up to the moment of his assassination in 1956 had been rewarded, as soon as Luis Somoza was sworn in, with the honorific post of Minister of Education. Later, the President had reassigned him to the Foreign Ministry, whence Schick had dutifully translated into proper legal terminology the cold war rantings that had made Luis Somoza one of Washington's anti-Castroite darlings. Now René Schick was to be promoted to nothing less than the Presidency.

The Conservatives, who had nominated Fernando Agüero as their candidate, decided that the best tactical approach to the elections was to hold Luis Somoza to his word. Agüero demanded that the President, as proof of his sincerity, should invite a team of O.A.S. observers to supervise the polls. Luis Somoza rejected the suggestion out of hand, claiming that it would amount to accepting 'foreign interference in Nicaragua's internal affairs'. Undaunted, Agüero organised a demonstration to show the extent of public support for his demands. Like René Schick, he too had his reward : the Guardia kept him under house arrest until after the elections. And when the Conservative party protested by announcing that it would boycott the event, Luis Somoza again called on the rubber-stamp Partido Conservador Nacionalista to provide him with the semblance of an Opposition. When the votes were counted in February 1963, the results showed that René Schick had achieved a ten-to-one victory over his 'rival', Diego Manuel Chamorro.

Schick's immediate reflex action as successor to the Somozas was to rush off to San José, Costa Rica, to join his fellow Central

American Presidents and John F. Kennedy in signing the 'Declaration of Central America', in which Castro was again denounced as an aggressor. But the new President of Nicaragua went on to make a number of decisions which liberalised his country's political life far more than anyone had expected. Detainees were released, the press was allowed to express itself freely, and the Guardia ceased to throw dissidents into prison on the smallest provocation.

Under Schick, however, there was also a blooming of two new segments of the population : the State and the entrepreneurial class which had appeared to take advantage of the recently-created Central American Common Market. Government expenditure increased fourfold, and jobs were created in the public sector at about three times the rate prevailing in the rest of the economy. Nicaragua's universities were disgorging an ever-increasing number of graduates, and most of them were finding ready employment in the dozen-or-so new agencies the government had established in order to cope with the demands of 'development' as conceived under Kennedy's Alliance for Progress. Joining the government, in whatever capacity, also meant joining the Partido Liberal Nacionalista, if only for reasons of expediency, thus greatly swelling the ranks of the régime's 'paycheck supporters'.

The rise of a class of apparently independent industrialists suggested that the younger Somozas had drifted away from their father's policy of having a finger in every pie, having discovered that their control over the country's administrative apparatus allowed them to tolerate economic diversity. After all, these new enterprises were born under the shadow of a special tariff treatment, tax exemptions and preferential credit lines, all of which were granted by the State, or in other words by the Somoza régime.

Luis Somoza was quite sure that he had made the right decision in extricating the family from direct responsibility for the Presidency. True, Tachito was still in charge of the Guardia, but Luis was convinced that the time would come when even that last overtly dominant position could be abandoned; all that they would need to retain were the party reins. As the public administration was virtually synonymous with the party, that would give them effective but discreet control over everything else.

Tachito disagreed. His understanding of the mechanics of power was far more straightforward and unvarnished. Like his father before him, Tachito believed that the Somozas' only reliable constituency was the Guardia, and that to delegate any power at all was an exceedingly dangerous game. The brothers clashed often on this issue, Luis insisting that Washington's current mood ruled out any return to old Tacho's style of government, Tachito insisting that at least one segment of the Opposition was increasingly committed to wiping out all trace of the Somoza dynasty.

At this point the newborn Frente Sandinista de Liberación Nacional made its real debut, with a series of sloppily organised guerrilla raids. Tachito's Guardia, a far more efficient force than anything his father had ever known, cracked down hard on the would-be revolutionaries, easily picking up many of their none-too-clandestine supporters in the universities and chasing the raiders round the countryside, taking time off only for the occasional 'exemplary' reprisal against suspected collaborators. This repressive campaign took an unexpected twist which left observers of Nicaraguan politics with a strange sensation of *déja vu*. It started with the great hubbub which was raised at the discovery of the corpses of three suspected 'subversives' in the vicinity of Chinandega. Instead of hushing up the matter as Tachito would have wished him to do, President Schick demanded an investigation and the punishment of who ever was found responsible for the killings. For the first time in the history of the Guardia, a senior officer, Colonel Juan López, was taken to court and sentenced to a stretch in prison. Tachito's indignation had not died down when, a few months later, the Guardia landed a prize catch : Carlos Fonseca Amador, the leader of the Frente Sandinista. President Schick's intervention saved Fonseca from almost certain death at the hands of his interrogators, and later, once he had been tried and sentenced, gave him the opportunity to choose between prison and exile. For Tachito this was the last straw.

Turning a deaf ear to Luis's entreaties, the younger of the Somozas let the party leaders know that in 1967, when Schick's term ran out, he would claim the Presidency for himself. It was the Sacasa and Argüello episodes all over again. Well in advance of the elections, Tachito began to take the reins of power into his own hands. First the Guardia—a purge, dismissals, new postings— then local government. Municipalities had long since lost the right to elect their own authorities, and it was an easy matter to replace unreliable appointees with new, ambitious and above all subservient flunkeys. Fascists were no longer fashionable nor acceptable, so instead of *camisas azules,* young Somoza armed a dedicated group of former Guardsmen to act as his party's 'dirty tricks' department.

Also long before the elections, Tachito was given a most welcome opportunity to increase his Guardia's combat-readiness. A rebellion had broken out in the Dominican Republic, with the overt purpose of toppling the military-backed government and reinstating Juan Bosch, one of the veterans of the 'Caribbean Legion', in the Presidency. Although President Lyndon B. Johnson first adopted a hands-off attitude, his embassy in Santo Domingo began to claim, on the basis of documents later proved to be false, that the rebels' real aim was the establishment of a Cuban-style Communist régime. So, in order 'to protect American lives and properties', in went the Marines. Their immediate embroilment in a civil war which refused to end, and moreover on what an increasing body of international opinion considered to be 'the wrong side', moved Johnson to seek some way of shifting responsibility away from Washington.

He hit upon the idea of getting the O.A.S. to take over nominal control of the invading troops, and accordingly an 'Inter-American Peace Force' was hurriedly put together. The 22,000 U.S. Marines and paratroopers still formed the bulk of this army, but they were soon joined by over 1,000 Brazilians and 450 Central American soldiers, prominent among whom was a unit eagerly despatched by Tachito. In September 1966, once Trujillo's heir Joaquín Balaguer was safely back in power in Santo Domingo, the Nicaraguan veterans returned to a rousing welcome. All, that is, except one—their commander, Colonel Julio Gutiérrez, who followed Rigoberto Reyes and Francisco Gaitán into the limbo reserved by the Somozas for senior officers of the Guardia who became too efficient or popular.

On August 1st, 1966, the government-owned radio station informed the nation that 'Nicaragua's new apostle', General Anastasio Somoza Debayle, had accepted the Partido Liberal Nacionalista's nomination as candidate for the Presidency. 'His name,' the people were told, 'beats already in the hearts of young Liberals and peasants. . . . Our faith is his faith, our love is his love, our destiny is his destiny.' His only enemies were the enemies of the nation : the Communist 'subversives' and the 'Conservative capitalists'.

The electoral campaign was far from peaceful. A renewed Frente Sandinista, fresh from training in Cuba, surfaced in the mountainous department of Matagalpa, bent on turning the area into 'Nicaragua's Sierra Maestra', a rural guerrilla *foco* which would soon spread out over the whole country. Although they managed to stage several impressive coups, the task looked easier on paper than up in the hills. Far from rallying to their call, the peasants of Matagalpa remained indifferent or actually denounced them to the Guardia. And the Guardsmen, themselves fresh from special training (U.S. military advisors had led them in a couple of massive counter-insurgency exercises earlier that year), proved more than a match for the young rebels. Nonetheless, the new *sandinistas* were a worrisome addition to Somoza's troubles.

President Schick died of a heart attack only two days after Tachito's candidacy was announced, and Congress appointed the Interior Minister, Lorenzo Guerrero, to complete his term. Nicaraguans were treated to another throwback to thirty years earlier when Tachito made a great show of respecting the Constitution by resigning his command of the Guardia, only to keep on turning up at his office in mufti, to dictate the orders which would be signed unquestioningly by President Guerrero, to whom the reins of the institution had been formally entrusted.

Ironically, this same hypocritical quest for respectability was what achieved the seemingly impossible task of uniting the Opposition against Somoza. A law had been passed establishing severe penalties for anyone advocating a boycott of the elections, basically in order to show the world that the electoral process was not a charade, but an honest, open competition between all of Nicaragua's political parties. The Conservatives joined the *social-cristianos* and the 'Independent Liberals' in the Unión Nacional de Oposición, and chose Fernando Agüero to stand as their candidate. Pedro Joaquín Chamorro acted as co-ordinator of the alliance.

Campaigning against Somoza was no easy task. Tachito had again thrown the largely fictitious Partido Conservador Nacionalista into the fray, mainly in order to sow confusion in the minds of uninformed voters, with Alejandro Abaunza Marenco as their candidate. Opposition rallies and meetings were often broken up by Tachito's armed bands of ex-soldiers, and harassment of the Opposition candidates by the Guardia was frequent. The atmosphere of bitter confrontation grew steadily heavier through the last months of 1966, and was so charged with tension by the first days of 1967 that some sort of violent outcome seemed unavoidable.

Fernando Agüero stated publicly that in the circumstances then existing impartiality in the elections was a near impossibility, and called upon President Guerrero to postpone the elections for a year until the situation had calmed down, and then to hold them under international supervision. Quite foreseeably, the request was denied. Agüero then applied for permission to hold a mass rally in downtown Managua. Overtly, it was his intention to call for a general strike in support of his demand for a postponement of the elections, but he himself later admitted that he had hoped that the size and the determination of the crowd would encourage the Guardia to stage a coup against the régime.

Authorisation was granted, and Opposition leaders throughout the country were asked to bus to the capital as many supporters as they could muster. It was an open secret that this was to be something more than the run-of-the-mill rally—the invitations included, under quite transparent euphemisms, a suggestion to come armed. On January 22nd more than 40,000 people gathered to listen to Agüero and other speakers in the centre of Managua.

Enthusiasm was such that when the officially authorised time-limit was reached, the meeting showed no sign of ending. The Guardia, however, had been issued strict instructions. The crowd was ordered to disperse. Unwilling to let this splendid political opportunity go to waste, the organisers began to lead the bulk of the demonstrators on an unauthorised march up the Avenida Roosevelt. Before they had gone far, a series of gunshot reports cut through the chanted slogans. Unidentified snipers, posted on the roofs of public buildings, had opened fire on the Guardia.

The troops responded by firing into the crowd, and pandemonium broke loose. Pistols and revolvers began to appear in the demonstrators' hands, a bomb shook the portal of the National Telegraph Office, and people started storming the National Palace, the seat of Congress. Guardsmen and demonstrators ran for cover and began a shooting match, raking the streets of downtown Managua with a deadly crossfire.

The gunbattle continued through the night, casualties on both sides mounting to well above 200. Instead of doing as Agüero had expected, and turning on their master, the Guardia closed ranks in defence of the régime and brought increasing pressure to bear on the groups of snipers and rioters who held the centre of the city.

The following day General Somoza decided to put an end to the mini-rebellion by ordering the tanks into the downtown area. Many of the insurgents scattered, but a hard core of about 600 followed Fernando Agüero and Pedro Joaquín Chamorro into the Gran Hotel, where they prepared to sit out a siege, holding the 100-odd startled guests as hostages.

The Papal Nuncio and the U.S. ambassador offered to mediate, and by the evening of January 23rd managed to convince the rebels to lay down their arms and release their hostages in exchange for a government promise that they would be allowed to go free. According to the official casualty list, thirty-four people had died and at least 100 had been injured, but the Opposition drew up a much longer list which they asked the International Red Cross to investigate.

Tachito blamed the incident on the Cubans and threw a tight security net over Managua, but rioting began again two days later. A much stricter clampdown followed, now clearly aimed at the domestic Opposition. It was in this atmosphere that Nicaragua went to the polls on February 5th, 1967. No one was greatly surprised when the official results showed that Anastasio Somoza Debayle had won handsomely, with about 70 per cent of the vote.

Somoza III was now President of Nicaragua.

CHAPTER XVIII

NICARAGUA IN THE LATE NINETEEN-SIXTIES

Four hundred and forty-five years had elapsed since the first *conquistador* arrived in Nicaragua, and the country had grown and changed a good deal in the meantime. In one aspect, however, it had remained the same. The population had clung to the narrow strip of land to the west of the volcanoes and the two great lakes, and the enormous region of wooded lowlands which stretched towards the Atlantic coast—the dreaded Tologalpa of the Spaniards—was still empty. There were by now close to two million Nicaraguans in this country of about the same area as England and Wales, the largest of the small republics in Central America, but nine out of every ten lived in this corridor along the Pacific seaboard.

The biggest concentration, some 300,000 people, was clustered around the hybrid, *parvenu* capital city of Managua, the town born of a mid-nineteenth century compromise between the rival claimants to primacy, Granada and León. Most of its early attempts at Frenchified splendour had been destroyed by the 1931 earthquake; restoration, reconstruction and new building in a hodge-podge of styles had given the downtown district, the hub of Nicaraguan life, a unique, if incongruous personality of its very own. The solid, twin-towered Metropolitan Cathedral, once the highest edifice in Managua, still overlooked the central plaza, but now dwarfed by the Palacio Nacional, with its façade of four-storey-high columns and its warren of legislative and executive offices occupying an entire city block. In recent years, rival exponents of more modern ugliness had begun to spring from the ground: the bunkerlike Rubén Darío National Theatre down towards the lake, and the towering new banks up towards the hill that housed the seat of Nicaraguan power.

Every Latin American capital has its equestrian statue of the Liberator, usually Simón Bolívar in the northern republics and José de San Martín in the south. Managua too has its bronze hero on horseback, but the features are those of General Anastasio Somoza García. There was also the unfailing baroque monument to culture, in the person of the great poet Rubén Darío, looking taller and slimmer than he ever was in real life, draped in an improbable toga, a winged angel at his back, and at his feet an ornate barque full of cherubs and muses.

Just a few crowded, noisy blocks away from the city centre Managua faded out into a miserable periphery which only those who did not live there could ever describe as 'colourful'; a jumble of boarded shacks with palm leaf roofs, unpaved roads and the advance guard of the lush greenery that stretched away as far as the eye could see.

Nicaragua's older, more sedate urban centres had lagged well behind Managua's rapid, disorganised growth. The university city of León was still the country's 'intellectual capital', but had remained a cluster of mainly one-storey buildings around the Parque Jerez, dominated by the massive, squat cathedral (Central America's largest)—its most precious treasure, a topaz-covered shrine donated by Philip II of Spain, locked away out of sight. Only slightly more than 50,000 people inhabited this enclave surrounded by volcanoes and not infrequently enveloped by a shower of cinders from the nearby Cerro Negro. The volcanoes, especially the perfect conical shape of Concepción, on Ometepe island, can also be seen from lakeside Granada, the thrice-sacked city which once housed a haughty merchant class with high hopes of running a great port on the inter-oceanic canal that was never built. The double-decked lake steamers moored at the jetty were all that remained of that dream, and Granada's population seemed to be stagnating at close to 40,000 souls.

South of Managua, the town of Masaya, with a population of some 35,000, had become the country's crafts centre, producing skilfully-knotted hammocks, rocking chairs and the smallish Nicaraguan *marimbas*. Further down the scale, only four cities (Chinandega, Diriamba, Rivas and Matagalpa) had more than 20,000 inhabitants.

Taken as a whole, more than half of Nicaragua's population lived in the country. In the most highly urbanised departments (Managua, Masaya and Granada), for each city dweller there were two who lived off the land; up in Matagalpa, an area which was only then being reached by the coffee planters and the cattle ranchers, the ratio was three country dwellers to one urbanite. But this was changing rapidly : the population was increasing at an annual rate of about 3 per cent, and out of every ten people born in the country, seven were making their way to the cities in search of a better life. Demographers were already calculating that by the early 1980s Nicaragua could well have a predominantly urban population.

Cotton had already replaced coffee as Nicaragua's most important crop, and sugar and cattle ranching were becoming increasingly significant. In terms of employment, it was still a rural country, with just under two-thirds of the population employed in agriculture. But agriculture's contribution to Nicaragua's gross domestic product had dwindled to about 25 per cent, while that of industry (which employed only 11 per cent of the population) had risen from next to nothing to more than 18 per cent.

Emigration to the cities and the growing importance of manufacturing were not, however, the result of the exhaustion of the country's agricultural potential. Only about 7 per cent of the country's surface was under permanent cultivation, and a similar area was devoted to pastures and meadows. Leaving aside the wastelands, which made up a third of the total, a full half of Nicaragua's territory remained covered in largely idle forests.

Most of the land that was being exploited had been concentrated in very few hands. Registered landholdings numbered only about 60,000, but even this figure disguises the fact that the bigger landowners—and Somoza was the biggest—had a large number of units to their name. The vast majority of the one million Nicaraguans who lived off the land were plantation hands or subsistence farmers, eking out a very precarious existence. Cold statistics showed that Nicaragua's *per capita* income was only slightly more than 350 U.S. dollars, an average that included the handful of millionaires who lived the good life commuting between Managua and Miami. Except in the cities, social security was real only on paper, as were the 'minimum legal wages' of the rural workers. Health care was almost non-existent in many parts of the country, and the general state of sanitation is best illustrated by the fact that, after old age, the main causes of death in a country with an average life expectancy of about fifty years were gastritis, duodenitis, enteritis, colitis and malaria.

The valiant aborigines encountered by the Spaniards had all but vanished. The smattering of isolated Sumos, Miskitos and Ramaiques in the eastern lowlands added up to a mere 4 per cent of the population. War and disease had certainly taken their toll over the years, but the main cause of their disappearance was miscegenation. A full 70 per cent of Nicaragua's population had mixed blood : mestizos (European and Amerindian), zambos (black and Amerindian) and mulattos (European and black). Only 17 per cent could claim to be of pure European stock, and about 9 per cent were blacks. As such, racial discrimination was not a trait of Nicaraguan society, but social discrimination based on wealth was very much in evidence, and the European minority could easily be spotted at the top of the pyramid of affluence.

Nicaraguan politics had been affected by miscegenation of a different sort. Whatever real differences there may have been between Liberals and Conservatives in the early years of the country's independent life, they had succumbed—as elsewhere in Latin America—to the personalistic approaches of the *caudillos,* charismatic or providential leaders whose appeal to the masses is almost impossible to define in terms of ideologies. They mobilised support through empathy with popular demands, plus skilful manipulation of deeply rooted familial and regional loyalties. Allegiance was to them personally, rather than to their 'causes', and they were perfectly able to cast aside principles and ideologies, to change alliances once and again, without alienating their followers. What the *caudillo* would do with power when and if he obtained it was completely unpredictable.

All the big names in Nicaraguan history belong to the *caudillo* tradition : José Santos Zelaya, Emiliano Chamorro, and José María Moncada—even Sandino and Tacho Somoza himself. Tachito had already become a *caudillo* in his own right, and shortly before he stepped into the Presidency the last of the old-school rival *caudillos,* Emiliano Chamorro, died at the age of ninety-six.

Many would readily have cast Pedro Joaquín Chamorro as the new *caudillo* of the Opposition. But he rejected that role, in the belief that the era of 'personalism' in Nicaraguan politics should come to an end with the hoped-for ouster of the Somozas. Pedro Joaquín felt that the growing attraction of Marxism could only be countered with another, equally appealing ideology. And he was convinced that such an ideology could be gleaned from the social teachings of the Church.

His critics, especially those on the left, held that this was just a smokescreen, and that the young Chamorro was in fact treading a well-worn path, appealing to the almost atavistic Catholicism of the Nicaraguans and to their deep-seated fear of Communism. Although Roman Catholicism was no longer the country's official religion, more than 90 per cent of the population professed it. The Nicaraguan Church's tradition was as old as the Spanish colonisation itself. As in the rest of the world, it was a rich and varied tradition, from which a whole range of differing emphases could be drawn at different points in time. It was the tradition of Friar Bartolomé de las Casas, the 'Apostle of the Indies' who preached in Granada and León against the enslavement and exploitation of the aborigines in colonial times. It was the tradition of the Church that supported the *status quo,* standing by the order imposed by the oligarchs and the personalistic *caudillos*. It was the tradition of popular devotions blended into very secular carnivals : the week-long festival of Santo Domingo in Managua, the masques and mummery of Christmas in Granada, the splendour of Holy Week in León, the celebration of the miraculous in the feast of the Saint of Esquipulas at La Conquista.

By the time Tachito Somoza became President, it was above all a Church that had swung around to the tune of Pope John XXIII's encyclical *Pacem in Terris,* and of a Vatican Council which proclaimed, 'If the demands of justice and equity are to be satisfied, vigorous efforts must be made . . . to remove as quickly as possible the immense economic inequalities which now exist.' In the very year of Tachito's accession to the Presidency, Pope Paul VI was quoting, in his encyclical *Populorum Progressio,* the message of St Ambrose : 'The earth was made for all, not just for the rich.' And the bishops of Latin America were preparing for the meeting they were to hold at Medellín, Colombia, the following year, an event which would be to the Latin American Church what Vatican II was to the Church universal. Even Pedro Joaquín Chamorro's brand of 'social Christian' ideology, a rather mild echo of the Christian Democrat experience in Chile and Venezuela, was about to be overtaken by this unforeseen wave of Catholic militancy.

CHAPTER XIX

PRESIDENT AND BUSINESSMAN

Tachito Somoza did not wait out the three months until he was formally sworn in to display his style as a ruler. A few days after the elections he closed down the Opposition radio stations, suspended publication of *La Prensa* and threw Pedro Joaquín Chamorro in prison on the charge of having provoked the recent disorders by spreading 'irresponsible' information. These repressive measures did not, however, have effect for long. When an International Red Cross representative, Jacques Jacquier, turned up to interview political prisoners and investigate the many unexplained 'disappearances' that had taken place during the January riots, and the Archbishop of Managua, Alejandro González, joined forces with other members of the Church hierarchy to call for the release of all political detainees, Tachito allowed President Guerrero to push through Congress an amnesty bill before he himself took office.

In April, also before Tachito's inauguration, Luis Somoza died of a heart attack. The main import of this event was not merely the disappearance of the only member of the ruling family who could presumably have 'moderated' Tachito's use of power; it also signalled the concentration of the entire family fortune in Tachito's hands. Estimates of the Somozas' wealth at the time vary enormously; different sources placed it anywhere between 50 million and 300 million U.S. dollars. Somoza III enjoyed being mysterious about it, and turned enquirers away with remarks such as, 'In your place, I'd start by asking how rich the British Empire is', or 'Without counting the land, 40 million would get you into the ball park.'

The lands Somoza so nonchalantly omitted from this calculation occupied an area about equal in size to the neighbouring republic of El Salvador; they represented about half of all registered landholdings in Nicaragua, and a quarter of the nation's best arable soil. In the countryside, they were administered by two firms, Compañía Agropecuaria and Sucesores del General Somoza; in urban areas they were mainly registered in the name of Salvadora Debayle de Somoza, Tachito's mother. In his largest *fincas* he produced the country's main export commodities: cotton, coffee and beef—and also sugar, an important newcomer which was introduced in the Nicaraguan economy when the Somozas' anti-Castroism was rewarded by Washington with a sizeable chunk

of the old Cuban sugar quota. Other, smaller units offered a stag-
gering variety of produce : cocoa, tobacco (Havana-type cigars
made by Cuban exiles were another of his anti-Castro conquests),
bananas, pineapples, maize, beans, rice, sorghum, sesame and all
kinds of vegetables.

A score of industrial and service companies completed the picture. The Somozas owned Mamenic (the Nicaraguan shipping line),
Lanica (the country's airline), the cement plant, textile factories,
sugar mills and the local concession of Mercedes Benz.

As Tachito stepped into the Presidential Palace, the State itself
became much more of a family concern. The Guardia's best-trained
corps, the Batallón de Combate Somoza, and its armoured unit,
were placed under the command of 'Papa Chepe', the President's
half-brother José. Relations with the United States remained in
the hands of his brother-in-law Guillermo Sevilla Sacasa, who had
received the ambassadorship in Washington as a wedding present
from old Tacho, and who by now also represented Nicaragua in
the United Nations and the Organisation of American States. The
Instituto de Fomento Nacional, which as Nicaragua's development
bank held the lifeline to most of the country's industries, was run
by a cousin, Noel Pallais. Another cousin, Luis Pallais, was editor
of the Somozas' newspaper, *Novedades*. Nicaragua's power utility,
Enaluf, was in the hands of 'Tío Luz', the President's uncle, former
Colonel Luis Manuel Debayle.

Modernisation of the family's widespread business interests had
called for the provision of all sorts of services to hitherto isolated
parts of the country. Paradoxically, this left many rural towns
worse off than before, their hopes of progress dashed by the
orientation of most public works schemes towards their glittering
'twins', the neighbouring Somoza *fincas*. San Miguelito lost its
chance when electricity, telephone lines, water and air links were
all directed to the nearby *finca* 'Morrillo'; Masachapa lost out to
the *finca* 'Montelimar'. Moyogalpa and Altagracia, on the island
of Ometepe, became also-rans when the railways' boat service was
routed through the *finca* 'Mérida'. The development funds which
San Rafael del Sur had been yearning for were channelled instead
to the nearby cement factory.

Tachito's administration, unlike that of his older brother, got off
to a good start. World prices for Nicaragua's main export commodities, combined with the rapid enlargement of the Central
American Common Market, made for heady growth. 'There are
great opportunities in our country,' Tachito would tell a class of
graduates in economics. 'We have a good base in that wealth is

properly distributed. Our *per capita* income is higher than in any other Central American nation, really. If we divide the number of agricultural units into the total population, we find that we have ten people per agricultural unit. We can proudly claim that we have peace, stability, tranquillity and freedom. Because of that, we can proudly claim that we are the only country, the only political unit in Latin America with a homogeneous race, without any pressures. And because of that we can proudly claim that any Nicaraguan can become President, as long as he is given the opportunity and has the right qualifications.'

Somoza's remarkable claims were soon backed by another, more believable one. After a nationwide manhunt by the Guardia, he was able to announce that the Frente Sandinista had been wiped out.

But storm clouds were looming over the horizon, and the winds of change sweeping through Latin America were whipping them into quite unexpected shapes. Pope Paul VI's encyclical *Populorum Progressio* had been taken to heart by a large segment of the Latin American Church, and when the Episcopal Conference met at Medellín, Colombia, its adaptation of these and other Vatican II teachings to local conditions sent a shockwave of seismic proportions through most Latin American capitals. Gone suddenly was one of the hitherto safest assumptions in Latin American politics : that the Church as well as the Army would stand squarely behind the oppressive régimes of the landowners and other privileged minorities.

'Latin America,' said the bishops, 'appears to live still under the tragic sign of underdevelopment, which makes it impossible for our brothers not only to enjoy material goods, but also to fulfil themselves. Despite all the efforts that are made, we are faced with hunger and poverty, massive diseases and infant mortality, illiteracy and marginalism, profound inequalities of income, and tensions between the social classes, outbreaks of violence and a scanty participation of the people in the management of the common good.' The answer to all this, the road to fulfilment, to salvation, lay in committing the Latin American Church to the easily understandable task of *liberación*.

Nicaragua's Church would produce a host of ardent advocates of *liberación*, the best known of whom is the priest-poet Ernesto Cardenal ('How much longer, Lord, shall you remain neutral/ And continue to watch all this as a mere spectator?').

That same year, in distant Bolivia, Che Guevara was putting

full stop to the first, disastrous chapter in the history of Latin American guerrilla warfare. His own original theories, born of a romantic reading of the Cuban experience, of creating peasant-based guerrilla armies and advancing from the countryside onto the cities, had given way to a more militaristic approach, best expounded in Régis Debray's *Revolution within the Revolution*. After a long, mysterious absence, Guevara himself had surfaced to lead a small band which, from the jungle area where Bolivia met Argentina and Paraguay, hoped to spark off the 'one, two, many Vietnams' that would rid the continent of *yanqui* imperialism.

His inglorious death at the hands of American-trained Bolivian Rangers brought about, instead, much heart-searching among the Latin American left. On the one hand, many turned their backs on the gospel of armed struggle and concentrated on the 'electoral way'. On the other, it persuaded the more radical elements to dump the old theories of rural insurrection and adopt the newer notion of urban guerrilla warfare which had been expressed in writing by the Brazilian Carlos Marighela.

The Frente Sandinista was among the pioneers of this latter trend. As early as September 1968 it had created an urban unit in Managua, under the command of Julio César Buitrago. Although activities in rural areas, most notably in Matagalpa, did not cease, they became increasingly confined to the training of cadres recruited in the cities, while the urban guerrillas began to raid banks and stores in Managua. Somoza's *orejas* were not working as effectively as they had done in the past, mainly because these young rebels moved in circles far removed from the Guardia informers' usual haunts. Nonetheless, by mid-1969 the urban band had been identified.

Buitrago and six other members of his team were tailed to a house in the Barrio Frixione, just west of the town centre. A cordon was thrown around the hideout, but action was delayed until Colonel Samuel Genie, the Guardia's Director of Security, arrived on the scene to conduct the operation in person. Genie was taking no chances; the troops had been issued machineguns, and a Sherman tank had been brought up to back them. When the guerrillas refused to surrender, a fierce gunbattle ensued. Tear gas failed to flush them out, and two Guardsmen were killed before the tank settled the score by shelling the house. Only two of the seven *sandinistas* were captured alive; among the dead was Buitrago.

A number of successful police raids elsewhere in the city allowed Tachito to claim once again that the Frente had been smashed, and a few weeks later his victory seemed complete when the Costa Rican authorities apprehended the *sandinistas'* exiled leader, Carlos Fonseca, and jailed him on a charge of robbery.

But trouble was already brewing in other quarters. A faction within the ruling Partido Liberal Nacionalista had united behind Ramiro Sacasa to revive Luis Somoza's theory that the Somozas should relinquish the overt trappings of power and 'institutionalise' the régime by delegating in the party the conduct of government affairs. Sacasa was obviously trying to pre-empt Tachito's still unrevealed plans to modify the Constitution in order to secure for himself another term of office. The fact that he was a distant relative of Tachito (by reason of old Tacho having married into the Sacasa family) and a member of Tachito's cabinet to boot, made it look as if the split reached all the way into the heart of the régime.

Another seam in the Somoza power structure burst when a Guardia captain was murdered by a fellow-officer in broad daylight. The killer, Major Oscar Morales ('Moralitos'), had been sentenced to imprisonment a year earlier for having tortured to death a suspected 'subversive', himself a former Guardia officer. The victim of this daylight killing was Captain Fernando Cerdeño, a key witness in the court case against Moralitos. The fact that the murderer was roaming about free instead of serving his prison sentence, and that he had openly flouted his impunity by killing an active Guardia officer in front of many witnesses, caused not only a public outcry but also a deep rift within the Guardia. Moralitos was locked up, and for the first time it became evident that even in the Guardia's officer corps there were those who were no longer prepared to justify the régime's worst excesses.

Tachito wriggled out of these incipient political troubles in a style befitting a true heir of old Tacho. He summoned his old rival, Fernando Agüero, and offered him a new version of 'historic compromise' between Nicaragua's two major political parties; a sharing of power in almost every imaginable branch of the State. It was a tempting platter : three of the seven seats on the Supreme Court, one seat in each Court of Appeal, two representatives on the boards of each autonomous government agency, the Social Security boards and collegiate bodies, an advisor in each Ministry and in the General Directorate of Central American integration, the Directorate of Planning, the Attorney General's office, the Pacific Railways, Customs, the Labour Dispute Settlement Boards, the Directorate of Communications, the Directorate of Sports and the Managua Water Company, and even a member in each diplomatic mission sent abroad.

That was not all. On acceptance of the offer, a constituent assembly would be convened and Tachito would step down, transferring executive power to a Triumvirate, one of whose members was to be designated by the Conservatives. Then came the final touch, craftily designed to assuage Agüero's conscience: the Organisation of American States would be invited to supervise the first Presidential elections under the new Constitution.

Agüero swallowed it whole. Tachito's triumph became even more complete when the new American ambassador, Turner B. Shelton, an enthusiastic Somoza fan, arranged for him to be invited to the White House for a meeting with President Nixon. Ever since their father's celebrated meeting with Franklin D. Roosevelt, the younger Somozas had been striving for similar recognition from the United States, and had actually taken to intervening in the American electoral process in the hope of assisting sympathetic politicians on their way to power. In 1959 Luis had sent a Guardia colonel with a 200,000-dollar contribution to support Lyndon B. Johnson's bid for the Democratic nomination (against John F. Kennedy), and Tachito later contributed to Nixon's campaign funds through their common friend Bebe Rebozo. If Roosevelt's friendship with the older Somoza was largely a fiction of Tacho's propaganda, Nixon seems to have been a genuine ally.

This rosy picture was not without its blemishes. In October 1970 the Frente Sandinista had finally managed to attract world attention by hijacking a plane belonging to L.A.C.S.A., the Costa Rican national airline, and forcing the Costa Rican authorities to free Carlos Fonseca Amador and fly him to Cuba. On top of that indirect blow to Somoza's prestige came a far more direct threat at home. Incensed by Agüero's 'betrayal', dissident Conservatives and *social-cristianos* joined forces with Ramiro Sacasa's breakaway Liberals and the older type of 'Independent Liberals', and even with the P.S.N. (the local pro-Moscow Communist party), in denouncing the Liberal-Conservative deal as a travesty of democracy. To crown it all, the new Archbishop of Managua, Miguel Obando y Bravo, led the Nicaraguan Church in an open protest against the agreement, pointedly refusing to accept the President's invitation to attend the circus he had organised to celebrate its formalisation on paper.

As was to be expected, none of this deterred Tachito. In August 1971 Congress voted to dissolve itself, vesting its powers in the President until such time as the constituent assembly had been elected. The Opposition, faced with a mock contest in which, irrespective of the number of votes they received, Somoza's Liberal Nationalists would take sixty of the 100 seats in the assemby (the other forty going to Agüero's Conservatives), decided to break the law and announced a boycott of the elections. In May 1972 Tachito formally handed over the Executive to the Triumvirate, on which he was represented by General Robert Martínez Lacayo and Alfonso López Cordero, and the Conservatives were represented by none other than Fernando Agüero. Just in case, Tachito retained command of the Guardia.

The new power-sharing club could not know that Nicaragua was only a few months away from a major upset, for which neither Tachito nor the Opposition, nor even the *sandinistas* would be responsible. This was to take place on December 23rd, 1972.

CHAPTER XX

THE EARTHQUAKE AND THE SPECTRE OF SANDINO

Most of Managua was fast asleep. Thirty-four minutes after midnight all hell broke loose. The city was lifted, heaved, rattled, torn apart by a sudden, major earthquake. The downtown area collapsed to the ground in chunks and pieces; even up on La Loma the shock-waves ripped up the Presidential Palace. Private houses and ministries, barracks and hospitals, hotels and banks cracked and crumbled. Fires had already begun to rage through the wreckage when the Managuans, pursued by aftershocks, streamed out of the town in search of safe open spaces. Though no one knew it at the time, about half-a-million people had been made homeless, at least twelve thousand had died and three-quarters of the city's buildings had been damaged beyond repair.

For about forty-eight hours there was anarchy. The Guardia soldiers had followed the civilians' example and run off to safety. Most of the diplomats fled to San José, Costa Rica, leaving only the U.S. ambassador's residence, amazingly intact, as a rallying point for the authorities. Looting broke out on a grand scale, and here too the Guardsmen followed the civilian example, eventually surpassing the civilian pillagers by using Army vehicles to ransack the abandoned city centre more systematically, and their arms to dissuade resistance and competition.

By the third day Tachito had managed to muster a small unit of Guardia with which he could begin to restore some sort of order. The downtown area was cordoned off and a complete evacuation was ordered. Veritable flocks of *gallinazos* were circling over the stricken city when troops moved in to start removing the thousands of already foul-smelling corpses, often improvising mass pyres in order to speed the clean-up before disease had a chance to spread. U.S. Army engineers were flown in from the Panama Canal Zone to help raze the city centre to the ground.

An impressive stream of relief supplies started to arrive at the airfield from all over the world. But huge quantities of these urgently needed wares were grabbed, as soon as they were unloaded, by greed-crazed Guardia officers, who were already running a thriving black market in looted goods, food, medicine and blankets throughout the sprawling tent cities that had sprung up around Managua.

Politics were revived almost instantly. The U.S. ambassador, Turner B. Shelton, had urged Tachito to take all the reins of power back into his own hands, but Somoza found the time to engineer a disguised takeover, indulging in formalities which looked doubly grotesque in the circumstances. He rounded up the constituent assembly and demanded the creation of a Ministry of National Reconstruction with sweeping powers, including that of overruling any decision made by the other branches of the Executive. The new agency would, of course, be headed by Tachito himself.

His Liberal majority was only too happy to oblige, but Fernando Agüero ordered the Conservatives to oppose the initiative. The bill was passed, but only after the Conservative representatives had walked out of the Assembly. Unwilling to permit such a visible split in his bipartisan setup, Somoza pushed through another bill, laying down new rules for the replacement of members of the ruling Triumvirate. No sooner had it been approved than Agüero was booted, and a more compliant Conservative leader, Edmundo Paguaga Irías, was appointed in his stead.

Then 'reconstruction' got under way. Unlimited greed prevailed over common sense, and instead of writing off the devastated capital and planning a new one in a safer location, Tachito decided to rebuild Managua on the same earthquake-prone site. His own extensive holdings of urban land had benefited from Nature's demolition job, and would benefit even more from the future reconstruction.

Peripheral *barrios* of quickly built houses started springing up around the old city; also a ring of motorways and bypasses to link them and a cluster of brand-new commercial centres at the exits to Masaya and the south. Well before construction had actually begun, the entire government hierarchy embarked on a land-buying spree and scrambled to secure concessions for new bus lines and services. Tachito's own business interests were surfacing everywhere; his were the cement used for construction work, and the hexagonal, earthquake-resistant paving blocks used for the new highway system, and his were the antiseismic roofs for the new dwellings and a sizeable stake in the new building concerns that began to flourish in Managua.

The larger industries were not much affected by the earthquake; it was the small industrial and commercial sector that had borne the brunt of the destruction. And when the time for reconstruction came, many hitherto independent businessmen found that they were competing with a Somoza who was once again expanding his empire, apparently no longer content with the indirect control he had hitherto wielded through the State apparatus. Somoza began now to take a firmer grip on the private financial sector, and on an expanding construction industry. The rules of the game had changed; where earlier many were quite prepared to tolerate minor exactions as the price for a relatively autonomous existence, and to support the Somoza régime in its role as protector of Nicaraguan capitalism, there now appeared bitterness and resentment at this shameless profiteering with the country's distress. The tacit 'social contract' between the Somozas and the independent businessmen had been broken.

The private citizen's urgent need to replace houses and personal belongings lost during the earthquake implied a drastic change in the pattern of spending. Rising inflation was almost inevitable, but Somoza added insult to injury by placing himself and his family interests at the receiving end of the price increases. Life in Managua became intolerably expensive; so much so that at one point only New York had a higher cost of living in the entire hemisphere. 'After the earthquake,' Tachito later explained with astounding candour, 'money did not remain in the hands of the powerful; that is why they are angry at me.'

Anger and resentment were not, however, confined to business-men. The universities had become intensely active centres of radical discontent. The intellectual José Coronel Urtecho described this process as follows : 'At least since 1950, and especially after 1950, most young intellectuals have been leaning towards Marxism. Those of us who were the "reactionaries", and consequently con-servatives, now feel practically, if not intellectually, defenceless before Marxism. And what is really significant is that those of us who used to find ourselves standing none too comfortably on the right, now find ourselves, without having moved from our places, standing none too comfortably on the left.' Pedro Joaquín Chamorro put it more bluntly : 'The students are all against the government; 70 per cent of them are Marxists, about 25 per cent are *social-cristianos,* and the remaining 5 per cent are nothing at all. For these youngsters, to be a Conservative or a Liberal is like going out into the tropical sun wearing a bowler hat.'

Student organisations like C.U.U.N. and F.E.R. had become recruiting centres for the Frente Sandinista; owners of small *fincas* were beginning to turn a blind eye when they discovered that their children were converting their farms into weekend guerrilla train-ing camps. Soon the whispered rumours about a *sandinista* buildup in the department of Matagalpa received confirmation : a fresh wave of guerrilla raids forced Somoza to send a still disorganised Guardia back into the field.

On March 14th, 1974, the Assembly approved a new constitution which included all the old injunctions against re-election and the candidacy of the incumbent's relatives. As it was the Triumvirate, and not Somoza, that formally wielded power in Nicaragua, there was no real objection to Tachito becoming a candidate once more. He resigned his post of *Jefe Director* of the Guardia in order to accept the Liberal nomination, but retained his other title of *Jefe Supremo* of the armed forces. Thus in effect he relinquished nothing. The Conservatives announced that Edmundo Paguaga Irías would run against Tachito; with the bipartisan power-sharing agreement still in force, it was clear to all that the elections would be a mere formality.

Pedro Joaquín Chamorro and twenty-six other Opposition leaders signed a petition addressed to the Electoral Tribunal, asking for the disqualification of both candidates on constitutional grounds. The Tribunal, a body set up under the terms of the Liberal-Conservative pact, rejected the motion, and when the Opposition parties announced a boycott of the elections, promptly declared them illegal and suspended their leaders' political rights. The Nicaraguan episcopate issued a blistering joint statement attacking the régime, and the Archbishop of Managua, Obando y Bravo, stated publicly that he would not even vote under the prevailing conditions.

Nonetheless, Tachito went ahead with the charade, and his electoral 'victory' was only marred by the news that Washington was recalling its ambassador, Turner B. Shelton—an event most observers interpreted as a withdrawal of American support for the régime. Somoza showed just what he thought of the American decision by organising a series of demonstrations and parties in honour of Shelton. The last one of these, a private party on December 27th of which a former Minister José María Castillo Quant was host, he did not attend, though he was well represented by his brother-in-law Guillermo Sevilla Sacasa, his cousin Noel Pallais Debayle and his nephew Leonel Somoza Abrego. It was a jolly, carefree occasion; none of these present had any way of knowing that it had been chosen by the Frente Sandinista as the best possible opportunity to pull off a spectacular coup—the kidnapping of the U.S. ambassador.

The 'Comando Juan José Quezada', led by young Eduardo Contreras Escobar, got its timing wrong. When the *guerrilleros* burst into the Castillo Quant residence, guns blazing, shortly after ten o'clock at night, Shelton and a number of prominent guests were no longer there. It was, however, a remarkable catch : members of the Somoza family, ministers, ambassadors, leading businessmen and their wives. Tachito was not even in Managua when it happened; he had taken off to the lazy beaches of Corn Island with his mistress, Dinora Sampson. But his half-brother, General José Somoza, turned up instantly with a contingent of heavily armed Guardsmen, determined to end the raid with a lightning assault on the house. His men had already started firing when a telephone message from the residence informed him that there were members of his family among the hostages.

The attack was called off while a startled, angry Tachito flew back from Corn Island. The siege lasted for sixty-two hours, while Archbishop Obando y Bravo, the mediator chosen by the *sandinistas,* talked Somoza into accepting the raiders' demands. An indignant, helpless Tachito was forced to broadcast the communiqués of the *guerrilleros,* to pay them a couple of million dollars ransom, and to allow them to be driven along a route lined by cheering Managuans to the airport, where a number of comrades released from prison were waiting to fly with them to the safety of Havana.

Somoza was not only furious at his humiliation; he was completely bewildered by the fact that his network of *orejas* had failed to pick up the least sign that a coup of this importance was in the offing. Although the actual perpetrators of the raid were well beyond his reach, countrywide repression began almost immediately. A state of siege was decreed, press censorship was introduced, military tribunals were set up. Suspects who were considered to be important enough in the Frente Sandinista to provide valuable information were taken away to interrogation centres and brutally tortured. Less important 'subversives' and mere sympathisers, especially in rural areas, were dealt with in 'exemplary' fashion, which usually meant being killed. American Catholic missionaries found three mass graves in wooded areas near Siuna, in the north, containing 109 bullet-ridden bodies. The Capuchin monks of Estelí and Bluefields prepared a report for the Episcopal Conference listing at least ninety-three disappearances, a number of known murders and an inventory of the methods employed by the Guardia to torture their prisoners. Church sources alone recorded close to 400 'disappearances' in the aftermath of the December 27th raid, while Amnesty International spoke of 200 peasants who had disappeared, 'as many as 500 political prisoners', and 'cattle corrals used for the relatively short-term detention of large groups of people'.

'The unprotected rural population,' says an Amnesty report, 'bears the brunt of abuses of human rights incurred as a result of counter-insurgency operations . . . Local leaders reportedly are tortured and murdered as a routine method to uncover F.S.L.N. guerrillas and to discourage local support.'

From Havana, the Frente Sandinista announced that the December 27th raid marked the beginning of a 'prolonged people's war' against the régime, while its units in the departments of Matagalpa and Zelaya began to 'execute' police informers and rural magistrates known to be collaborating with the Guardia.

Somoza did not confine his repressive efforts to the *sandinistas*. Very soon after the December raid he was accusing Pedro Joaquín Chamorro and the newspaper *La Prensa* of having instigated the whole affair. '*La Prensa*', he claimed, 'was trying to create an atmosphere of hatred so that, when the time was ripe, it could place the government in a shameful position. Well, there you are : all the editorials that were written and all the articles that were published have yielded their fruit—the deaths of four innocent men and another four men wounded.' Tachito was clearly trying to twist facts in such a way that Chamorro and *La Prensa* could be taken to court under the provisions of Article 500 in the Penal Code he had recently imposed. That remarkable piece of legislation stipulates : 'If it is not possible to find out who committed [an] act of terrorism, its promoters or instigators will be held responsible for it.'

Chamorro took up the challenge and deliberately broke the censorship law by distributing a mimeographed 'open letter' to Somoza, in which he countered : 'The regrettable deaths and injuries caused by the raid on Dr José María Castillo's house are not the fruits of my harvest, but of the violence your régime has institutionalised for many years.' Somoza threatened to have him tried by a military court, but backed away when the press throughout the world rushed to Chamorro's defence. Not that he actually gave up the idea of making Chamorro answer for his impudence, for, as he would confide later, 'We have introduced censorship and on more than twenty occasions he, Pedro Joaquín, has sent clandestine letters to his subscribers, always in the hope that the authorities would take reprisals against him, so that he could play the role of the victim. After careful consideration we arrived at the conclusion that those letters would not, let us say, provoke a demonstration on the streets. So we have let him be. But we have it all in his record ! He has broken the law, and we are keeping it all in his record until this insubordination is translated into action. And when that happens, he will have to face our justice.'

CHAPTER XXI

CRACKS IN THE EDIFICE

For all Tachito's 'investigative' efforts, in six months the Guardia were only able to come up with thirty-seven indictments, most of which were against people who had left the country. However, the massive scale on which repression was conducted dealt the Frente Sandinista what appeared to be a crippling blow. In the process, purely political opposition to the régime was strengthened. Pedro Joaquín Chamorro emerged as the leader of a united Opposition front, the Unión Democrática de Liberación (UDEL), which was a coalition of all the illegal parties and the major labour unions. One of the clearest indicators of the prestige acquired by UDEL was the bitter attack the new force evoked from the *sandinistas*. 'UDEL,' they declared, 'born in the bosom of the bourgeoise Opposition, is an organisation that hides under revolutionary terminology, but which is essentially venomous. It has been formed by bourgeois parties and labour unions controlled by pro-Soviet parties; UDEL pretends to be an alternative to imperialism for the sole purpose of prolonging its domination should the time come when the Somozas prove to be an encumbrance.'

Some *sandinistas* were quick to pick up signals of growing dissent within the ruling circle itself, and particularly within the Guardia Nacional. During his much-publicised trial, the F.S.L.N. leader René Núñez told the military prosecutor : 'The Frente is not aiming at the total destruction of the armed forces, because the repressive apparatus will only be our enemy inasmuch as it protects anti-popular interests—the F.S.L.N. could well strike up an alliance with the armed forces if these took up the defence of the people's cause.'

Far more than the intensity of repression and the alienation of former allies, what was worrying the inner circle of the Somoza régime was the suspicion that Tachito was cracking up under the pressure of events. His family life was a shambles, and he no longer seemed to care. The rift with his American-born wife, Hope Porto-carrero, once billed as Nicaragua's answer to Evita Perón, was nothing new, but Tachito had now taken to appearing in public with his mistress Dinora, whom he allowed to hold court in her residence, dispensing government favours and appointments, while Hope was quite openly shipping her belongings abroad. There were whispers about the circumstances in which two of his sons, Roberto and Julio, had been committed to New York hospitals. His daughter Carolina's marriage with socialite Víctor Orcuyo was on the rocks, and his daughter Carla had fled to London in disgust after the Guardia broke up her romance with Alejandro Lacayo, a member of the Frente, by torturing him and forcing him into exile. And young Anastasio, groomed to be Tachito's successor in the Guardia, had first been dismissed from Sandhurst, and later created a wave of resentment among the Guardia career officers by the high-handed manner in which he flaunted his premature promotion to the rank of Major (a new version of the 'Minor Major' ditty began to make the barrack rounds). Nephews and nieces were accused of involvement in drug scandals, or of conspiring with the *sandinistas*.

Always a hearty drinker, Tachito had begun to exceed himself. As he puffed out to a bloated caricature of his former self, his behaviour became more and more unpredictable. However, when by the end of 1975 he came across the first hard evidence of a plot between members of his own family and certain high-ranking Guardia officers, he still managed to make the purge a surgically neat and discreet affair. The plotters' mistake had been to suppose that he would actually welcome the notion of a 'coup from within' which would have enabled him to cut his losses and go into exile after liquidating a sizeable share of his assets. But Tachito was never in a mood for this sort of 'defeatism'. As he put it, 'The choice here is between free, *socialising* private enterprise, and State-run Communism. Anyone who does not see that just isn't looking properly.'

What Tachito's messianic confidence did not allow him to see was that the mood of the country was changing rapidly, and that he himself was responsible for the change.

'Apolonio Estrada' is as good an example as any of a typical middle-aged, middle-ranking official in the Somoza administration. Until 1972 he and his family lived, together with his parents and his unmarried brother, in a spacious old house in downtown Managua. After the earthquake, thanks to the good offices of a cousin in the Guardia, he was among the first to secure a newly-built house in the Colonia Salvadorita, a development lying south-east of the old city which had been named after Tachito's mother. The company that built his house is half-owned by the General, and both the cement they used and the antiseismic roof were provided by Somoza firms. Every morning, the Estrada family breakfasts on Presto instant coffee, another Somoza product, milk pasteurised by the General's dairy products company, and sugar which might have come from Montelimar, Santa Rita or Dolores, all owned by Somoza. Yesterday's rubbish will have been carted away in a Mercedes truck (bought at the Somoza agency, which also supplies vehicles for the Guardia and top government officials).

Apolonio's pre-lunch drink is usually a Somoza-distilled rum with Somoza ice cubes; lunch itself is Somoza-slaughtered beef and a salad dressed in Somoza oil. As Señora Estrada retreats into the kitchen to wash the dishes while listening to Somoza radio, Apolonio's youngest son switches on the set to watch Somoza television, and Apolonio himself sinks into an armchair to smoke a Somoza cigarette (lit by a Somoza match).

What he no longer does is read the Somoza newspaper. He is fed up with the Somozas, even if they did get him his job when he joined the Partido Liberal Nacionalista years ago. And not only because his salary is buying him much less than before (he is now spending almost half of it on the monthly instalments for the new house). He knows what the Somoza police did to his niece Carmen, who was not even involved in this *sandinista* business. So now he pretends not to notice when his eldest son locks himself up in the back room with his schoolmates for secret discussions, and he is actually eager to hear from his cousin Jaime, who owns a *finca* not far from Granada where the boys spend weekends listening to political lectures and learning to handle pistols and machineguns.

Not only were the Estradas of Managua changing, but they were not the only ones who were aware of the changes taking place around them. At the popular Coliseo restaurant, one of the victims of the December 27th kidnapping, the picturesque Colonel László Pataky, a veteran of the French Foreign Legion and the Israeli army who is a close friend of Tachito and of his Chief of Internal Security, could complain bitterly at the impunity of the higher-class *guerrilleros* and point out, at nearby tables a bank director whose daughter was a *sandinista,* and a financier whose son had been indicted for 'subversive' activities but never arrested, even though he was often seen on the streets of Managua. 'You cannot trust anyone any more,' said Pataky, 'not even your own sons and daughters.'

As 1976 advanced, it began to seem as if Tachito was winning the little war against the *sandinistas.* The founder of the *Frente,* Carlos Fonseca Amador, was killed in action in November, but few believed Somoza when he announced it; they thought he was lying as he had done three years earlier, when he even produced a body and brought in Fonseca's mother to identify it.

Then in December, the accumulated tension, plus the excesses to which he had resorted to stave it off, caught up with Tachito. At a meeting with Central Bank officials he collapsed with a heart attack. A ripple of panic ran through the establishment, but Somoza III soon recovered to hear that his wife Hope was setting up residence in New York and reportedly considering a divorce.

A few months later a second, more severe heart attack forced his immediate evacuation to a hospital in Miami. The Interior Minister, Antonio Mora, took over the Executive, as was usual whenever the President was temporarily absent, but as it became clear that Tachito was not pulling through as rapidly as on the previous occasion, the more ambitious Liberal leaders and Guardia officers began to press for a more permanent replacement. Cornelio Hueck, the veteran Secretary-General of the party and President of the Chamber of Deputies, held that the time had come to invoke the constitutional provisions regarding the President's incapacitation—Hueck's position in Congress made him one of the three men constitutionally eligible to step into Somoza's shoes. Guardia General Roger Bermúdez appeared to go along with Hueck, but retreated when the President's half-brother, General José Somoza, took a firm stand against any changes. Rumours of an impending Guardia coup began to circulate, and Tachito's old crony General José Ivan Allegret was mentioned as a leading plotter.

After a nerve-racking absence of three months, a haggard Tachito returned to Nicaragua. Close behind him, his aging mother Salvadora flew down from her Miami residence to preside over an emergency meeting of the Somoza clan at the Montelimar sugar estate. Although the meeting was secret, Nicaragua came alive with rumours, that as a precaution against a third, fatal heart attack, Tachito had signed over his holdings in the Somoza business empire to the rest of the family. For the first time, it was murmured, a notarised statement listed the full extent of the family fortune. The most frequently mentioned figure was 600 million dollars for Tachito alone, and more than 1,000 million if one took into account the joint holdings of all branches of the family; the Sevillas, Debayles, Sacasas, Pallais and their multiple permutations. An anonymous inventory circulating at the time in Managua listed 346 companies covering every imaginable field of activity: coffee, sugar, cotton, agriculture and commerce in general, textiles, shipping, customs agencies, travel agencies, fishing, meat packing, cattle ranching, warehouses, a harbour, air transport, construction, aluminium products, oil refining, match manufacturing, tobacco, publicity, recreation centres, banking, real estate, cement, consulting firms, auto sales, furniture, electrical appliances, cine parlours, dairy products, footwear, distilleries, publishing houses, radio, television, geothermal energy, pipelines, fertilisers, rice, shipbuilding, mining, recording, computing, boutiques, laundromats, even exports of human blood and plasma.

Whatever was decided at the family conclave, it was certainly not Tachito's early retirement. He was soon back at the Presidential desk, making a show of confidence by lifting the state of siege which had been in force since December 1974, and purging his establishment of those whose behaviour during his absence had been less than reassuring. The first head to roll was that of Cornelio Hueck, who was replaced by the President's cousin, Luis Pallais Debayle. General Allegret was arrested when he refused to accept an uncomfortable field command, although he did not remain out of favour for long; confirmed as chief of operations, he was soon handling a two-million-dollar fund for hiring mercenaries in the United States.

Everyone had been expecting a major guerrilla offensive during Tachito's illness, when internal squabbling had weakened the government. But it did not materialise, and for a very good reason : the Frente Sandinista was having internal problems of its own. After the heavy beating suffered by the Frente in 1975 and 1976, two conflicting lines of thought had developed within the rebel movement. One favoured instant, spectacular military action, and eventually a political alliance with the rest of the Opposition, while the other adhered to the theory of a 'prolonged people's war' and intransigent Marxist proselytising. The Frente split into not two, but three factions, each of which claimed to be the standardbearer of authentic *sandinista* tradition and accused the others of treason.

The bulk of the *sandinista* fighting forces sided with the 'Tercerista' or 'Historic' faction, which favoured an immediate strike against the régime. These *guerrilleros* were divided into three 'War Fronts' : 'Carlos Fonseca Amador' operating in the far north, 'General Benjamín Zeledón' in charge of the extreme south, and 'Rigoberto López Pérez' in the centre and west. On October 13th, 1977, they launched a countrywide offensive.

The southern 'War Front' attacked La Fortaleza barracks in San Carlos, close to the Costa Rican border; the northern unit ambushed a Guardia patrol near Ocotal and later briefly occupied the town of Mosonte; and the central forces made a series of raids on Masaya, Altos de Masaya and Esquipulas. By the time the Guardia mounted a counter-offensive the *guerrilleros* had disappeared. In the new, predictable wave of repression that ensued, a Guardia unit followed the *sandinista* trail to the island of

Solentiname, where the priest-poet Ernesto Cardenal had his hitherto peaceful commune. The place was overrun and destroyed. Cardenal was abroad at the time, and when news of the event reached him, he sprang a surprise on everyone. For quite some time, he declared, he had been a secret member of the Frente Sandinista's National Directorate.

Somoza's major public response to the guerrilla offensive was a new version of the ploy so favoured by his father and brother : 'bring in the Americans'. Tachito had been experiencing trouble with the Carter administration, which had condemned his régime for violating human rights, but he had managed to come out of it with much more credit than other Latin American military governments; although Washington announced at first that it would 'defer' a 12-million-dollar aid package granted to Nicaragua, it later disbursed 2.5 million dollars in *military* aid. And after the October outbreak Washington was influential in persuading the CONDECA (the Central American military alliance) to hold the mammoth 'Aguila Six' counter-insurgency exercises on Nicaraguan soil. American, Guatemalan and Salvadorean troops joined the Guardia for these war games, which were held in the *sandinistas'* usual stamping grounds.

The Nicaraguan Opposition had repeatedly accused Washington of duplicity on the issue of human rights in their country, and the *sandinistas* claimed that the Americans were doing somewhat more than turning a blind eye to the recruitment of mercenaries (both Americans and exiled South Vietnamese) by Somoza in the United States. The Frente also insisted that Tachito had hired the services of Brazilian interrogation experts and of a Colombian general with experience of anti-guerrilla operations in his own country.

Following their October attacks, the Frente issued a call to the formation of a 'Broad Anti-Somoza Front' comprising all Opposition forces, regardless of their political persuasion. The reply was soon on its way. Twelve prominent Nicaraguans met in Guatemala to sign a joint statement. They represented an interesting cross-section of Nicaragua's middle classes : two businessmen, two Catholic priests, two lawyers, an agronomist, a teacher, a writer, an economist, a dentist and an architect. Their manifesto, soon to become known as *El Documento de los Doce* (Document of Twelve), said : 'For more than a decade the Frente Sandinista de Liberación Nacional has fought generously for change in Nicaragua, and the blood shed by so many youths is the best witness of the permanence and presence of this struggle, which is carried out with ever-increasing political maturity. We, the signatories of this document, do not hesitate to call on all conscientious Nicaraguans to provide a national solution to Nicaragua's pressing problem, a solution which cannot exclude the participation of the Frente Sandinista de Liberación Nacional if it is to guarantee a permanent and effective peace.' When Archbishop Obando y Bravo chimed in with a call for a 'national dialogue', it seemed that everyone was speaking the same language.

CHAPTER XXII

ONE MAN AGAINST A NATION

The offer of the Frente Sandinista to enter an alliance with the rest of the Opposition, and its acceptance by 'The Twelve' on behalf of Nicaragua's more traditional political forces, remained a largely theoretical proposition until January 10th, 1978. On that fateful day a gang of hired killers ambushed and shot Pedro Joaquín Chamorro, the outspoken editor of *La Prensa* who appeared to the world as the most plausible head of the non-violent Opposition groups. The ensuing uproar shook all sectors of Nicaraguan society. As enraged crowds took to the streets, Tachito promised to track down and punish the assassins. The gunmen were arrested almost immediately, and they confessed to their crime, but their identification of the paymasters was vague and contradictory, and did not dispel the widespread suspicion that the régime, however indirectly, had been its ultimate instigator.

Nicaragua's business community crossed ranks against Somoza and ordered a nationwide lock-out until he stepped down from the Presidency. In Congress, the bipartisan power-sharing agreement came to an abrupt end as the Conservatives joined in the general clamour for Tachito's resignation. When Somoza ignored these demands and went ahead with the municipal elections he had scheduled for early February, fifty-two candidates withdrew from the race and only one-third of Nicaragua's 700,000 voters bothered to turn up at the polling stations.

Somoza still seemed unruffled. He made an appearance in public (behind a screen of bullet-proof glass) to announce that he had not the slightest intention of relinquishing power before his term expired in 1981. He went on to announce a fresh package of social benefits for the workers, including a juicy annual bonus, in an unsuccessful attempt to deflate the Opposition campaign for a general strike which, added to the lock-out, would bring the whole country grinding to a halt.

Tachito's deliberately restrained response to the challenge ended when Frente guerrilla units launched a couple of raids in Granada and Rivas, and when particularly violent rioting broke out in Masaya, León, Matagalpa, Jinotepe and Diriamba. The Guardia was ordered to suppress the uprisings swiftly and completely; at least thirty people were killed in armed clashes, and scores were arrested. The lock-out-cum-general-strike fizzled out after three weeks, but the country did not return to normal.

The rebellious mood continued to spread unevenly, infecting one segment of society after another. First the construction workers went on strike, to be followed soon afterwards by the municipal and hospital employees. University and secondary students walked out of their classes in Managua, then Diriamba, Matagalpa, Rivas, Boaco, Estelí, until schools all over the country were empty. Riots erupted here and there, introducing a new element in the conflict : the readiness of ordinary *muchachos* (youngsters) unconnected with the Frente Sandinista, to risk an unequal armed confrontation with the Guardia. Somehow the fear which had underlain the many years of *pax somociana* seemed to have vanished. This was never more evident than when the usually subservient judiciary threw out the charges of 'illegal association' and 'delinquency' brought by the government against 'The Twelve', and announced that they could return to Nicaragua unmolested.

Not that repression had eased. Dozens of people were still being arrested, held without trial, tortured, or sent away to the remote prison camps of Río Blanco, Dú Dú and Waslala. So six months passed but dissent was still spreading.

Then, all of a sudden, came an entirely unexpected shock for the Opposition. President Jimmy Carter wrote Tachito (the selfsame man who had earlier told Washington, 'Those who historically have beaten up blacks and kept Indians as second-class citizens have nothing to teach us') a letter congratulating him for his promises to restore human rights in Nicaragua. Democratic Opposition leaders were aghast. The directorate of the Frente Sandinista interpreted the letter as a sign that the United States were still committed to supporting Somoza. The Church answered indirectly, through a joint statement of the Episcopal Conference calling once more for Tachito's resignation.

But Somoza's moment of triumph was shortlived. On August 22nd, 1978, a group of twenty-five uniformed *sandinistas* drove into the heart of Managua and marched unopposed into the Palacio Nacional, the seat of Congress and a number of government agencies, and captured 1,500 hostages, including the Interior Minister José Antonio Mora and the President's cousin Luis Pallais Debayle. The government was to release fifty-nine political prisoners, pay a ransom of 10 million dollars, broadcast a revolutionary communiqué on the radio and give them a safe conduct to leave the country. Forty-five hours later, having obtained all their demands except the full amount of the ransom money, the *sandinistas* were waved off at Las Mercedes airport by a delirious crowd.

Before Tachito could recover his bearings, the 'Broad Opposition Front', a coalition of all anti-Somoza parties and labour unions, called a general strike. The Federation of Chambers of Commerce followed suit by voting in favour of a lock-out to reinforce the strike. Groups of armed *muchachos* took to the streets in Masaya, Matagalpa, León, Granada, Estelí and Chinandega. The government's reaction was still sluggish, and the reason for this became apparent on August 29th, when it was announced that Tachito had crushed an attempted putsch, placing twelve senior Guardia officers and nearly 200 men under arrest. His explanation was typical : these were extreme right-wing elements who had panicked at the prospect of an imminent Communist takeover.

Repression now began in earnest. Guardia units were ordered to move into the rebellious towns, and dissenters were rounded up by the hundred. A Guardia spokesman declared : 'What is at stake is the survival of Nicaragua, not just of the Somoza dynasty.' By September 9th, however, the spontaneous fighters had been joined by Frente units who seized the centre of León and launched a simultaneous offensive in Masaya, Estelí, Chinandega, Diriamba and Granada. Martial law was imposed, and heavy fighting broke out on both sides of the Costa Rican border, as Guardia units intercepted *guerrillero* columns and followed them in 'hot pursuit' into the neighbouring state.

By mid-September it looked to the outside world as if a full-scale civil war was raging in Nicaragua, and there were ominous signs that the conflict might acquire an international dimension. Venezuelan President Carlos Andrés Pérez supplied aircraft and weapons to Costa Rica to halt the Nicaraguan army and air force raids across the border. He also called upon the Organisation of American States to intervene; Washington took up the idea and suggested O.A.S. 'mediation', but Pérez was reportedly more inclined towards sending an Inter-American Peace Force into Nicaragua to halt the fighting. Other Central American governments, notably Honduras and Guatemala, offered instead to send their own troops in aid of Somoza, while hundreds of civilians in Panama offered to join the anti-Somoza forces as volunteers.

In Tachito's brilliant tactical mind, however, there was no such thing as a civil war. He saw the situation quite differently. He was facing, on the one hand, an attempt at armed insurrection by no more than 700 hard-core *sandinistas* and a host of ill-equipped *muchachos,* who had managed to entrench themselves in the town centres of León, Masaya, Chinandega and Estelí (the capital city, Managua, remained relatively unaffected). On the other hand, there was this strike-cum-lock-out organised by disgruntled and misguided labour leaders and businessmen. Even taken together, they did not add up to an immediate threat to himself.

He refused to play into the *guerrilleros'* hands by spreading his forces thin and attempting to check all the outbreaks at once. Instead, he tackled one rebel stronghold at a time, ordering heavy airborne attacks which had the instant effect of isolating the combatants from the panic-stricken bystanders, and then following up with assaults by mobile Guardia units. It was a slow, costly operation. The last rebel-held city was not cleared until late September, and in the process the town centres were destroyed and some 1,500 people lost their lives. Most of the *guerrilleros* managed to slip away before each of the final Guardia onslaughts, and the spontaneous *muchachos* discarded their masks and kerchiefs and blended again into the population.

The ferocity of the Guardia's mopping-up operations was only partly picked up by the television crews who had been following the revolt day by day (in each case, just before the Guardia closed in for the *coup de grâce,* the area was cleared of journalists), but for whole weeks television sets the world over had carried images of barricaded town centres held by masked gunmen—precisely the image on which Tachito wanted to play for propaganda purposes. It seemed to confirm his argument that he, Somoza, was the only remaining barrier to a takeover of Nicaragua by Communist hoodlums. The destruction caused by the Guardia's bombing, strafing and shelling was dealt with in pure Goebbels style : it was simply blamed on 'the Communists', who were also accused of committing a number of atrocities, including the inevitable emotion-laden charge of raping innocent women.

The general strike he ignored, admitting freely that he would wait until the businessmen felt that their losses had become more intolerable than the continued presence of Somoza in the Presidency. On the international plane, his skilful playing of the Communist bogey was highly successful. A number of U.S. Congressmen and Senators wrote to President Carter urging him to support Somoza's brave anti-Communist stand. In the Organisation of American States this same propaganda theme was enlarged into a Central American 'domino theory' : a Communist takeover in Nicaragua would be followed by similar coups in El Salvador, Guatemala and Honduras—a most convincing notion, given the fact that many political analysts agreed that Somoza's replacement by even the mildest form of democratic government would encourage the overthrow of the neighbouring military or military-backed régimes. The South American military rulers indirectly accepted Somoza's reading of the situation, and ganged up to block even the most timid attempt at 'mediation' by the O.A.S., on the grounds that it would constitute unwarranted intervention in the internal affairs of a sovereign state (which had been their line of defence against Washington's human rights offensive).

Only after recapturing the rebel-held towns and carrying out swift, bloody reprisals against suspected *sandinista* collaborators did Tachito concede that Washington might mediate between his régime and the Opposition, making it clear that by Opposition he meant practically everyone . . . except the *sandinistas*.

Another battle for survival had been fought and won, but as the summer of 1978 ended, it was clear that the Somoza régime was threatened as it had never been threatened before in the forty-two years since Anastasio Somoza García took power, after having ordered the assassination of Augusto C. Sandino. Tachito Somoza, already perhaps the wealthiest man in Central America, had allowed his insatiable greed to alienate the support he once enjoyed among the Nicaraguan moneyed classes, and his lust for power had pushed even the most accommodating of his political adversaries into an alliance with a left-wing revolutionary organisation. Not even the Somozas' very own 'constituency', the 8,000-strong Guardia Nacional, remained an entirely trustworthy ally.

Thousands of his fellow-countrymen had been killed, tortured, imprisoned or driven into exile so that Nicaragua might become his own private business concern, his *finca*. Whichever set of ideas became fashionable in Washington (anti-Nazism, anti-Communism) had been skilfully played upon in order to build up an armed force which existed for the sole purpose of keeping the dynasty in power. 'The alliance of money and the machinegun', as the Nicaraguan poet Pablo Antonio Cuadra used to call it. Cuadra once gave the warning : 'Do not believe in the alliance of money and the machinegun, for your children will inherit not the money, but the machinegun.' The late 1970s seemed to be proving the poet right.

Tachito often claimed that he was more of a 'true' Liberal than the European or American variety, and that he had used private enterprise and agrarian reform to 'socialise' Nicaragua's economy. The fact is that a full third of Nicaragua's income goes to the top 5 per cent of the population; that this same 5 per cent of the population owns more than half the country's arable land (the top one per cent owns about 41 per cent of the land and sells a full 85 per cent of the country's agricultural exports). Seven out of every ten Nicaraguans cannot read or write; only three in every thousand manage to make their way through a university career. Infant mortality is high, tuberculosis is widespread, goitre is endemic, blindness and brain damage through malnutrition are common in northern rural areas; all of which is not very surprising in a country where most people's calory intake is only slightly more than half of what the World Health Organisation considers a safe minimum, and where there are only five doctors for every 10,000 inhabitants. Small wonder, either, that more murders are committed every year in Nicaragua than anywhere else in the world, and that there are more chronic alcoholics there than anywhere else in Central America.

On the other hand, one Nicaraguan in every 250 is a soldier of the Guardia Nacional (if the police and Treasury Guard units are taken into consideration as well, the ratio is one Nicaraguan in every 166). The Guardsmen are very much a privileged caste, with access to housing, schooling and health services, subsidised food and clothing, lower tax rates and special credit facilities. Because the Somozas have traditionally turned a blind eye towards graft and corruption in the service, Guardia officers have usually been able to count on retiring as pretty affluent men (especially as they continue to draw their full salary in retirement, and in addition tend to walk straight out of the barracks into well-paid positions in government or industry).

Over forty-two years, however, the relatively unchanged power structure has become top-heavy, and access to the more lucrative positions in the Guardia has become slower and more difficult to obtain; so much so that Tachito finally resorted to forcing entire classes of officers into retirement in order to ease the pressure from below.

By 1978 the Guardia had become an entirely professional military force, with General José Somoza, the President's half-brother, as the only visible reminder of the old days of political appointments. Tachito was not even able to push his son Anastasio up through the ranks fast enough to become, from a key command position, the obvious heir to the throne. Within the Guardia, over the years, devotion to the Somozas has begun to be replaced by devotion to the system; loyalty to the *caudillo* by loyalty to the more abstract notion of 'national security'. Political ambition is not unknown among the senior officers, nor are their juniors immune to the ideological and political uncertainties that have swept through other Latin American armies.

It was once said that Nicaragua would be the easiest country in the world to turn socialist; a victorious revolution would only need to expropriate the holdings of a single family. But even if this were to happen, it would not mean the end of the Somoza fortune. Although a considerable share of the family's assets are in Nicaragua (it could almost be said that they *are* Nicaragua), and are by their nature immovable, their holdings abroad are just as impressive, and out of the reach of any would-be expropriator. Anything less than a socialist régime would, equally, be unable to touch the bulk of the family's properties within the country.

Though he certainly tried hard enough with young Anastasio (and at one time had high hopes of a military career for his son Julio), Somoza has tended to disguise his failure to produce a recognisable successor by claiming that, unlike his father, he did not groom his children for the Presidency. 'My only heir', he is fond of saying, 'is the Partido Liberal Nacionalista.' But the many possible heirs who appeared within the party, or within the Guardia, were always cast away as soon as they began to look right for the job, because the Somozas were always quicker to see in their qualifications the potential threat of the present than the vague promises for the future. With young Anastasio's ascent blocked by a sensitive officer corps, and the other boys showing little promise, Tachito might well have been as childless as Perón— indeed, his position has seemed uncomfortably similar to that of old Trujillo, the Dominican *Benefactor,* who left behind only his playboy son Ramfis and a couple of ineffectual, blood-thirsty brothers.

Not that Tachito was ever fond of meditating on these matters. 'After me the deluge', was the way the American press summed up his attitude to the mounting opposition in 1978. But even that would be far too defeatist a motto for the real Tachito; when fighting raged in all major Nicaraguan cities, when a united domestic Opposition, the Church and several foreign governments were clamouring for his resignation, he told a visiting journalist : 'If they push me out, I'll fight; out of office I would still be the most powerful man in Nicaragua.'

GLOSSARY OF SPANISH TERMS
USED IN THE TEXT

Auxiliares. Auxiliary; name given to the irregular forces recruited by the Guardia Nacional to fight against Sandino (formerly *voluntarios*).

Barbudos. Bearded ones; Fidel Castro's guerrilla fighters.

Barrios. Quarters, neighbourhoods.

Cabildo. Town or city councils; local authorities in Spanish colonial America.

Calderonistas. Followers of Costa Rican President Rafael Angel Calderón Guardia.

Camisas azules. Blueshirts; Fascist shock force armed by Tacho Somoza.

Caudillo. Leader.

Comuneros. Commoners; advocates of the rule of 'the common' in colonial times.

Concón. Name given to the rifles used by the Liberal rebels, after the Mexican ship *Concón* in which they were transported to Nicaragua.

Conquista. The Spanish conquest of America.

Córdoba. Nicaraguan currency unit.

Corsarios luteranos. Literally, Lutheran corsairs; name given to English raiders and traders.

Cortes. Cuts.

El pirata. The pirate.

El Pulpo. Literally, the Octopus; name given to the United Fruit Co.

Finca. Farm or plantation; rural property.

Foco. Focus; initial point of guerrilla activity.

Gallinazo. Buzzard.

Gamonal. Small town strongman.

Guayabera. Loose shirt used in tropical regions of America.

Gringo. Foreigner, particularly British or North American; said to be a corruption of 'green grass'.

Jefe Director. Director-in-Chief; the highest rank in Nicaragua's National Guard.

Machete. Long, broad-bladed knife; the tool of the canecutters.

Muchachos. Young men; kids.

Orejas. Literally, ears; police informers and spies.

Peninsulares. Spanish-born inhabitants of the colonies.

Pipe. Typical Nicaraguan appellative; mate, friend.

Somocistas. Followers of the Somozas.

Voluntarios. Volunteers; irregular forces recruited by the Guardia Nacional to fight against Sandino.

Yanki, yanqui. Yankee; North American.

SELECT BIBLIOGRAPHY

Adamson, David, *The Ruins of Time; Four and a Half Centuries of Conquest and Discovery among the Maya*. London: George Allen & Unwin, 1975.

Alemán Bolaños, Gustavo, *Un Lombrosiano: Somoza 1939-1944*. Guatemala: Editorial Hispania, 1945.

————, *Sandino, El Libertador*. Mexico: Ediciones del Caribe, 1951.

Amnesty International Report 1975-1976, London.

Amnesty International Report 1977, London.

Belausteguigoitía, Ramón, *Con Sandino en Nicaragua*. Madrid: Espasa-Calpe, 1934.

Borah, Woodrow, *Early Colonial Trade and Navigation between Mexico and Peru*. Berkeley: Univ. of California Press, 1954.

Burland, C. A., *Peoples of the Sun: The Civilizations of Pre-Columbian America*. London: Weidenfeld and Nicholson, 1976.

Calderón Ramírez, Salvador, *Ultimos Días de Sandino*. Mexico: Ediciones Botas.

Chamorro, Pedro Joaquín, *Estirpe Sangrienta, Los Somoza*. Buenos Aires: Editorial Triángulo, 1959.

————, *5 P.M.* Managua, 1967.

Debray, Régis, *Revolution in the Revolution? Armed Struggle and Political Struggle in Latin America*. New York, London: MR Press, 1967.

Díaz del Castillo, Bernal, *Historia de la Conquista de la Nueva España*. México: Editorial Porrua, 1960.

Floyd, Troy S., *The Anglo-Spanish Struggle for Mosquitia*, 1967.

Fonseca Amador, Carlos, '*Rigoberto López Pérez, En la Lucha por la Liberación*'. Havana, 1972 (mimeographed).

Hamill, H. M., *Dictatorship in Latin America*. New York: Knopf, 1965.

Herring, Hubert, *A History of Latin America*. London: Cape, 1968.

Ibarra Grasso, Dick E., *Lenguas Indígenas Americanas*. Buenos Aires: Editorial Nova, 1958.

IBRD, *The Economic Development of Nicaragua*, 1953.

Jarquín Calderón, Edmundo, '*Reflexiones sobre la Situación Actual*'. Managua: *ca* 1975 (mimeographed).

Johnson, Haynes *et al.*, *The Bay of Pigs; The Leader's Story of Brigade 2506*. New York: W. W. Norton, 1964.

Madariaga, Salvador de, *Hernán Cortés, Conqueror of Mexico*. London: Hodder and Stoughton, 1942.

————, *The Fall of the Spanish Empire*. London: Hollis and Carter, 1947.

Meneses, Enrique, *Fidel Castro*. London: Faber and Faber, 1968.

Millett, Richard, *Guardians of the Dynasty*. Maryknoll: Orbis 1977.

Munro, Dana G., *The Five Republics of Central America*. Oxford University Press, 1918.

————, *The United States and the Caribbean Republics 1921-1933*. Princeton Univ. Press, 1974.

Obando y Bravo, Miguel, *Golpe Sandinista.* Managua: Editorial Unión, 1975.
Palacios, Alfredo L., *Nuestra América y el Imperialismo.* Buenos Aires: Editorial Palestra, 1961.
Parry, J. H., *The Spanish Seaborne Empire.* London: Hutchinson, 1966.
Pataky, László, *Llegaron los que no estaban Invitados.* Managua: Editorial Pereira, 1975.
————, *Nicaragua Desconocida.* Managua: Editorial Universal, 1957.
Perkins, Dexter, *A History of the Monroe Doctrine.* Boston: Little, Brown, 1955.
Picón-Salas, Mariano, *De la Conquista a la Independencia.* Mexico: Fondo de Cultura Económica, 1958.
Ramírez, Sergio (ed.), *El Pensamiento Vivo de Sandino.* San José: EDUCA, 1976.
Ramos, Jorge Abelardo, *Historia de la Nación Latinoamericana.* Buenos Aires: A. Peña Lillo, 1968.
Republic of Nicaragua, The: an Amnesty Intenational Report, London: AIP, 1977.
Rojo, Ricardo, *Che Guevara: Vie et Mort d'un Ami.* Paris: Editions du Seuil, 1968.
Romero, Ramón, *Somoza, Asesino de Sandino.* Mexico: Ediciones Patria y Libertad, 1959.
Salvatierra, Sofonías, *Compendio de Historia de Centroamérica.* Managua: Tipografía Progreso, 1960.
Salvatierra, Sofonías, *Sandino o la Tragedia de un Pueblo.* Madrid, 1934.
Scroggs, W. O., *Filibusters and Financiers.* New York: Macmillan, 1916.
Selser, Gregorio, *El Pequeño Ejército Loco.* Buenos Aires: Editorial Triángulo, 1958.
————, *Sandino, General de Hombres Libres,* Vols I and II. Buenos Aires: Editorial Triángulo, 1958.
Somoza García, Anastasio, *El Verdadero Sandino o el Calvario de las Segovias.* Managua: Tipografía Robelo, 1936.
Soustelle, Jacques, *La vie quotidienne des Aztèques a la veille de la Conquête Espagnole.* Paris: Hachette, 1955.
Squier, Ephraim, *Travels in Central America, particularly in Nicaragua,* Vols. I and II, 1853.
Stimson, Henry L., *American Policy in Nicaragua.* New York: Charles Scribner's Sons, 1927.
The Military Balance 1975-1976. London: International Institute for Strategic Studies, 1975.
Townsend Ezcurra, Andrés, *Las Provincias Unidas de Centroamérica; Fundación de la República.* San José: Editorial Costa Rica, 1973.
von Hagen, Victor W., *South America called them: Explorations of the Great Naturalists.* New York: Knopf, 1945.
————, *The Aztec: Man and Tribe.* New York: New American Library, 1958.

INDEX

Abaunza, Gustavo, 78, 80, 81
Abaunza Marenco, Alejandro, 133
Accessory Transit Company, 30, 32
Acosasco, Fort, 80, 87, 92-4
Acosta, José de, 18
Adams, John Quincy, 29
Aguado, Enoc, 71, 105, 119
Agüero, Fernando, 129, 133, 134, 145, 146, 147, 149
Alfonso XIII, King of Spain, 120
All-American Anti-Imperialist League, 61
Allegret, José Ivan, 158-9
Alliance for Progress, 128, 130
Altamirano, 'Pedrón', 68, 69, 71, 75, 86, 98
Alvarado, Pedro de, 17-19
Amador, Edmundo, 119
'American Phalanx of Immortals', 32, 33
Amnesty International, 152-3
Andrade, Dina, 115
Andrade (de Rivera), Miriam, 115
Antonelli, Batista, 18
A.P.R.A., 61
Arauz (de Sandino), Blanca, 55, 57
Arbenz, Jacobo, 111-12
Arévalo, Juan José, 8, 110-11
Argentina, 8, 61, 67, 93, 102, 118, 144
Argüello, Leonardo, 94, 97, 105-7, 117, 133, 148, 160
Ariel, 60
Army, U.S., 63, 103, 107, 108, 117, 133, 148, 160
Assembly, see Constituent Assembly, National Assembly
auxiliares, 76, 80, 83
Aztecs, 12-18

Balaguer, Joaquín, 132
Balladares, Manuel, 77
Batista, Fulgencio, 4, 8, 90, 123
Beals, Carleton, 61, 63
Beaulac, Willard, 76
Belize (British Honduras), 29, 33, 34

Bermúdez, Roger, 158
Betancourt, Rómulo, 8, 104
Blandón, Pedro, 71, 75
Blewfields, 20, 21
Bluefields, 35, 38, 39, 50-3, 75, 152
Boaco, 163
Bolaños, Gustavo Alemán, 68, 76, 77, 82, 86
Bolivia, 93, 143-4
Bonilla, Policarpo, 35
Borah, William, 61
Bosch, Juan, 8, 132
Bosque, Romero, 67
Brazil, 93, 108, 132, 144, 160
Brenes Jarquín, Carlos, 94-5
'Brigade 2506', 126-7
Britain, 24-30, 33, 35-9, 42, 51 (see also England)
Broad Opposition Front, 160, 162, 164
Buccaneers, 19-23
Buitrago, Julio César, 144
Bustamante y Guerra, José, 28
Butler, Smedley, 38, 44

Calderón, Augusto, 36-8 (see also Sandino, Augusto C.)
Calderón, Margarita, 36
Calderón Guardia, Rafael, 109
'calderonistas', 109-13
Calderón Ramírez, Salvador, 77
California, 29, 30, 103, 117
Calles, Plutarco Elías, 51
'camisas azules' (blueshirts), 92, 99, 131
Campeche, Gulf of, 21
Campo de Marte, 49, 75, 84, 86, 88, 89, 107
Canal, interoceanic, 15, 18, 23, 25, 30, 31, 34, 36-8, 44, 52, 67, 80, 99
Canning, George, 28-9
Cannon, Lee Roy, 38
Caracas, 112
Carazo Hurtado, Evaristo, 76
Cardenal, Ernesto, 2, 7, 143, 160

Caribbean, 10, 12, 18-21, 23, 52, 54, 55, 59, 71, 75, 80, 99, 104, 120, 123
Caribbean Legion, 8, 101, 103, 104, 109, 110, 117, 126, 132
Caribs, 20
Carter, Calvin, 49-51, 53
Carter, Jimmy, U.S. President, 160, 163, 165
Casas, Bartolomé de las, 139
Castillo Armas, Carlos, 111-12
Castillo Quant, José María, 151-3
Castro, Fidel, 6, 8, 123-7, 129-30
Castro Wassmer, Carlos, 55, 77
Central American Common Market, 130, 142
Central American Court, 38, 45
'Central America, Declaration of', 130
Cerdeño, Fernando, 145
Chamorro-Bryan Treaty, 45, 80
Chamorro, Emiliano, 5, 37-8, 40, 42-52, 62, 79, 81, 93-4, 108, 110, 112, 119, 139
Chamorro, Diego Manuel, 46, 129
Chamorro, Fruto, 5, 31
Chamorro, Pedro Joaquín, 2, 5, 7, 119, 124-5, 133-4, 139-41, 150-5, 160
Charcas, 25
Central Intelligence Agency (C.I.A.), 111, 126
Chiang Kai-shek, 61
Chibchas, 11, 13, 14
Chichigalpa, 75
Chile, 61, 140
China, 18, 61
Chinandega, 51, 53, 59, 131, 137, 164
Chiriboga, José R., 113
Chontales, 55, 56, 75
Christian Democrats, 125, 140 (see also 'Social-cristianos')
Church, Roman Catholic, 6, 16, 18, 37, 126, 134, 139-41, 143, 146, 151-2, 163, 168
Clarence, 'King' Robert Henry, 35
Clayton-Bulwer Treaty, 30, 33

Cocibolca, Lake, 10-14, 16 (see also Lake Nicaragua)
Cockburn, Adolfo, 75
Coco, River, 23, 55, 59, 73, 75, 80, 82, 83, 98, 120
Colindres, Juan J., 75
Colombia, 8, 13, 37, 61, 111, 140, 160
Colonia Salvadorita, 156
'Comando Juan José Quezada', 151
Comintern, VI World Congress, 61
Comité Manos Fuera de Nicaragua, 65-6
Comité Pro-Liberación de Nicaragua, 77
Comité Pro-Sandino, 61
Communism, Communists, 47, 51, 71, 108-9, 111-12, 118, 123, 125-7, 132, 139, 146, 155-6, 164-6 (see also Marxism)
Compañía Agropecuaria, 141
'Company M', 72
CONDECA, 160
Congress, Nicaraguan, see National Assembly
Conservative Party ('historic'), 5, 6, 28, 30-8, 40, 44, 46, 49-58, 62, 64, 70-1, 76-84, 89-95, 108, 110-11, 117, 119, 124-9, 132, 133, 139, 145-51, 162
Conservative Party, Nationalist, 95, 105, 119, 129, 133
Conservative Party, Republican, 46
Constabulary, Nicaraguan, 49-53, 58
Constituent Assembly, 89-93, 98, 107-10, 146, 149, 151
Constitution, 88, 90, 95, 98, 101, 102, 108, 110, 117, 133, 145, 146, 151
Contreras, Rodrigo de, 17
Contreras Escobar, Eduardo, 151
Corinto, 44, 49, 52, 53, 78
Coronel Urtecho, José, 150
Corn Islands, 39, 45, 152
Cortés, Hernán, 15-17
Costa Rica, 8, 15, 22, 28, 31, 33, 45, 61, 65, 103, 108-12, 117, 119,

123-6, 129, 145, 146, 148, 159, 164
Cuadra, Pablo Antonio, 166
Cuba, 1, 8, 43, 61, 123, 125-8, 132, 142, 144, 146
C.U.U.N., 150

Dallas-Clarendon Treaty, 33
Dalling, General, 25
Darién, 11, 13, 15, 22
Darío, Rubén, 2, 36, 45, 136
Dávila, Miguel, 38
Davis, C. H., 33
Dawson, Thomas, 40
Debayle, Luis Manuel, 103, 105, 142
Debayle (de Pallais), Margarita, 2-3
Debayle (de Somoza), Salvadora, 47, 88, 105, 141, 158
Debray, Régis, 144
de Graaf, 'Captain', 22
Democratic State Journal, 31
Dennis, Lawrence, 51
Díaz, Adolfo, 38, 40-4, 49, 52-3, 62, 64, 70-9
Díaz, José León, 68
Díaz del Castillo, Bernal, 10, 16, 17
Díaz Lanz, Major, 125
Dickinson-Ayón Treaty, 34
Diriamba, 126, 137, 162-4
Dominican Republic, 8, 17, 37, 40, 42, 47, 108, 123, 132, 168
Drake, Sir Francis, 20
Dú Dú, 163

Eberhardt, Charles, 50
Echandi, Mario, 124
Ecuador, 114
Eisenhower, Dwight D., 116, 126
El Bálsamo, 69
El Bramadero, 64
El Chaparral, 123
El Chipote, 59-60
El Jícaro, 54
El Salvador, 3, 8, 15, 30, 33, 38, 45, 61, 67, 77, 83, 91, 93, 94, 101, 111, 114, 118, 119, 141, 160, 165

El Tiempo, 8
Enaluf, 142
England, 19, 20, 22, 23, 136 (*see also* Britain)
Episcopal Conference, Latin American (CELAM), 143
Escamilla, Juan, 67, 80, 83
Escondido, river, 38, 52
Española, island (Hispaniola), 21
Espinosa, Rodolfo, 94
Esquipulas, 159
Estelí, 59, 66, 152, 163, 164
Estrada, Francisco, 85-6
Estrada Cabrera, Manuel, 38
'Ethelburga Syndicate', 38

Fascism, fascists, 89, 92, 99, 131
Federation of Chambers of Commerce, 164
Feland, Logan, 65
F.E.R., 150
Figueres, José, 8, 109-13
Fonseca Amador, Carlos, 123, 128, 131, 145, 146, 157
Fonseca, Gulf of, 45
France, 19, 25, 27, 28, 37
Frente Sandinista de Liberación Nacional, 1, 5, 6, 128, 131, 143-6, 150-66
Freylinghuysen-Zavala Treaty, 34

Gaitán, Francisco, 118, 132
Gallegos, Rómulo, 104
Garrison, Cornelius, 32
Garro, Pedro de, 16
'Generation of 1944, The', 119
Genie, Samuel, 144
Germain, Lord George, 25
Germany, 99
González, Alejandro, 141
González Dávila, Gil, 15, 16, 20
'Good Neighbour Policy', 77, 90
Grace, Leonard, 38
Gracias a Dios, Cape, 23, 25, 75
Gracias a Dios province, 120
Granada, 2, 16, 18, 19, 21-3, 25, 28, 30, 31, 33, 44, 76, 77, 136, 137, 139, 140, 157, 162, 164

Grant, Gen. Ulysses S., 34
Gresham, Roger, 35
Greytown, 30
Grognier, 'Captain', 22
'Grupo Solidario', 65
Guanacaste, 110
Guapinol, 69
Guardia Nacional, *see* National
    Guard
'Guardias de Hacienda', 96
Guatemala, 8, 15, 17, 28, 31, 33,
    38, 47, 67, 68, 82, 86, 101, 110-
    12, 117, 126, 160, 164, 165
Guayaquil, 23
Guerrero, Lorenzo, 133, 141
Guevara, Ernesto ('Che'), 8, 111,
    112, 123, 143, 144
Gutiérrez, Francisco, 35
Gutiérrez, Julio, 132
Gutiérrez, Policarpo, 87

Haiti, 42, 47, 123, 127
Hanna, Matthew, 78
'Happy Valley', 126
Hatfield, Gilbert D., 57
Havana, 1, 8, 61, 123, 142, 152,
    153
Hawkins, Sir John, 20
Haya de la Torre, Víctor Raúl, 61
Hernández de Córdoba, Francisco,
    16, 17
Hernández Martínez, Maximiliano,
    93
Herring, Hubert, 114
Hitler, Adolf, 89, 92, 99
Honduras, 3, 10, 15, 17, 20, 30, 31,
    33-5, 38, 46, 47, 54, 58-61, 65-9,
    82, 84, 91, 111, 112, 120, 123,
    127, 128, 164, 165
Honduras Sugar and Distilling
    Company, 46
Hoover, Herbert, 61, 63, 67
'Huasteca Petroleum Company',
    47, 54
Hueck, Cornelio, 158-9
Hull, Cordell, 99

Indians, American, 11-26, 29, 31,

34, 35, 72, 138
Instituto de Fomento Nacional
    ('Infonac'), 142
Instituto de Occidente, 64
International Anti-Imperialist Con-
    gress, First, 61
International Club (of Managua),
    50
International Conference of Ameri-
    can States, VI, 61
Isabelia, Cordillera, 64
Italy, 99

Jackman, 'Captain', 21-22
Jacquier, Jacques, 141
Jagger, Bianca, 1
Jamaica, 21, 22, 25, 26, 35
Japan, 99
Jefe Director, 78-95, 105, 118, 120,
    151
Jenkins, Robert, 24
Jeremy I, 'King', 23
Jerez, Máximo, 31
Jinotega, 53, 55, 56, 61, 62, 66, 88
Jinotepe, 126, 162
Jirón Ruano, Manuel, 67
John XXIII, Pope, 5, 140
Johnson, Lyndon B., 132, 146
Jovellanos, Gaspar M. de, 25
Judson, Frederick, 104
Jueces de Mesta, 96

Kellogg, Frank, 67
Kennedy, John F., 5, 126-8, 130,
    146
Knox, Philander, 39, 43, 64
Korea, 111

Labour Party, 65
Labour; strikes and union activity,
    91, 92, 101, 102, 128, 138, 155,
    162-5
Lacayo, Alejandro, 156
Lacayo, Miguel, 28
Lacayo Farfán, Enrique, 124
Lacayo Sacasa, Benjamín, 107-8
La Condamine, Charles-Marie de,
    25

La Cruz, 110
L.A.C.S.A., 146
La Loma, 43, 49, 50, 53, 77, 80, 87, 105, 148
La Luz y Los Angeles Mining Company, 38, 40, 64
Lane, Arthur Bliss, 85, 86, 90-2
Lanica, 142
'Lansing Plan', 45
La Paz, 32
'La Pólvora', 77
Lara, Escolástico, 65, 77
La Salle Military Academy, 103, 117
Las Flores, 59
La Unión, 67
Leblanc, Admiral, 29
'Legation Guard' in Managua, U.S., 44-52
León, 2, 7, 8, 16-19, 22, 25, 28, 30, 31, 53, 65, 71, 75, 80, 82, 87, 92-4, 114-16, 118, 136-40, 162, 164
Leoni, Raúl, 8
'liberación' (theol.), 143
Liberal Party ('historic'), 28, 30-6, 39-47, 50-8, 64, 71, 76-87, 89, 91-5, 106, 139, 150
Liberal Party, Independent, 101, 102, 105, 123, 133, 146
Liberal Party, Nationalist, 95, 97, 101, 102, 105, 106, 129-32, 145, 147, 149-51, 157, 158, 168
Liberal Party (Ramiro Sacasa faction), 145-6
Liberia, 110
Lindberg, Irving, 102
Loans, foreign, 32, 38-46, 128
Logtown, 75
López, (Col.) Juan, 131
López, (Lieut.) Juan, 89-90
López, Santos, 86
López Cordero, Alfonso, 147
López Irías, 'General', 55
López Pérez, Rigoberto, 7-9, 114-16, 119, 123
Luz y Verdad (manifesto), 74

McCoy, Frank R., 63

Machado, Salvador, 35
Madriz, José, 39
Malvinas (Falkland) islands, 29
Mamenic, 142
Managua, 1, 2, 4, 7, 31, 33, 35, 36, 42-5, 47, 49, 52, 53, 64, 65, 75-7, 80, 82, 84-6, 89, 91, 94, 98, 102, 104, 106, 107, 116, 118-20, 124, 126, 133-8, 140, 144, 148-50, 152, 156, 158, 163, 164
Managua, Lake, 11, 56, 78, 99 (*see also* Lake Xolotlán)
Mansvelt, Edward, 21-2
Maracaibo, 22
Marighela, Carlos, 144
Marín, Luis, 16
Marines, U.S., 37, 38, 44, 49-65, 69, 70, 72, 74, 76-9, 132
Maritime Canal Company, 34, 36
Martínez, Bartolomé, 46, 47
Martínez, Maximiliano, 101
Martínez, Tomás, 33-34
Martínez Lacayo, Robert, 147
Marxism, Marxists, 6, 128, 139, 150, 159 (*see also* Communism)
Masachapa, 142
Masaya, 30, 36, 43, 44, 126, 137, 149, 159, 162, 164
Matagalpa, 6, 53, 55, 56, 66, 75, 132, 137, 144, 150, 153, 162-4
Matthews, Calvin, 78
Maximilian of Austria, 29
Mayas, 12
Medellín, 140, 143
Mena, Luis, 40, 42-44
Mendieta, Salvador, 36
'Mérida' (*finca*), 142
Mérida (Yucatán), 68
Mexico, 12-16, 19, 29, 31, 32, 37, 39, 41, 47, 51, 52, 54, 61, 65-9, 72, 77, 107, 125
Miskitos, 20-6, 29, 31, 34, 35, 138
Mistral, Gabriela, 61
Moctecuzoma Xocoyotsin (Montezuma II), 13, 15
Mokorón, 120
Moncada, José María, 40, 42, 50-7, 62-79, 83, 93, 97, 102, 138

Monroe Doctrine, 29, 31, 35-7, 40, 41, 52; 'Roosevelt corollary', 37; 'financial corollary', 40-1
'Montelimar', 142, 157, 158
Mora, José Antonio, 158-63
Morales, Oscar, 145
Morgan, Charles, 32
Morgan, Sir Henry, 21-3
'Morrillo', 142
Morris, 'Captain', 21-2
Moseley, Benjamin, 26
Mosonte, 159
'Mosquito Coast', 20-5, 29, 31, 35-8, 120
Moyogalpa, 142
Muñoz, José Trinidad, 31
Murra, 63
Mussolini, Benito, 89, 92, 99
Muzo, 13

Naco, 16
Nahuatl, 11, 13
Napoleon III, 29, 30
Naranjo, 64
Nation, The, 61
National Assembly, 49, 50, 52, 87-90, 94, 98, 99, 102, 107, 111, 117, 133, 134, 141, 146, 158, 162
National Bank (of Nicaragua), 43, 52, 97
National Guard, 6, 7, 37, 42, 43, 47-53, 58-65, 69-72, 77-113, 117-20, 123-6, 131-4, 142-67
Nationalist Party, 64
'National Sovereignty Defence Army', 60, 71
Nau, Jean David (L'Olonnais), 22
Navy, U.S., 32, 39, 44, 52, 63, 126
Nazis, 99, 100, 166
Nelson, Horatio, 25-6
New York, 40, 42
Nicaragua: economy, 24, 34, 36, 40, 41, 45, 46, 96-9, 113, 114, 120-2, 127-30, 136-8, 141-3, 149, 150, 156, 157, 166, 167; geography, 10, 11, 136, 137; population and social structure, 11, 27, 34, 41, 96, 97, 121, 122, 130,

136-9, 143, 156, 157, 166, 167
Nicaragua, Lake, 10, 11, 18-22, 27-30, 35, 45, 55, 56
Niquinohomo, 36, 46, 54
Niquiranos, Nicarao, 13-17
Nixon, Richard M., U.S. President, 146
Nombre de Dios, 18
Northcott, Elliot, 40-1
Novedades, 142
Nueva Prensa, La, 85, 87
Nueva Segovia, 54, 55, 57, 62, 66

Obando y Bravo, Miguel, 146, 151, 152, 161
Ocotal, 58-60, 63, 159
Ojoche, 63-4
Old Man I, 'King', 23
Old Man II, 'King', 23
Old Providence, 21
Olds, Robert, 52
Ometepe island, 10, 137, 142
Orcuyo, Víctor, 156
Organisation of American States (O.A.S.), 110, 113, 119, 120, 127, 129, 132, 142, 164-6
Ortez, Miguel Angel, 64, 71, 75

Pacem in Terris, 140
Pacific Ocean, 10, 12, 18, 23, 28-30, 53, 55, 99, 100
Paguaga Irías, Edmundo, 149, 151
Palacagüina, 75
Palace, National, 90, 106, 107, 134, 136, 163
Palacios, Alfredo, 61
Pallais Debayle, Luis, 142, 159, 163
Pallais Debayle, Noel, 142, 151
Panamá, 4, 8, 13, 15-18, 22, 37, 93, 113, 116, 118, 123, 148, 164
Pan-American Conference, Tenth, 112
Paraguay, 25, 144
Parajón, 'General', 55
Paredes, José de, 66
Partido Conservador (*'histórico'*), see Conservative Party ('historic')
Partido Conservador Nacionalista,

see Conservative Party, Nationalist
Partido Conservador Republicano, see Conservative Party, Republican
Partido Laborista, see Labour Party
Partido Liberal ('histórico'), see Liberal Party ('historic')
Partido Liberal Independente, see Liberal Party, Independent
Partido Liberal Nacionalista, see Liberal Party, Nationalist
Partido Nacionalista, see Nationalist Party
Partido Revolucionario Institucional (P.R.I.), 125
Partido Socialista Nicaragüense (P.S.N.), 146, 155
Pedrarias de Avila, 15-17
Peking, 61
Peralta, Ismael, 71
Pérez, Carlos Andrés, 164
Pérez Jiménez, Marcos, 8
Perón, Juan Domingo, 8, 9, 102, 168
Perón, Eva, 155
Perú, 18, 19, 61, 93
Philip II, King of Spain, 18, 20, 137
Picado, Teodoro, 108, 109, 112
Picado, Teodoro (Jr.), 112-13
Picón-Salas, Mariano, 10
Pigs, Bay of, 127
Pineda, Laureano, 31
Pis Pis, 64
Pizarro, Gonzalo, 18
Playa Girón, 127
Pochtecatl, 12-13
'Populorum Progressio', 140, 143
Portes Gil, Emilio, 66-69
Portocarrero, Horacio, 77, 85
Portocarrero (de Somoza), Hope, 155-8
Port Royal, 21, 25
Prensa, La, 2, 119, 141, 153, 162
Prinzapolca, 54-5
'Provisionales', 63
Pueblo Viejo, 22

Puerto Cabezas, 52-5, 75
Puller, Lewis B., 72

Quiboto, 64
Quintana, Julio, 129

Rama, 52, 75
Ramas, 20, 138
Raveneau de Lussan, 'Le Sieur', 22-3
Rebozo, 'Bebe', 146
Red Cross, International, 134, 141
Reyes, Rigoberto, 88, 94, 95, 100, 132
Río Blanco, 163
Río Grande, 51
'Rio Treaty', 110, 113
Rivas, 9, 28, 33, 116, 137, 162, 163
Rivas, Alfredo, 49-50
Rivas, Luis, 49
Rivas, Dagoberto, 46
Rivas, isthmus of, 18
Rivas, Luis, 49
Rivas, Patricio, 32
Rivera, Abraham, 73, 75
Rockefeller, Nelson, 104
Rodríguez, Carlos, 126
Rojas Pinilla, Gustavo, 8
Román y Reyes, Víctor, 50, 108, 110, 111
Roosevelt, Avenida, 99, 134
Roosevelt, Franklin D., 77, 90, 98, 99, 146
Roosevelt, Theodore, 37, 38, 43

Sacasa, Antioco, 87
Sacasa, Juan Bautista, 46, 47, 50-4, 76-95, 99, 105, 131
Sacasa, María de, 89-91
Sacasa, Ramiro, 145-46
Sacasa, Ramón, 87, 92-4
Sacasa, Roberto, 35
Sacramento, 31
Salgado, Carlos, 59-60
Salvatierra, Sofonías, 65, 79, 82, 85-6
Sampson, Dinora, 132, 155
San Albino, 54, 57

San Carlos, 119, 159
'*Sandinistas*', *see* Sandino, Augusto C., and Frente Sandinista de Liberación Nacional
Sandino, Augusto C., 36-8, 45-7, 53-87, 90, 98, 112, 120, 128, 139, 166
Sandino, Gregorio, 36, 38, 57, 85, 86
Sandino, Sócrates, 86
San Francisco, 32
San Isidro, 80
San José, 8, 109, 112, 113, 119, 123, 129, 148
San Juan, castle of, 26-7
San Juan, river, 10, 18, 20, 23, 26, 27, 30, 38, 45, 99
San Juan del Norte, 30
San Juan de Ulúa, 29
San Marcos, 36, 51, 54
San Miguelito, 142
San Rafael del Norte, 53, 55, 57, 66, 82, 83
San Rafael del Sur, 142
Santa Anna, Antonio López de, 29
Santa Catalina island, 21-2
'Santa Rita', 157
Santo Domingo, 17, 29, 132
Santo Domingo (Nicaragua), 75
Santo Tomás, 124
Schick, René, 129-131, 133
Scull, Greg, 43
Segovias (region), 23, 54-9, 64, 65, 69-71, 75, 80
Sellers, David Foote, 65
Selva, Salomón de la, 65, 77
Sevilla Sacasa, Guillermo, 104, 142, 151
Shelton, Turner B., 146, 149, 151, 152
Sierra Maestra, 123
Simon, 'Le Sieur', 22
Smith, Adam, 25
Siuna, 152
Social-cristianos (Social Christians), 128, 133, 140, 146, 150
Solentiname island, 2, 7, 160
Solórzano, Carlos, 46-50

Somoza, Bernabé, 30, 36, 47
Somoza, José, 103, 142, 152, 158, 167
Somoza Abrego, Leonel, 151
Somoza Debayle, Anastasio: 1-7, 103-7, 111, 117, 118, 120, 124, 128, 130-5, 139-68; begins first Presidency, 135; begins second Presidency, 151
Somoza Debayle, Luis: 9, 103, 105, 111, 117-31, 141, 145, 146; begins Presidency, 117
Somoza fortune, 96, 97, 99, 100, 127, 130, 138, 141, 142, 149, 150, 156-9, 168
Somoza García, Anastasio, 7-9, 30, 36, 45, 47, 51, 53, 54, 70, 71, 79-120, 123, 129-31, 136, 139, 145, 146, 166; becomes *Jefe Director*, 78; begins first Presidency, 95; begins second Presidency, 98; begins third (interim) Presidency, 111; begins fourth Presidency, 111; assassination, 7-8, 112-16
Somoza Portocarrero, Anastasio, 156, 167, 168
Somoza Portocarrero, Carla, 156
Somoza Portocarrero, Carolina, 156
Somoza Portocarrero, Julio, 156, 158
Somoza Portocarrero, Roberto, 155
Somoza, Sucesores del General, 141
Southerland, Admiral, 44
South Pennsylvania Oil Company, 47
Spain, Spaniards, 11, 13, 15-29, 43, 99, 136, 138
Standard Fruit and Steamship Company, 34
Stimson, Henry L., 52, 53, 56, 70, 74, 76
'Studer, Carl', 111
Suchiate, river, 67
Sumus, 20, 138
Sweden, 113

Taft, William Howard, 40

Tegucigalpa, 60, 65, 68
Telpaneca, 59
Tenochas, 12 (*see also* Aztecs)
Tenochtitlán, 11-14
'*Terceristas*', 159
Tierra Azul, 124
Tijerino, Toribio, 64
Tiscapa, Explana de, 99
Tologalpa, 20, 136
Tortuga, 21
Townley, 'Captain', 22
Treaty, Peace and Friendship, 47
Triumvirate, 146-9, 151
Trujillo, 20, 21
Trujillo, Rafael Leónidas, 8, 9, 37, 108, 123, 132, 168
Trujillo, Ramfis, 168
Truman, Harry S., 104, 107
Turcios, Froylán, 60-68
'Twelve, The' ('*Los Doce*'), 160, 162, 163

Ubico, Jorge, 8, 9, 82, 101
Ulate, Otilio, 109
Umanzor, Juan Pablo, 75, 86
Unión Democrática de Liberación (U.D.E.L.), 5, 155
Unión Nacional de Oposición, 133
United Fruit Company, 34, 35, 47, 111
United Nations, 110, 142
United States of America: 7, 8, 28-72, 74-80, 83, 84, 90, 91, 93, 98, 99, 102-13, 117, 118, 121, 125-9, 132, 133, 142, 146, 151, 159, 160, 163, 165; intervention in Nicaragua, 38-72, 74-80
University students, 101, 102, 150
Uruguay, 127

Vanderbilt, Cornelius, 30, 32, 33
Varilla, 6
Vasconcelos, José, 61
Vatican Council II, 140, 143
Venezuela, 8, 104, 140, 164
Veracruz, 47, 69
Veragua, 15
Villa de Mosa, 21
'*Voluntarios*', 67-70, 76

Walker, William, 8, 31-33, 116
Warren, Fletcher, 104
Washington, D.C., 35, 38, 42, 44, 49-52, 57, 61, 74, 76, 87, 91, 93, 99, 102, 104, 107, 108, 111, 113, 117, 120, 123, 129, 132, 141, 142, 151, 160, 163, 164, 166
Waslala, 163
Weitzel, George, 43-44
West Point Military Academy, 103, 105
Wheeler, Senator, 61
Wilson, Woodrow, 44
Wiwilí, 83, 85, 86, 98
World War, Second, 99-100

Xolotlán, Lake, 10 (*see also* Lake Managua)

Yalí, 57, 69
Yrigoyen, Hipólito, 67
Yucatán, 13, 68

Zelaya, 6, 153
Zelaya, José María, 77-8
Zelaya, José Santos, 35-42, 45, 93, 139
Zeledón, Benjamín, 44
Zepeda, Pedro, 65-9
Zúñiga, Juana de, 15